AN ENTIRELY DIFFERENT GAME

AN ENTIRELY DIFFERENT GAME

The British Influence on Brazilian Football

AIDAN HAMILTON

With best wishes

MAINSTREAM
PUBLISHING

EDINBURGH AND LONDON

For my mother Cynthia

In memory of my father Joseph, and Hilary Bubear

First published in Great Britain in 1998 by
MAINSTREAM PUBLISHING COMPANY (EDINBURGH) LTD
7 Albany Street
Edinburgh EH1 3UG

ISBN 1 84018 041 2

A CIP catalogue record for this book is available from the
British Library

The front cover shows (clockwise from top): Jack Barrick;
Entrada pela Praça Charles Miller (Charles Miller Square
entrance); Charles Miller; Harry Welfare; Leônidas da Silva
scoring for São Paulo FC against AC Juventus at Pacaembú,
circa 1948; match-card cover for CA Paulistano v Rio de
Janeiro
The back cover shows Bangu Athletic Club, 1906

Typeset in Bembo and Stone
Printed in Great Britain by Butler & Tanner Ltd

Contents

They were all footballers in the team – eleven footballers, where British football then never used to be. You played to the position you were in. We had footballers who were good kickers of a ball but couldn't beat a man to save their life. And that was playing for England as well. It was a different kind of game [that the Brazilians were playing]. It was an entirely different game.

Ted Ballard, Southampton FC, 1947–51

Preface

I can picture myself now, returning to São Paulo in November 1994 to prepare a radio piece on Brazilian football's centenary. I took with me a copy of the Brazil entry from an A–Z of World Football. It begins: 'Charles Miller, a keen soccer player in England, arrived in Brazil in 1894, and immediately set about popularising the game at São Paulo Athletic Club . . .'

There are, of course, discrepancies between this statement and others on the origins of the Brazilian game. So Miller was English, was he? And his football lessons – did they really begin the moment he arrived in Brazil? It was after meeting Miller's daughter Helena that I decided to investigate.

What started out as a biographical study of Charles Miller swiftly embraced other connections between British and Brazilian football – in particular the remarkable career of Harry Welfare. With Charles it was a case of separating fact from legend; Harry, on the other hand, had been almost completely forgotten. Today, while Charles is widely revered in Brazil, the only trace of Harry is the Welfare in Rio whose grandfather adopted the name to commemorate his favourite player.

The framework for this story of Miller and Welfare is provided by Tomás Mazzoni's *História do Futebol no Brasil 1894–1950*. The period covered is almost identical; there is emphasis on the development of football in Rio and São Paulo, and Brazil's performances internationally; and, as in Mazzoni, the highlights of key games are given.

For half a century, Britain influenced aspects of the Brazilian game. And it's taken British football nearly as long to begin to analyse just how Brazil mastered that legacy.

My heartfelt thanks to all who contributed to the preparation of this book.

In Brazil, I am especially grateful to Helena Miller and the late Charles Rule for freely sharing with me their memories of Charles

Miller, and the Gregori family for their friendship and hospitality. *Obrigado* and *um abraço*, also, to João Lopes da Silva and Watanabe at the *Gazeta Esportiva* archives; Rubens Ribeiro at the Federação Paulista de Futebol; Silvana Fontanelli at CA Paulistano; John R. Mills for the copy of Mazzoni; Robert Turner; Márcia and Fátima at the Biblioteca Mário de Andrade (São Paulo); Marli Olmos at O *Estado de São Paulo*; Sonia and Tony; Paulo Couto at the Biblioteca Nacional (Rio); Zezinho at Fluminense FC; Carlos Santoro and fellow football statisticians Heber, Mário and Moretzsohn; Roberto Assaf for material from his archives; and Cláudio Christóvam de Pinho, Flávio Costa, Zezé Moreira and Segundo Villadoniga for invaluable recollections.

In Britain, I would like to express my gratitude to Harold and Norman Welfare for supplying information about Harry and his family; Dave Juson, discoverer of the Miller letters, for his help and hospitality; David Bull for generously providing me with accommodation and for suggesting the title; Ray Barnes at the Hampshire FA; Tony Mason for his comments on the manuscript; David Barber at the FA; Gary Chalk for the copy of Willy Meisl's *Soccer Revolution*; my brother Nick; Arthur Smith at the Referees' Association; Simon Clifford; staff at Colindale and the libraries of Liverpool, Paisley and Southampton; Norman Gannaway; Brian Truscott at Southampton FC; Roger Barrick, Jess Lay, the late Fred Chaplin and P.M. Barker; Judy Diamond at Mainstream Publishing; Ted Bates, Bill Ellerington, the late Eric Webber, George Swindin, Don Roper, Laurie Scott and Sir Tom Finney for sharing their memories of playing in Brazil and for lending memorabilia; and, finally, Doreen for all her support and encouragement.

ONE

Banister Court

On the quay in Santos, solemn, as if he were at a funeral, my father was waiting for me to disembark holding my degree certificate. But in fact I appeared in front of him with two footballs, one in each hand . . . The old man, surprised, enquired:
– What is this Charles?
– My degree, I replied.
– What?
– Yes! Your son has graduated in football . . .
The old man, in good spirits, laughed. I was off the hook . . .

From an interview with Charles Miller, *O Imparcial*,
21 October 1927

There is an element of theatre about the above family reunion; the scene is at once one of tension and comedy. This is Charles Miller's account of his return to Brazil in October 1894. It matters little whether or not a similar conversation actually took place between Miller and his father. Football historians in São Paulo and Rio had already decided that it was this event that represented the birth of the game in Brazil. Consequently, on Brazilian football's one hundredth anniversary it was not, as is more usual, the founding of a league or club, or a particular match, that was celebrated; it was the return of Miller bringing with him the two footballs. No wonder he felt entitled, obliged even, to describe his home-coming in dramatic terms.

Miller probably recounted this episode in Portuguese. But when it came to explaining why the footballs were a form of diploma, he used English to refer to his graduation. At any rate, this is how the dialogue appeared in print. The English words are striking and give importance to the idea that Miller, while in England, had attained mastery of one activity in particular. He was a football graduate. His father must have been aware of his son's footballing achievements, but what he did not know was that the two balls had been presented by a leading administrator of the game. Miller's declaration to his father may have been light-hearted. But, as we shall see, he was fully justified in making this assertion.

Charles William Miller was born in the Brás district of São Paulo on 24 November 1874. He was the second son of John Miller and Carlota Alexandra Fox, a Brazilian of English descent. John Miller, a Scot, had come to Brazil to take up the position of engineer with the São Paulo Railway Company. Backed by British capital, the company was set up in the late 1850s to provide transportation for coffee from the pioneer farming areas around Jundiaí, up on the plateau behind São Paulo, to the port of Santos at the foot of the mountains. Construction of the first track was completed in 1867, and, with further profits assured, plans were soon under way for an expansion of the service. Miller's skills were in demand, and he was not alone in opting to settle in Brazil.

As São Paulo's British community continued to grow, the city assumed an increasingly British character. An Anglican church was built near the Luz station, and a wide range of consumer goods was imported. Afternoon tea was among the traditions that were kept up. In the nearby town of Paranapiacaba a replica of Big Ben still stands on the platform of the now disused station, a symbol of former prosperity amid current squalor and neglect. In the 1870s, any sense of distance from the old country was eased by the steamships which regularly plied the route between Santos and the ports of Southampton and Liverpool. Charles was made aware of his father's heritage from an early age. He must have been no more than five years old when he posed for a painting wearing traditional Scottish dress.

In 1884 Charles Miller, aged nine, was sent to boarding school in England. His elder brother John and cousin William Fox Rule accompanied him on the SS *Elbe*. When the boys disembarked in Southampton on the evening of 29 July, it was only a short distance to Banister Court, a Georgian mansion which lay directly south of the town's main common. The school had been set up by the Peninsular and Oriental Steam Navigation Company in the 1860s for the sons of ships' officers. But although the scheme was short-lived, the first headmaster, the late Rev. George Ellaby, had ensured the school survived. It was being run by Ellaby's widow and eldest son.

Arriving in the heat of an English summer, the new pupils lost no time in exploring the large country house, its landscaped gardens and surrounding area comprising Banister's Park. They watched and played cricket, and perhaps visited the Antelope Ground where, in the week after their arrival, Hampshire County Cricket Club had matches against Sussex and Somerset. But all too soon lessons began, and as the season changed so did activity on the sports fields. For Charles Miller, those first months in England would leave a lasting impression:

> Much more than the voyage itself, I was enchanted by the enormous opportunity for recreation at the school. Just as a schoolboy, in the Garden of Childhood, listens to the teacher, so I, fascinated, saw my first game of Association football.

It is significant that Miller actually specifies the football code, for during that first term rugby union was still an important winter sport at Banister Court. An example of the co-existence of the two codes of play occurs in November 1884 and was reported by the *Southampton Times* in a column headed 'Football Matches'. One Saturday the school had an association fixture with Temperance, followed, four days later, by a Union rules game against Southampton Grammar School. It was noticeable that in the Banister's teams masters played alongside boys. This was a feature of sport in the Victorian era, a case of schools strengthening their sides to face opposition that was for the most part grown-up.

Seeing him turn out for the football XI, Miller must have noticed his headmaster's passion for the sport. Not long after he had taken up the headship in the summer of 1883, Christopher Ellaby formed an association football club at Banister Court. He had learnt the game during his undergraduate years at Oxford; but it was not so much his ability with a ball that was important – he was, we are told, a moderate player. What counted was Ellaby's whole-hearted enthusiasm and, later, his determination to be involved in running the game in Hampshire. Not surprisingly, his writings on this period are peppered with references to football.

Already, in the autumn of 1884, while established clubs in the north of England were at loggerheads with the FA over the question of professionalism, attempts were being made to organise the game on the south coast. One of the men behind the formation of the South Hants and Dorset Football Association was William Pickford, a journalist based in Bournemouth. With rules derived from a set obtained from the Lancashire FA, the committee began recruiting members. Pickford later recalled this stage of what he termed 'real amateurism':

> Players chosen to represent the new Association in county matches went as far as Brighton, Portsmouth, Salisbury and Reading and paid their own fares. They did more, they purchased their own county shirts and on one splendid occasion all the team solemnly paid their sixpences at the gate to see themselves play!

According to Pickford, he and his colleagues were amateurs 'from serious conviction that football should be a mere pastime'. It was precisely this ethos that underpinned Miller's experience of football in England and which he eventually took with him to Brazil.

In 1885 two events occurred which would have important repercussions for Charles's sporting aspirations. The first was Hampshire CCC's move to Banister's Park, the official opening taking place on 9 May. The bounds of Charles's school extended to the boundary line of the new County Ground. Not only did the boys have a privileged viewpoint on match days, they also had the use of the nets for practice. Many years later an Old Boy fondly recalled that 'when there was a match on the County Ground and anything exciting was happening they would somehow forget to sound the bell after morning break'. Such lenience was understandable, especially when, during Miller's schooldays, a player of W.G. Grace's calibre was at the crease.

The second event was the formation in November of St Mary's, a football club which took its name from a local church. St Mary's, the forerunner of the present Southampton FC, played only a handful of games in their inaugural season, the first of these not far from the County Ground, on land on which the County Bowling Club now stands. The Saints got off to a bright start, and did not lose a game until a year later. For that defeat Miller almost certainly would have been a spectator, for it was his school, playing at home, which inflicted it by two goals to one. The match took place three days after his twelfth birthday.

Earlier, in June 1886, Charles had been present at an athletics festival held in a neighbouring park. His name appears in a report in the *Southampton Observer*, and among the other competitors are his brother John and cousin William. Towards the end of the following summer the name crops up again, this time in the cricket columns. The occasion was a match at the Antelope in which Miller and his brother were guesting for Cavendish College, a private school in the locality. These are early examples of Charles's involvement in sport. But it was football that he preferred, and it was now that the game in Hampshire acquired a fresh purpose and direction.

With football growing in popularity, there were calls for a change in the regional governing body. East Hampshire members in particular felt that the South Hants and Dorset FA was too remote. What they were seeking was the creation of an association that would operate from a central point in Hampshire. On 13 April 1887 their lobbying was rewarded when delegates at a special meeting voted to dissolve the existing association. A week later, a general meeting of a new Hampshire FA was held in Southampton. Pickford informs us that he was unable to attend, 'having met with a football accident', but in his absence he was elected honorary secretary. Of the 17 clubs represented there were two schools, one of which was Banister Court.

The fact that Christopher Ellaby participated in that historic meeting dispelled any doubts as to which code of play his school gave its allegiance. From this moment, Banister's headmaster, to use his own words, 'took a rather prominent part in the Hampshire FA'. Membership of the association entitled the school to enter one of two cup competitions and ensured that its players were eligible to be picked for the full county side. A representative selection was soon achieved when, in October, W.P. Cole, a goalkeeper, was included in Hampshire's first ever XI. There was also the opportunity for members to submit teams for a six-a-side tournament over Easter 1888. Charles was not included in Banister's two sixes, but he most probably attended the event at the nearby venue, the increasingly popular County Ground.

By this time Charles had won at least one prize for his school work. But when he looked back on this period he was loath to mention personal success in the classroom. Naturally it was his sporting ability that he emphasised:

> While my classmates revealed their talents for the different branches
> of study, I revealed mine for football . . . I took a course in this sport,
> playing in every position.

This clearly indicates that Banister's boys were encouraged to gain a thorough knowledge of the game. Credit for this must go to Ellaby, but also to a man recruited in the autumn of 1888, Cambridge graduate Arthur Denning. During the coming football season the new master successfully took over the running of the team when Ellaby sustained an injury. Ellaby wrote of his replacement: 'In a short time he infused such spirit into the boys that they became equal or superior to some of the best teams.' Denning was also adept at demonstrating football technique. According to Pickford, he was 'an untiring and skilful half-back and a tower of strength', qualities which led him to captain the Hampshire XI. Miller might have had Denning in mind when referring to a course in football.

Charles's first appearance for Banister's football team, it seems, came the season after he made his cricket début for the school in the summer of 1888. Ten weeks after his 14th birthday he may have worn the school's red and black against St Mary's at the Antelope on 9 February 1889. But there is lingering doubt as the Miller at half-back bears no initial. A month later there was clarification. The Banister's XI was at Totton, and, in what appears to be an unchanged midfield trio, the centre-half was C. Miller. If the line-ups are accurate, successive reports show that the boy from Brazil was indeed given different roles on the field before gravitating to the left wing.

In April 1889 for the second Hampshire FA sixes tournament Banister Court increased their entry to three sides. Both Charles and his brother were selected for the C team. In winning their opening match this young side, we are told, 'completely danced round their opponents to the amusement of the spectators'. Throughout the summer, the brothers turned out for the school cricket XI, and at the start of the new football season they continued as team-mates – but not for long. During a cup match in October John broke his collar-bone. It must have been a particularly physical game as another of the school's forwards was reportedly 'badly knocked about'. Charles, however, came out of it unscathed and, for his efforts, earned praise in the local press.

Five months later, the elder Miller was back in the fray, once again competing alongside his brother in the sixes event. But soon, during the summer, the boys' names were listed in a team for the last time. John had just turned 17, and at this point it appears that he left Banister Court. He would have received his last book for good work, dated midsummer 1890, shortly before he made his way back to Brazil. Intriguingly, of the cuttings that Charles kept of his stay in England, the only football one to survive shows the brothers' names in the list of players who participated in that 1890 sixes tournament. The relevant side was pinpointed with a red mark.

In October 1890 Banister Court held its annual prize-giving

ceremony. Masters and boys were joined by parents and a group of local dignitaries which included most of the town's clergy. Successes in the examination room and on the playing-field were noted, before the Dean of Winchester handed out the prizes for academic achievement. Charles was one of the recipients of a valuable book. For the address which followed, an apposite theme had been chosen on the role of sport in boys' education. A newspaper report conveyed the tone of the speech:

> By doing the very best they could in their games they were strengthening not only their muscles, but their brain power as well, and the whole of their bodies and mental functions, and they were also learning to bear with one another – a very important lesson – to stand hard blows without making a row about it, to take a second place, and to continue in well-doing . . .

The Dean's words tell us something about the principles that were central to Charles's schooling. At Banister Court the values of muscular Christianity were adhered to, and a strong feeling of *esprit de corps* prevailed.

By Christmas 1890 Charles had a regular place in Banister's football team. He had for company Frank Ellaby, one of the headmaster's younger brothers. Charles usually appeared on the left wing, Frank either as a half or in the forward line. In the new year the boys contributed to a string of victories, but, in mid-February, for the school's most important game of the season, both were omitted from the line-up. For this Senior Cup semi-final, and with St Mary's the opponents, it was felt that older, stronger players should be used. The tie was played on the County Ground, and Miller saw his school go down 3–0. The goalkeeping of W.P. Cole saved the Court from a heavier defeat, one newspaper reporting that he 'threw the ball out like an expert labourer, with pints of beer in him, excavating a trench'.

By the end of the 1890–91 season St Mary's had confirmed their supremacy in Hampshire football. Having won the Junior Cup three years in succession, they secured victory in the Senior competition at the first attempt. Added to that, in April 1891, the club lifted the sixes trophy for the third time. With the aim of broadening their horizons a decision was taken to enter the English Cup in the following season. Playing resources now needed to be bolstered to cover entry in several competitions, and so a pre-season trial match was arranged for 19 September. Charles's inclusion in the St Mary's B team was the first indication that his talent had been recognised outside the confines of the Court. He appeared in the line-up at inside-left, with Frank Ellaby one of the halves. It was a high-scoring game, and Miller was quick to make an impression:

ST MARY'S A *v* ST MARY'S B

These teams tried conclusions at the County Ground on Saturday. The weather was very inclement, which of course militated against a large 'gate'. The A's kicked off, but the B's soon secured the ball, and taking it up past Carter, Miller sent in a shot which Fry failed to stop. The A's now began to considerably press their opponents, and got into pretty dangerous ground until Richardson relieved by a smart bit of play. For some time the game was of a give-and-take character, Richardson, Hughes and Miller doing some useful work for the B's. Presently the A's again got into dangerous proximity to the B's goal, and Nicholls obtaining the leather sent it through, thus equalising matters. Delamotte added another goal within a few minutes, but the B's now played up, and from a splendid pass by Miller, Wilkins sent in a shot which Ruffell failed to stop. Almost immediately after another goal was obtained from a scuffle, the teams changing over with the B's leading by a goal. The A's, however, soon equalised, and Delamotte scored the leading point after about 20 minutes' play. The juniors were not to be beaten without a hard fight, and presently another goal fell to them, thus making it four all. Two more goals were scored in turn by the A's and the busy B's, but after this the senior eleven showed some superior play, and two goals in quick succession fell to their credit, the game ultimately ending in a victory for them by two goals.

(*Southampton Times*, 26 September 1891)

What with twelve goals and encouraging displays from several of the Saints' newcomers, those who had braved the bad weather certainly got their money's worth. They must have marvelled at the sight of a fragile-looking schoolboy cheekily taking the ball round St Mary's skipper George Carter and then beating the keeper – all this in the opening minute of the game. Not only did Miller score, he shone sufficiently to be given two other mentions by the reporter. Admittedly it was a practice match, but the 16-year-old from São Paulo had seized his opportunity.

When Banister's began their list of friendlies Charles turned out on the left wing and, with new-found confidence, continued to catch the eye. He was already showing the qualities of a creator and a scorer of goals. In the game against Weymouth College on 10 October we are told 'Miller put in some beautiful centres', and ten days later, when Winchester visited the County Ground, he notched a hat-trick. St Mary's, of course, had been following his progress, and for the B's Junior Cup tie against Andover on 7 November he and Frank Ellaby were summoned, making up 'a strong side'. We do not know if Miller was one of Saints' six first-half scorers, but with the visitors replying just twice after the break, his St Mary's début was a winning one.

Turning his attentions to the Hampshire Senior Cup, Charles helped his school to reach the semi-final stage. Avoiding St Mary's in the draw, the Courtiers were paired with one of the army sides, the Medical Staff Corps. As usual, the County Ground was ear-marked for both semi-finals, giving the school team automatic home advantage. But this was of no benefit to Banister's who, with Miller and F. Ellaby forming the left side of the attack, were defeated 5–2 on 10 February. One verdict was that the Courtiers 'had excellent individual players, but many of them were utilised for the occasion only, and combination told its tale . . .' The school really had no option but to enlist guest players for important games; as Pickford later recalled, 'Its weakness lay in not having a big staff of masters and in having to match under-grown boys against hefty opponents.' But it was exactly these conditions that allowed Miller an early start in senior football.

With the season drawing to a close, Charles was picked for Banister Court B, the school's strongest six, in the now familiar Easter tournament. In goal this side had the current Cambridge Blue, Corinthian and future England international L.H. Gay – a notable coup for Christopher Ellaby's recruitment skills. Having brushed aside two opponents in early rounds, Banister's B were faced with a semi-final against Royal Engineers B. The school triumphed in what was described as a 'rare good battle', but not before the organising committee had dismissed a protest by the Engineers over Gay's eligibility. Ellaby was familiar with the rule regarding birth qualification, and the illustrious keeper merely had to affirm that Banister's was indeed situated within a six-mile radius of his birthplace.

As regards the final, the Hampshire FA records confirm that later that day, 2 April 1892, Banister Court B defeated St Mary's A by 4 points (one goal) to 1 (one corner). Dashwood netted the all-important goal, and we can only speculate as to how Charles fared against Saints' backs Carter and Marshall. There were mixed reactions in the press to the unexpected outcome – a 'popular victory' for some, 'disappointing' for those who believed St Mary's had a divine right to silverware. But it was Banister's first trophy for football, of the association variety at least, and for Charles Miller there was a winner's medal to treasure. Little did he know that a fortnight later events would conspire to offer him an even bigger stage on which to perform; in terms of his football education it was to be the first serious test of his ability.

TWO

Corinthian, Saint and Cricketer

Probably the best goalkeeper of the period was L.H. Gay, who also achieved distinction as a wicket-keeper. He was wonderfully clever with his hands and took a football almost as readily as a cricket ball. He was a strong, heavy man who, when taking a goal-kick, nearly always drove the ball 70 or 80 yards.

. . . G.O. Smith . . . is accepted as the greatest centre-forward of his time . . . The secret of his consummate skill, his adroitness in trapping and controlling the ball, his mastery in dribbling, his precision in passing, and his deftness in shooting, was an altogether uncommon faculty of balance . . . Most unselfish of players, he got most of his goals by his own individual finishing efforts, and no forward was ever more artfully adept at drawing his opponents before passing.

From *A History of the Corinthian Football Club*,
F.N.S. Creek, pp.34–37

I played for a number of English amateur clubs, all from Southampton. I battled against teams from other towns, but I especially enjoyed playing against the Corinthians from London because of the superb exhibition given by their stars.

From an interview with Charles Miller, *O Imparcial*,
21 October 1927

A former Hampshire player introducing football to Brazil? It didn't take long for the idea to sink in. Ray Barnes, Hampshire FA Secretary, was soon helping me with my enquiry, initial incredulity fast turning to excitement. The Hampshire FA headquarters is tucked away off a cul-de-sac near the northern fringes of Southampton Common. I had made my way there on a steaming afternoon in August 1996 with the hope of being allowed access to the Association's minute books for Charles Miller's period in England. The minute books, I was told, were there, but before I reached them I made an unexpected discovery.

When Barnes opened the door of one of the cupboards containing his organisation's archives, several mounted photographs tumbled out in front of us. Two were of teams containing Miller; the other was a portrait of Fred Mouncher, a Saints player of the early 1900s. On the reverse side there was a signed dedication: 'To C.W. Miller Esq. of St Paulo' (*sic*). Whether Charles ever received this photo will never be known; it was dated October 1924 and was a gift from F.G. Mouncher – 'in remembrance of my son Fred, who died on February 19th 1918'. Charles's friendship with the Mounchers is another mystery that must remain unravelled.

One of the team pictures, paling with age, shows the victorious Banister Court six of 1892; the other is of the Hampshire XI that faced the Corinthians in 1894. In the photo of the county side Miller occupies one of the seats as does Banister's master, A.W. Denning; and standing at the far left is Ray Barnes's distinguished predecessor, William Pickford. Barnes had been storing his Association's archives in the recently completed office extension of the Hampshire FA building. It was a matter of days before this annexe would be officially opened and the house named after Pickford.

Combing the contents of the cupboards I found a collection of Pickford's newspaper articles – 'The Veteran', as he styled himself in the early years of this century, reminiscing on Hampshire football. If the Sixes Tournament of 1892 provided Miller with a first taste of success, another high point was his selection not long after for St Mary's A team. The 17-year-old was one of Saints' scorers in a 3–1 defeat of the army's Aldershot Division, one report stating that Charles 'gave unmistakable evidence of becoming a very useful wing player'. Forty-eight hours later and both of these achievements had been eclipsed. The circumstances surrounding Miller's representative début are truly anomalous. Pickford, in a piece entitled 'Famous Hants Forwards', explains why:

> Hampshire were playing the Corinthians at Southampton, and the latter had arrived with only four forwards. Miller, then a schoolboy at Banister Court, was recommended, and so well did he adapt

himself to the style of the famous amateurs that he was one of the features of the match.

The XI to which Charles belonged on that Wednesday afternoon, 20 April, despite being under-strength, contained players of the top order. In goal there was L.H. Gay, at half-back C.B. Fry and C. Wreford-Brown, and up front 'the nonpareil of Victorian centre-forwards' G.O. Smith. Some of them, on the previous Saturday, were part of a Corinthians side that had played and lost against Queen's Park, an annual fixture which brought back memories of former England *v* Scotland clashes. Had Miller's father been at the County Ground perhaps he would have playfully chided his son for turning out for a team that smacked of the auld enemy.

Pickford was not alone in providing a glowing summary of Charles's first performance as a Corinthian. Or could it be that he was the author of the report that appeared on the Saturday after the game in the *Bournemouth Visitors' Directory*? On learning that Hampshire right-back George Carter was 'in splendid form', the reader might have deduced that the visitors' left flank had been kept at bay. Several sentences later, though, it emerges that Miller was indeed outstanding. First, there is description of the Corinthians' inside-forwards:

> The forwards combined grandly, and the neat way in which Veitch, Gosling and Smith got rid of the ball and made progress was the subject of much commendation from the spectators. It did not strike us that Veitch particularly exerted himself, but when he did he generally got the better of the exchanges. He had as partner little Charlie Miller, of Banister Court, and the way in which the youngster fed him, and the accuracy of his passes, was as good as some of the more brilliant work of the others.

Veitch it was who scored the only goal of the match just before the final whistle. Perhaps it was during the course of the afternoon that 'little' Charles was given the nickname 'Nipper'. According to Pickford, Charles, having impressed the Corinthians' founder and Secretary N.L. Jackson, played at least one more game for the gentleman-amateurs. But for now he could concentrate on cricket.

Miller was already a regular member of the Banister's cricket XI. His performances may have been low-key in comparison to his exploits in the winter game; however, there were signs that he was equally at home with bat and ball. Certainly, his part in the Court's

historic win in June over their rivals from the Grammar School –
when chasing a total of 69, his side had lost seven wickets for 28 –
merited comment in the local press:

> Amidst great excitement C.W. Miller and W.H. Hodges pulled the
> match out of the fire, and the eighth wicket fell for 92. This is the
> first victory of Banister's over their opponents at cricket, and the
> greatest praise is due to the two batsmen who so pluckily won them
> the game.

Besides scoring a half-century Charles took five opposition wickets.
Displays such as this, which, as with football, took place in close
proximity to or on the County Ground, could not fail to be noticed.
What is more, there was a convenient link between the County
Cricket Club and St Mary's: both organisations had the ubiquitous
and influential Dr Russell Bencraft to administer their affairs. One of
Southampton's most prominent citizens, Bencraft had in the 1880s
run the County Club almost single-handedly; and it was through his
good offices that Miller would later play cricket at a higher level.

In the 1890s, football in Southampton did not resume until mid-
September – but not everyone welcomed its reappearance. In 1892 one
Freemantle resident wrote to the *Southampton Times* complaining about
'the resumption of the nuisance' – i.e. football – on one particular
street corner. 'Youths and boys of all ages – especially on Sundays –
lounge about for hours, and do not hesitate to insult respectable
passers-by.' Further police action was called for to put a stop to these
boisterous kick-abouts. Not only was the game increasing in
popularity – a fact that had necessitated change at national level that
included the introduction of the penalty-kick and the use of goal-nets
– but in the south a different attitude to players was in evidence.

Not surprisingly, on the south coast, ambitious St Mary's were the
first club to court controversy over the issue of professionalism. To
start with, they had shown solidarity with the south's first professional
club, Woolwich Arsenal, by playing a friendly with them in February
1892. For Arsenal, punishment for paying players a year before had
resulted in expulsion from the London FA. But in Hampshire the
governing body's line on 'inducements' was philosophical. In 1888,
three years after professionalism's legalisation in the north, the Hampshire FA had allowed a club in Winchester to field a professional:
'Nobody was a penny the worse,' wrote Pickford of the pioneering
decision. Yet, four years later, the signing of Saints' first professional was

not made public – despite transfer talk in the press.

On the day St Mary's kicked off the 1892–93 season, 17 September, it was reported in the *Southampton Times* that their attempts to register Freemantle's Ridges as a professional had fallen through. Ariel, doyen of the local sports correspondents, admitted he was at a loss to know 'what particular code of ethics should apply to a football player'. He did, however, express a view on recruitment methods when he wrote: 'A good deal of sharp practice is resorted to in many places in the case of professionals, but so far as amateurs are concerned I think a man should be allowed to please his own fancy as to which of any number of teams anxious to secure his services he should play for.' Doubtless there was cunning in the way Saints had persuaded Jack Dollin to join them from Freemantle – he was, so he later recalled, 'paid £1 a week and found a job'. Either Ariel was sworn to silence, or the details of the player's terms had somehow escaped his attention.

For St Mary's opening game, on the County Ground, Dollin was included in the forward line – as was Charles Miller. It was to be an inauspicious beginning to Saints' life as a professional club. A number of regulars were missing, among them Farwell who was 'prevented playing, owing to the alteration of the business hours at the establishment where he is engaged'. If the St Mary's directors saw the signing of Dollin as a necessary step for progress, the impression their players' appearance gave was misleading – 'a scratch lot' was how Ariel described them. 'Two of them played in white shirts, one in some other colour, and I believe there was still another uniform besides the cherry squares.' There may have been occasional 'brilliant work' put in by the home attack, but it had no bearing on the result, a 4–0 drubbing by the soldiers of the South Stafford Regiment.

When it came to Banister's fixtures, Charles and his fellow Courtiers fared little better. For the game at Freemantle on 1 October the school had intended to turn out with L.H. Gay in goal, but come the kick-off and Gay was missing from the line-up. Miller must have seen little of the ball for his side's defence was by far its busiest department. With a substitute keeper performing heroics, the loss was restricted to 3–0. Nevertheless, Ariel was at pains to point out that of the two teams Banister's had played 'the prettiest game'. Further consolation came when the line-up was announced for Hampshire's forthcoming match against Sussex. The Court's master in charge of football, Arthur Denning, had retained his place at half-back, and Miller, on the strength of what he accomplished in April, was to play left-wing.

Unexpectedly, it was Charles's partnership with a Freemantle player, Ridges, that proved to be the highlight of Hampshire's encounter with their easterly neighbours. Late withdrawals had meant a move for Ridges from full-back to inside-forward. During a 'finely contested' first half at the County Ground we are told that 'successive runs were made by the Hants forwards, Miller and Ridges playing well on the left'. It was scoreless at the interval. When play resumed, Hampshire laid siege to their opponents' goal, and after 30 minutes two opportune strikes put them in command. Study of both Bournemouth and Southampton reports is necessary in order to ascertain the identity of the scorer:

> Ultimately the ball was taken down in a fine run, in which most of the Hants forwards participated, and although they were repulsed on the first attempt Miller headed the ball right through, and thus obtained the honour of opening the score for the home county.
>
> (*Times*)

> No. 1 gained, No. 2 was not long in following. Out of a loose scrum the ball came to the feet of Miller, and with a neat screw shot he sent the ball through the corner, one of the visiting defence assisting it on its passage by an ill-timed head.
>
> (*Visitors' Directory*)

Still to turn 18, Charles had more than justified his selection, and before the game was over he had contributed to Hampshire's final goal in a 3–0 win. Ariel thought Miller was 'rather light to partner Ridges on the wing, but he played a fine game, and did good service'; while the report in the *Bournemouth Visitors' Directory* concluded with the words 'Ridges and Miller combined capitally'. For Charles, the County Ground in Southampton was beginning to feel like part of his second home at nearby Banister Court.

Ariel wasn't alone in referring to Miller's slight build. Perhaps this was something the Hampshire selectors discussed when they decided to leave Miller out of the team to play Surrey. At any rate, a 'strong side' was chosen, including the Old Carthusian and county cricketer Captain E.G. Wynyard at centre-forward. Although Hampshire romped to victory, there was further reorganisation for the next match – and a place found for Miller. For the *Hampshire Independent* journalist who had concluded that the Courtier was 'yet too light to be advantageously incorporated in a senior eleven', Charles had the perfect riposte. Significantly, it was Wynyard, a future Corinthian, who provided support. Berks and Bucks were the victims, and the newspaper that had suggested Charles be excluded from the Hampshire XI duly changed its tune:

> One of the most agreeable features of the game was that 'little Milier' was one of the finest forwards on the ground. He not only scored twice but assisted in getting a third. He and Captain Wynyard were fair 'teasers' for their opponents, who were quite outplayed by them.

With all the fuss being made over Miller's impact on football in Hampshire it would not have been premature had his 'graduation' in the game taken place at the end of 1892. After all, he had broken into the county side and was a member of St Mary's squad of players. But this year would not only be remembered for unrivalled sporting achievement. Assuming Charles was kept informed of events in São Paulo, two particular pieces of news would have reached him, each of widely differing import. One caused a door to close on the past and perhaps reinforced his resolve; from the other, parallels could be drawn with the furtherance of his football knowledge. First, there was the death of his brother John in March. Then, later in the year, Charles may have been sent the article that appeared in the *Diário Popular* describing the prodigious talent on the piano of his six-year-old cousin Antonietta Rudge. Her teacher enthused: 'What and how she plays . . . leaves the intelligent spectator immersed in a world of extraordinary meditations.' Charles's wing-play was provoking a similar search for superlatives.

In the spring of 1893 the Corinthians once again exhibited their skills on the County Ground. On this occasion Miller wore the crimson and blue colours of Hampshire. He renewed his partnership with Captain Wynyard; however, the two of them spent far more time watching their opponents than trying to give Gay a save to make. According to the *Southampton Times*, 'the Corinthians appeared to be always on the ball' and 'their passing was simply superb and quite baffled the home county forwards'. The visitors, numbering G.O. Smith, Veitch and Wreford-Brown in their ranks, won a 'very tame game' by four goals to nil. As Miller intimated in the interview quoted at the start of this chapter, it wasn't so much the results of these matches that mattered, it was the pleasure derived from sharing the same pitch with some of England's finest players.

Three weeks later, on 26 April, Stoke became the first English League club to visit Southampton. During the past season, St Mary's had managed a win and a draw against the professionals of Woolwich Arsenal. Victory against the men from the Potteries would be fresh evidence of the Saints' progress and an antidote to their debilitating defeat by Freemantle in the final of the Senior Cup. St Mary's were forced to make one change to the side that had beaten Cowes in the Hants CCC benefit competition. Price came in for the injured Carter; so Charles Miller kept his place on the left wing. In inimitable fashion, Ariel captured the mood at the County Ground:

> A stranger to the game might be pardoned if judging from the enthusiasm displayed on this notable occasion, he jumped to the conclusion that it was a great demonstration at the inauguration match of the national game. The people were packed round the ropes like peas in a pod, and the grandstand was full to overflowing. There was quite a distinguished company present. His Worship the Mayor started the ball for St Mary's, and I must congratulate Mr Lemon upon the scientific send-off he gave to the leather. When the Saints are hard pushed for a full-back they must next apply at the Municipal Offices.

But there the fun stopped as the writer proceeded to explain how the Saints, despite a 'plucky' performance, were overwhelmed 8–0. Miller had one of his toughest assignments, pitted against England right-back Tom Clare. Indeed, of Miller and his team-mates, only centre-forward Dorkin appeared to hold his own. We may wonder, therefore, what exactly St Mary's were subjected to that afternoon, what some of the differences were between the professional and the amateur game? Ariel provides us with an insight:

> The points which struck me in regard to the playing of the Stoke men were these. The backs never kicked the ball hard for the sake of showing how far they could kick, but used discrimination, and landed the ball where it could be used to most advantage if it were only ten yards away. The half-backs waited on the forwards like shadows, and the forwards themselves were in their places and understood each other's play as if it were done by rule of three. They passed most unselfishly, and never charged unless it were absolutely necessary to do so.

Not only did the game fire the public's imagination, it was 'all that could be desired financially'. From the point of view of the St Mary's directors, lucrative friendlies such as this would raise the club's profile and provide funds for buying new players. At this stage in his life, Charles Miller didn't think twice about turning out for a club whose professional aspirations were obvious. But ten years on, Miller, the leading light of Brazil's first football league, had strictly amateur credentials. And this adherence to amateur principles would harden as increased competitiveness in the Brazilian game led inevitably to professionalism. It was as a member of the Hampshire FA's executive committee that Miller first began to mull over the pros and cons of professional sport.

Each year, from the foundation of the Hampshire FA in 1887, one of Banister Court's senior boys, as football secretary, accompanied headmaster Christopher Ellaby to committee meetings. Charles was already fulfilling secretarial duties for his school's cricket team when, in July 1893, he attended the Association's AGM at the Adelaide Hotel in Southampton. One month later, Miller was elected onto the Hampshire FA Executive Committee. Of the four others chosen to represent the Southampton Division, two were from St Mary's – club secretary A.C. Knight and treasurer H.B. Johns. In his annual report, Pickford gave as a reason for the Association's 'sound financial basis' the record gate in the Senior Cup final; but he warned against the adoption of gate-sharing among clubs competing in the latter stages of the competition. 'Spoils to the victors is all very well,' he wrote, 'provided it be not at the expense of the efficiency of the governing body.' Another concern, unaired yet imminent, was the potential effect of St Mary's professionalism on the Association's coffers.

By the start of the 1893–94 season St Mary's had bought several new players. It might have been the club's advertisement in the sporting press that led to Angus moving from Ardwick and Offer signing from Woolwich Arsenal. Both were forwards, and so the services of Banister Court's 'little' winger were not required for the campaign opener. Undeterred, Charles 'showed that he was in splendid shooting form' with three goals in Banister's opening match. Moving from wing to inside-left he began to score goals at the same rate Romário has done in the 1990s for Flamengo in the Rio championship. Admittedly, in both cases, the strength of the opposition was variable. But in contrast to Romário, Miller, in a team still composed mainly of schoolboys, was usually up against heavier and harder opponents.

Thankfully, those details of Charles Miller's last football season for

Banister's were recorded away from the columns of the broadsheets, and survive to this day in a bound volume in the Southampton Special Collections Library. Reports and line-ups for the 'Christmas Term' appear in the first number of the *Banister Court School Magazine* published in December 1893. In the space of two months Miller notched three hat-tricks, twice he was on target five times and on one occasion, against Cavendish, he scored six. In assessing the team performances, the chronicler singled out a 3–2 win away to Portsmouth Grammar School, played in gale-force winds. Charles netted two goals, the first after he had made 'a magnificent run half the length of the field'.

Concluding the football content of the new magazine there were brief pen pictures of the Court's squad of players. For the most part, the description of C.W. Miller certainly chimes with reality – 'wonderfully quick dribbler and brilliant shot' and 'scores goals with great consistency'. But in an effort to provide balanced comment, the compiler also added the incongruous 'might work harder at times'. Two other senior players, full-backs Arthur Denning and Frank Ellaby, were treated in a similar vein. The former was 'inclined to overtrain', while the latter 'has improved greatly, but is still inclined to dribble'. Ultimately, in the miscellaneous section entitled 'School Notes', we learn that Miller has been awarded his county cap.

After the match with Sussex in October had been rained off, the Hampshire XI took to the field, Surrey's Guildford field to be exact, on 8 November. On opening the scoring, Hampshire then conceded five unanswered goals until, as the *Southampton Times* tells us, 'just on the close Miller put in a fine run and scored'. The selectors' reaction to the 5–2 reverse was to make six changes for the next game – but Miller retained his place on the left wing. On 6 December Berks and Bucks were the visitors to the County Ground, and although they brought a 'comparatively weak' team and had to borrow two players, Hampshire made hard work of victory, moving ahead 3–1 late in the game. The Banister winger's best moments were as creator: 'Miller made a splendid run down the field and centred to Evans, who sent in a shot which struck the crossbar . . .'; 'a pretty bit of play on the part of Miller and Lowman followed, the latter ultimately shooting over the crossbar.' Transferring his energies from the pitch to the committee room, Charles appears to have been cautious and restrained. Hardly surprising, given the imposing presence of skilled administrators such as Pickford and Dr Bencraft.

On 13 December the Courtier contributed to one of the items on an agenda being discussed by the Hampshire FA Executive. Once the season got under way, much of the committee's business was taken up with resolving protests. In this instance, Bournemouth Wanderers had written to the Executive asking to withdraw two protests. Consent was given, and another proposal made:

> The Hon. Sec. moved, and Mr Miller seconded, 'That the fees be returned, and that a warning be given that in future cases the Executive would take different action.' Mr Maberly proposed that the club be fined 10s. Mr Johns seconded, but the amendment was lost, and the resolution was carried.

Charles shows lenience in dealing with this case and his action suggests that he was not one of the money-motivated members. His input is relatively modest. But this, it seems, is the only reference in the published minutes to Miller actively participating in the proceedings of the Hampshire Executive. For that, it is significant.

So to 1894 and the months leading up to Charles's homecoming. Before Banister's resumed their fixtures he had a game for the Saints on 20 January. According to Ariel, Miller 'made an excellent centre-forward', a position he subsequently filled for his school and for Hampshire. He continued to get his name on the scoresheet with startling regularity, and in the run-up to the Easter programme he chalked up his sixth goal in six starts for the county XI. We are told that, with the Dorset defence hesitant, 'Miller quietly tipped the ball into the net – very gently, as if it was of no account'. A fortnight later, on 31 March, Charles found himself on the left-wing facing Corinthian and England international A.H. Harrison. This fixture at Dean Park, Bournemouth, turned out to be the first in a succession of swan songs.

This was the Hampshire *v* Corinthians match that Charles referred to in an interview with the São Paulo-based *Gazeta Esportiva* – 50 years on, almost to the day. He was pictured in his study, sitting at his desk, a framed photograph of that very same Hampshire side on the wall behind him. He probably dug out a report of the game to show the visiting journalist. If it was Ariel's version, then, in light of Charles's noted modesty, the phrase 'Miller was often brilliant' would not have been pointed out. An image, reinforcing Ariel's comment, was included in the *Southern Referee*:

> The left wing were by far the best, and the run-ups were almost
> always made by this wing. Miller played a beautiful game, and to see
> the way he got the best of Harrison (who could rest his arm on
> Miller's head) was a treat.

Indeed, of the three goals scored by Hampshire, two stemmed from
Miller gaining possession. On another day, beating England keeper
Gay three times might have resulted in a win. But the Corinthians ran
up six, centre-forward Sandilands, another England cap, helping
himself to four goals. The visitors' Easter tour had ended, their sixth
game in six days.

For Charles, the day was memorable in more ways than one. Before
the game, he had attended his final meeting of the Hampshire FA
Executive held on the terrace at the side of the Grand Hotel. Part of
the agenda entailed fixing dates for the next season's cup competitions; and as the members deliberated, Miller was most likely considering his own future. Later, following the 'pretty display of football', the
committee organised a dinner for the Hampshire players, reserves and
officials – 'an excellent menu' being complemented by speeches, toasts
and songs. As the *Southern Referee* recorded, there was a colourful conclusion to the evening:

> Last scene of all was that of 20 worthy members of the executive and
> of the team, who had to leave by train, clambering into the recesses
> and on to the roof of the hotel bus. A howl of despair from the
> interior when the weighty treasurer of St Mary's squeezed inside
> was drowned by the cheers of a small knot of locals, and so as the
> bus whirled away, with its sporting load, into the darkness, ended an
> eventful day.

When São Paulo's footballers first entertained their counterparts
from Rio, just after the turn of the century, the tone of the occasion
was not dissimiliar.

A week after the Corinthians game Charles Miller had a final taste
of competitive sixes action on his beloved County Ground. Along with
Denning and Frank Ellaby he formed the nucleus of Banister's best
side. But hopes of another trophy were dashed – inevitably by a six
representing St Mary's. The circumstances surrounding the Courtiers'
exit were controversial, and passions out of character were aroused. In
the Banister's magazine the facts are presented in incontrovertible
manner:

The B team were drawn against Freemantle B in the first round and had no great difficulty in defeating the latter by three goals and two corners to nil, or 14 points to none. Miller and Page did the scoring for us, Miller especially distinguishing himself by his tricky play. Mr Denning and Ellaby at back were very safe. In the next round our B team met St Mary's B the ultimate winners of the Cup. This tie was watched with the greatest eagerness by the crowd, the supporters of Banister's cheering on their representatives to the bitter end; and bitter it was, for we were beaten by two goals and one corner to one goal and one corner, or by nine points to five; but we had every reason to be dissatisfied as Miller shot at goal, the ball getting past the goalkeeper, who eventually scooped it out, the referee ignoring our appeal for a goal, and later on, Ward, who was lurking in our goal offside, put the ball through for Saints; this was given a goal. The referee was certainly inefficient, as he took no notice of one of the Saints' forwards fouling and eventually collaring by the back one of our backs. Thus our set for this year.

Press reports of the tournament do not state that a protest was lodged, so we may assume that defeat, when it occurred, was taken on the chin. Even so, there must have been substance to the allegations of bad refereeing and unsportsmanlike behaviour by the Saints. Had the account been spurious, Headmaster Christopher Ellaby, a respected Vice-President of the Hampshire FA, would surely have prevented its publication.

Ill feeling between Banister's and St Mary's, if it existed, must have quickly dissipated, for, on 18 April, Miller was included in the Saints team that faced the Lancaster Regiment in the semi-final of the Hampshire CCC Charity Cup. Ironically, with Ward away on holiday, it was the left-wing position that Charles occupied – Ward being the scorer of the disputed goal in the sixes event. Two games were needed to separate the teams, and in the replay, with Charles keeping his place, the soldiers were beaten 3–0. In the final, on Monday, 23 April, St Mary's met another army side, the 15th Company Royal Artillery. In what turned out to be his last competitive match in England, Miller was particularly conspicuous.

The County Cricket Club would have hoped for a decent attendance to boost the proceeds from the event, but bad weather put paid to that. Even so, we can take it that there was dutiful support from Banister Court at the County Ground to witness Charles's wizardry on the wing. In highlighting Miller's speed and fine crosses the *South-*

ampton Observer's correspondent saw fit to mention him by name seven times in a six-paragraph write-up – an impressive recognition, despite the writer's predilection for one adjective. Besides setting up chances, the Courtier displayed an ability to go it alone and test the opposing keeper. During one second-half attack we are told that 'Miller . . . made a splendid single-handed run on the left, and shot for goal with a splendid high 'un, but the goaly just reached it, and got it away safely'. It was the nearest Charles came to scoring in Saints' 5–1 triumph. On the following Saturday, 28 April, gold medals were given to the winners at St Mary's final 'smoking concert' of the season. (These social events or 'smokers' were opportunities for club members to gather and smoke, and usually comprised items of entertainment and monologues.)

The final act on the pitch had taken place three days before at the County Ground – a venue described by Ariel as 'popular and now historic'. For Charles, a page in his own history was turning, as he played his final match in St Mary's scarlet and white colours. For the return of 'Leaguers' Stoke, the Saints side was identical to the one that had claimed the Charity Cup. Playing before 'a large and enthusiastic concourse of spectators', the home team twice went in front; but eventually the professionals, albeit below-strength, prevailed 3–2. According to the *Southampton Times*, the Saints' second goal was provided by their left-winger – 'Miller doing the needful after some capital passing by Nineham, Angus and Dorkin'. The report ended with the view that St Mary's 'brilliant play . . . was a fitting termination to their very successful season'.

With another football season over, Charles may have been feeling that now was the time to return to South America. Indeed, on 5 May, one newspaper actually reported that he was 'about to sail for Buenos Aires' – although 'bound for Santos' would have been more accurate. If Charles had intended leaving, he had second thoughts, and was soon seeing to the smooth-running of Banister's cricket fixtures. During the coming months, Miller gave several notable performances for his school, including scoring a century in one match and having bowling figures of 9–41 in another. But, as with football, it was his inclusion in representative sides that marked him out as a specially gifted sports-man. The zenith arrived in mid-June when Charles appeared in the MCC and Ground XI which took on Hampshire at the County Ground.

Presumably Dr Bencraft, captaining the county side, was the one who recommended Miller to the MCC – the Londoners having arrived a player short. The *Hampshire Independent*'s report of the first day's play was among the cuttings Charles took with him to Brazil. It stated that 'Miller played confidently until at 94 he was c[aught] and b[owled] by Cave' – one of the Hampshire professionals. In the annals of the Marylebone Cricket Club a scorecard of the match shows that 'C. Miller Esq.' made a First Innings score of 16. But curiously, in direct equivalence to Miller's début for the Corinthians, his name is not in the club's list of participating players. MCC Curator Stephen Green has confirmed as much. Among the other cricket clubs with which Charles was briefly associated were South Hants, Hampshire Hogs and Hampshire Club and Ground – and all feature in his sadly depleted collection of clippings.

In August 1894 there is an indication that Charles considered prolonging his stay beyond the end of the cricket season. He had already attended a meeting of Hampshire FA Secretaries, in May, to arrange fixtures for the coming winter; and, at the end of July, he was present at the Association's AGM. One of the rule changes was the renaming of the governing body: the Hampshire FA Council. Soon, voting papers for new officers were being sent to clubs. Charles, it appears, was contesting one of four seats in the Southampton district. On 18 August, the *Southampton Observer* predicted that the 'duel' for representation would be between St Mary's and Freemantle, the assumption being that 'Charley [*sic*] Miller is not likely to be disturbed'. The count, however, revealed otherwise.

Southampton's two most powerful clubs, St Mary's and Freemantle, each had two candidates elected, 'Miller failing to secure a place'. We shall never know if this result influenced Charles's decision to pack his bags just over a month later. For the time being, he continued to play cricket; and when football clubs began their pre-season friendlies, tellingly, Miller persisted with the summer sport. There was talk in the press of him joining Freemantle. But this never materialised; and when St Mary's turned out for their opening game on 8 September, bizarrely, Charles was playing in one of two cricket matches on another area of the County Ground. The *Observer*'s Sir Bevis remarked: 'With the exception of the scorers and the umpires, hardly a solitary person took any interest in the cricket, attention being solely centred in the football match.' A 13–0 scoreline in the Saints' favour was the reason why.

When Charles finally did dust down his football boots it was for Banister's first match on 29 September. The Courtiers were defeated 5–0, and on the same day Sir Bevis touchingly bemoaned the fact that

Miller was on the point of returning home. At the beginning of the item, his proposed link to Freemantle is implied:

> I understood that Charlie Miller, the smart left-winger of Banister's, might help the team this season, but I now hear that to-day is likely to be his last Saturday in Old England, for on Friday next he purposes to sail for his South American home. We shall be sorry to lose this ardent and thorough sportsman from our games, which he has graced, and I shall only be voicing the wishes of my readers when I express the hope that he will have a pleasant voyage and abundant success in his new surroundings.

Charles played two more games for his school, before boarding the SS *Magdalena* on Friday, 5 October.

Two days before, the Hampshire Football Council had convened for the first time. At the end of the minutes it is recorded that 'the hon. sec. is authorised to write to Mr C. Miller (Banister Court), on his leaving Hants, expressing the thanks of the Association for his past services on the executive and in county matches'. Perhaps the two footballs that Charles bears with him to Brazil are a postscript to William Pickford's bittersweet note. Understandably, the mention in the Banister's magazine of Miller's return to Brazil is far more effusive. The 'Introductory' to the October 1894 edition declares that he is 'probably the best forward player in county football, and in cricket is not far from county form, while he has been a most efficient secretary of both cricket and football'.

When Pickford later recalls Charles Miller's début for the Corinthians in 1892, he makes several more comments:

> From that moment his name was made, and, what is more, he lived up to it. His work on the left wing was most artistic, and always better in good company.

How appropriate that the man credited with bringing football to Brazil is described as an artist by an esteemed and knowledgeable *aficionado*. Today, 'football art' is synonymous with the Brazilian game, the '*chaleira*' perhaps the oldest skill in a player's bag of tricks. Perhaps Miller's missing St Mary's Southern League première on 6 October wasn't so important after all. He sensed there was work to be done in São Paulo.

THREE

From Lore to League

'How do you play this game?' some of them asked.
'Which ball are we going to play with?' enquired others.
'I've got the ball. We just need to fill it,' answered Miller.
'Fill it with what?' they asked.
'With air,' retorted Charles.
'Then you go and fetch it, and I'll fill it,' someone replied.

Charles Miller's version of setting up his first kick-
about in São Paulo as told to *O Cruzeiro c.*1953

When we played the first inter-state game in Rio, in 1902, on
returning to São Paulo I asked the newspapers to publish
something about this match which we had won. But the reply of
O Estado de São Paulo, Correio Paulistano, Platéia *and* Diário
Popular *was unanimous: 'We're not interested in this subject!'*
And how different it is today!

Charles Miller, in an interview in the
Gazeta Esportiva, 11 March 1944

Bowls and the calmness the sport exudes (reference to an 'end' were among the first words I heard uttered there); carefully maintained flower-beds and a trellised path; the strong smell of polish in the entrance hall; shepherd's pie – a fixture on the list of culinary suggestions. Slap in the middle of South America's largest metropolis sits an enclosed area, at most, the size of three football pitches. It's a space which seems impervious to the heady pace of life outside its gates. São Paulo Athletic Club – or SPAC as it's popularly known – possesses an ambience that is the antithesis of that in the neighbouring streets. A bastion of bygone Britishness, it was here, at the beginning of this century, that one of the first competitive football games was played in Brazil.

There had been six matches in the inaugural Liga Paulista when São Paulo Athletic entertained SC Internacional on 8 June 1902. The British Club had been leasing the site, just off Rua da Consolação, one of the city's main arteries, for five years. Before that, its sporting activities had taken place at a property belonging to an American, Charles Dulley. Most likely it was on the Dulley estate that Charles Miller first encountered organised sport in São Paulo, following his return in October 1894. But at that time, among the British, it was cricket rather than football that held sway.

Even before he boarded the SS *Magdalena*, Charles had probably been reassured by his family that in São Paulo he would be able to satisfy his passion for sport. Since the 1870s, cricket matches had been organised by members of the Rio and São Paulo British communities and several clubs had been established. It must have been gratifying for Miller to learn that some of his relatives had participated in the founding of São Paulo Athletic Club – among them his cousin, a former pupil of Banister Court, William Fox Rule. Also present at the launch in May 1888 was William Speers, the Superintendent of the São Paulo Railway Company. Charles not only had an easy entry into SPAC; through a combination of his father and Speers he was found employment, a post in the railway stores department.

From playing two or sometimes three cricket or football matches a week, suddenly Charles had to make do with a game each weekend – if that. As if arranging meaningful cricket fixtures wasn't difficult enough, in 1892 the keenness of the SPAC devotees was sorely tested when the match against a visiting Argentine XI was washed out without a ball being bowled. A measure of the challenges facing these pioneering sportsmen can be glimpsed in a letter published in England in *Cricket: A Weekly Record of the Game* on 31 May 1894. The correspondent was a Mr A. Richards, the Honorary Secretary of Santos Athletic Club:

> Thinking it might interest you to hear how cricket is carried on in these warm regions by the 'balance' of the English and Americans left over from the ravages of the 'Yellow Jack', I take the liberty of sending you herewith our cricket fixture card for the coming season. As you will see, we have to arrange or rather manufacture matches between the members on account of the distance to any

other cricket-playing community, the only outside matches we are able to play being against Rio de Janeiro, São Paulo and Campinas. Our club was only started in August 1890, so is not a very old institution, but there is plenty of enthusiasm, cricket being looked forward to as only Englishmen can look forward to it, even with the great difficulties we have to overcome, the greatest being that we are obliged to play on the sea beach, which is luckily very hard and makes a really good and true pitch with cocoa-nut matting laid down.

As a member of the SPAC cricket XI, Charles may have encountered the Santos wicket during one of the matches on Mr Richards's fixture card. Twenty years later, the footballers of Exeter City, *en route* for the Argentine, would have an entirely different ordeal on the Santos sands.

In addition to cricket, the British Club promoted baseball games and athletics meetings which included bicycle races. In similar fashion, sporting events for São Paulo's German expatriates were organised by a Gymnastics Club. It appears that membership of these bodies was restricted to citizens of the required social standing and nationality. In the early-1890s, for the 'native' Brazilian seeking a sporting diversion, there were essentially three options: for the better off, a visit to the Jockey Club; for the wider populace, the sport of pelota, and later cycling.

It was the increasing interest in cycling that led to the powerful Prado family constructing a velodrome on their land on Rua da Consolação. Antônio Prado's Veloce Club Olimpico was the forerunner of the prestigious and still exclusive Club Athletico Paulistano. The first cycle races were held at the Velódromo from 1895, some of the events attracting 'Brazilian riders belonging to the São Paulo social élite' and 'the most famous champions of European cycling'. Inevitably, Charles Miller was among the participants. In March 1997, Helena Miller showed me a silver medal won by her father. On one side there was the outline of a bicycle with the name of Prado's club; on the other, laurels encompassing the words 'to the second winner in the ninth race'. It was dated '18-4-97'. In the first decade of this century the Velódromo became for Miller what the County Ground in Southampton had been.

Not long after returning to Brazil, Charles corresponded with his old school; and, round about the end of February 1895, he would almost certainly have received the fourth issue of the *Banister Court*

School Magazine. The Notes at the end, while mentioning the doings of Old Boys anywhere from the Cape to Canada, state that 'Charles Miller gained two prizes at some Athletic Sports on the voyage to Brazil, and has played in some cricket matches at Sao Paulo [*sic*]'. The magazine's first article is a report of the Annual Distribution of Prizes held in October. There is the usual mixture of compliments and thanks, and then, sandwiched between lists of examination successes and prize-winners, there is a rare, particularly touching, encomium:

> But the training of school life did not aim merely at success in examinations. They hoped to form men of firm and reliant character, and such a man he ventured to say would be found in one who had just left. Charles Miller was not only a splendid player, but he had managed the business in connection with the school games down to the very day before he sailed. He had also taken an interest in the management of county football. It was efficiency such as this, and what was far better, the unselfishness and industry that it implied, that made a man deserve success in life.

This comment not only underlines Headmaster Ellaby's enduring enthusiasm for football and appreciation for the work of a more than able practitioner, but it also serves as further evidence of the kudos that Charles enjoyed. Three pages on, there is a report of Miller's last game for the school at Weymouth on 4 October 1894. Banister's went down by the odd goal in three, the account concluding: '. . . C. Miller's . . . loss to the team will be very great indeed.' The writer then emphasised: 'For the last three seasons he has been one of the most brilliant and consistent forwards in the county, and last year obtained about 70 per cent of our goals.' A month after his copy of the magazine arrived, Charles was organising the historic 'first' football game in Brazil.

Of course, there are reports, in the 1870s, of kick-abouts between British sailors in Brazilian ports – and a version of the Eton wall game being introduced by a priest at a school in the town of Itu. But these instances of football – and there were others involving the employees of British companies in Rio and São Paulo – were inconsequential and transient. This is the conclusion drawn by historians such as Tomás Mazzoni and Paulo Varzea. What set Miller apart was his determination to create the conditions to play the game at which he'd excelled in England, to have the sport incorporated into the activities of an existing club and eventually to ensure that that organisation was at the forefront of football in São Paulo. It was March 1895, the onset of autumn in Brazil. After enjoying an extended cricket season, Charles's thoughts now turned to football.

Certain preparations were necessary before a recognisable game took place. Like the story of his arrival in Santos, Miller's charming account of preparing the ball for the first kick-about may well be apocryphal. But in the absence of detailed records, such episodes from football folklore assume importance. From the various versions of the game's inception in Brazil, several details ring true. To begin with, Charles persuaded a group of SPAC members – in the main British workers from the São Paulo Railway, the London Bank and the Gas Company – to give football a go. It was deemed inappropriate to use the Dulley property for the first familiarisation session. Instead, Miller and his friends opted to share a field with the mules which pulled the city's trams. This land, running alongside the River Tamanduateí, was the Várzea do Carmo, to the east of the city centre in the Brás district where Charles was born.

Two other features seem tenable: there were barely enough players for a six-a-side, and the ball used was one of the ones Charles had been given by William Pickford. Several kick-abouts-cum-practices were held on the Várzea do Carmo, culminating in a game between two denominated teams. Miller told Paulo Varzea what he remembered about this occasion:

> As soon as we felt more experienced and the number of players had increased, I got the group together for the first controlled confrontation, calling the sides The Gas Team and The São Paulo Railway Team, each made up of employees from these companies. It was 14 or 15 April 1895. When we got to the field, the first thing we had to do was to drive away the Viação Paulista's mules which were grazing there. Soon after, we started our game, which was interesting as, lacking the necessary strip, some of my companions played in trousers. The São Paulo Railway, the team I was playing for, won 4–2 – most of them were SPAC members. When we left the field, we'd already agreed to promote a second game, the general feeling being: 'What a great sport, what a nice little game.'

Charles also related that 'there were 22 players on the field, but only 16 took part and some of those were soon exhausted . . .' Perhaps if he'd been present, Charles's cousin Willie Rule might have felt obliged to join in. He was in Europe at the time, and while in England had visited Banister Court. When Rule returned to São Paulo he would have conveyed the news that one of the Banister's teams had won the Easter six-a-side tournament in Southampton. Also, Charles might have been wondering how the school's new sixes competition for juniors had gone – it was he who had presented the trophy for which six teams had been competing.

It is not clear how many more practices – if any – were held on the Várzea do Carmo before Miller was preparing a pitch, markings and all, on the SPAC sports ground. The move to the Dulley property signified the club's acceptance of the game, and soon a football section was established. Charles recalled that, henceforward, 'the games were watched with great interest' – and not only by the membership. In August 1896, a Rio journalist, in a letter to a colleague, attempted to describe his first encounter with football:

> There, near Luz, in Bom Retiro, a group of Englishmen, a bunch of maniacs as they all are, get together, from time to time, to kick around something that looks like a bull's bladder. It gives them great satisfaction or fills them with sorrow when this kind of yellowish bladder enters a rectangle formed by wooden posts.

Not long after England's World Cup triumph this extract was reproduced by the *Revista do Esporte* in an article entitled 'The English helped the Brazilians to be good at football'. In the wake of the champions' unceremonious exit from the 1966 tournament, it was an appropriate moment for retrospection – painful maybe, but tinged with irony. The Brazilian pupils had long since surpassed the best their British teachers could offer.

In the São Paulo of the 1890s, the first Brazilians to catch the football bug were the well-heeled students of Mackenzie College. Perhaps they began playing in 1896 when, allegedly, a basketball brought by a teacher from the United States was used for a kick-about. It's certainly possible that some of the students had seen or taken part in games being organised by Charles Miller, while others had been initiated during schooling in Europe. A pitch was marked out on their recreation ground, and, once an Associação Atlética had been set up in 1898, a football club was started. Contact with the British players was greatly facilitated by SPAC's relocation to its current home in 1897. The College was, and still is, situated a couple of hundred yards away, on the other side of Rua da Consolação.

When SPAC moved from the Dulley property the football pitch

there did not remain idle. A group led by German immigrant, Hans Nobiling, was waiting to make use of this ready-made facility. Nobiling had arrived in March 1897 with the necessary football paraphernalia, including the rules of the club which he had captained in Hamburg. It was the German colony's Gymnastics Club that pointed him in SPAC's direction. The fact that the British Club's policy towards sport was not open-door frustrated Nobiling:

> ... at the Dulley property ... I came across two São Paulo Athletic teams in the middle of a game, and it was clear that in Charles Miller and Jeffery the club had two quality players. I spoke with both of them and with Mr Crewe and came to the conclusion that the British kept the game very much to themselves ...

But Nobiling found an ally in Mackenzie's director of football René Vanorden. Players were recruited from within the German business community and later a number of the College's alumni were added. In March 1899 Nobiling's cosmopolitan side played out a goalless draw with the students at the Dulley field, presaging the ultimate test in the coming months – triangular matches involving Charles Miller's SPAC XI.

Defeats against SPAC – 1–0 and 4–1 – were neither deflating nor disastrous, and a fortnight after the second game Nobiling and his team-mates held a meeting on 19 August at which São Paulo's third football club was founded. Sadly for Nobiling, the name Sport Club Internacional was not his preference, and just days later, 'amicably' as he put it, he broke away with several colleagues to form Sport Club Germânia. Having campaigned for the expansion of the game, Nobiling had chosen an 'exclusive', colonial set-up – similar to the one he'd criticised at SPAC.

We do not know Charles Miller's reaction to football catching on in São Paulo. In a future letter to Banister's the inference is that he was surprised. The *School Magazine* continued to publish scraps from his dispatches, but in not one of them was there a reference to football. Any mention by Charles of the informal games at SPAC was likely to have been seen as unnewsworthy, paling totally in comparison to his exploits for Hampshire and St Mary's. On the other hand, cricket news was taken seriously, as the following entries attest:

> C. Miller was enjoying himself in June at Sao Paulo [sic] playing cricket and baseball. His batting average is at present, he writes, 52,

but I am afraid it will not last. Charlie Miller has been distinguishing himself by making 125 not out for the Sao Paulo [sic] Cricket Eleven; Rule was playing in the same match and made 17.

After the second note, included in the July 1898 issue of the magazine, there appears to be a lull in correspondence. Coincidentally or not, this was a period of great change in Charles's life. There were fresh surroundings at SPAC's new headquarters, and workwise a transfer in 1898 from the São Paulo Railway to the London and Brazilian Bank. It was also around this time that tragedy again struck his family. Helena Miller was told how her grandfather, John Miller, having sustained a serious back injury, never recovered from an operation in Britain. Apparently Charles hardly knew his father, and yet the evocation of his homecoming in 1894 provides evidence of his affection for him.

At the turn of the century Charles made what turned out to be his final career move when he joined the staff of the Royal Mail shipping company. In São Paulo, fuelled by British technology and capital, urbanisation was gathering momentum. The São Paulo Railway, Light and Power Company had been set up to provide the city with electricity, and in 1900 cables were laid for street-lighting and tram-lines. In a lengthy letter to his old school, some four years later, Charles made specific reference to the developments that had been taking place:

> The present population of S. Paul's [sic] is anything between 280,000 and 300,000 inhabitants, the greater part being Italians. The whole town has an European appearance, as you will see by a few photo cards I am sending you. Electric-cars or trams run all through the town and out into the suburbs, six miles or more. The force for the electric power is supplied by a large waterfall fifteen miles out of town; nearly all the factories are worked by electricity from the same fall. The centre streets of the town are paved with wooden blocks, the same as the High Street in Southampton, I am told.

The tram service that Miller mentioned began operating in May 1900, its inauguration described by a Light engineer as 'a major event'. 'It resembled a popular festival, with the streets along the route full of applauding, enthusiastic people ...' No one could have imagined that the 'British sport' of football would become a far greater magnet for popular feeling. But in 1900 the game lacked organisation – until a young Brazilian set about changing that. His name was Antônio Casemiro da Costa.

Rio-born, da Costa spent most of his childhood in Europe. He had attended a college in Switzerland, turning out for several football clubs there and, crucially, meeting up with other Brazilian-born youngsters. Once in São Paulo, da Costa soon found his way to popular SC Internacional where, with foresight, he instituted football games for children. Still in 1900, already the captain of his club, da Costa's strategy to popularise the game included throwing down the gauntlet to Mackenzie for a series of matches. Not only that, it is alleged that he talked a shoemaker into producing the first locally made football – the result, a lucrative sideline for the fortunate craftsman.

When football started to appear at the Velódromo's cycling meetings, here was a sign that the game was gaining ground. Miller and da Costa probably participated in an exhibition match there in July 1901. Club Athletico Paulistano had been formed six months before, the Prado's velodrome had been leased and now 'foot-ball' was being introduced – cautiously, so it seemed. Two 25-minute halves were played either side of one of the cycle races. The programme stated that '22 of the best players in São Paulo will take part, 11 on each side'. Cycling fever was passing; for football, in the eyes of Miller and da Costa, consolidation required the setting up of a league for São Paulo. But before this project was formalised there were matches to be played against their football brothers in Rio.

In terms of football progress, the capital city of Rio de Janeiro was lagging behind São Paulo. In 1900 there were just three teams playing football on the sports grounds of Paysandu Cricket Club and Rio Cricket and Athletic Association. Rio's equivalent of Charles Miller was an Anglo-Brazilian by the name of Oscar Cox. According to Paulo Varzea, Cox was an 'indefatigable propagator of the game', but for all his efforts the only noteworthy matches were between teams of Brazilians and British-born citizens. Apparently it was the success of these encounters – or was it more the relentless struggle to stimulate interest? – that led Cox to organise the first games between Cariocas (natives of Rio) and Paulistas. The idea was embraced by two school-fellows, Casemiro da Costa and René Vanorden.

'State of Rio versus State of S. Paulo.' This was how one newspaper described the two matches that consequently took place at SPAC's Consolação 'ground' on 19 and 20 October 1901. Incontrovertibly the event is a landmark, a turning-point in Brazilian football history. It was also one of the first instances of lengthy reports in a number of newspapers, and these reports became blueprints for football writing in Brazil. Descriptions in Portuguese of context and action on the field of play were punctuated by italicised English words and phrases, underlining Britain's influence on the Brazilian game and further emphasising the wider authority that Britain enjoyed. It was the first time, too, that Charles Miller's leading role in Paulista sport was expressed in print. Previously, it seems, this had been tacitly assumed.

In Brazil, football was and would remain for more than two decades essentially an amateur activity – for the most part played, watched and run by the privileged members of society. At SPAC on 20 October 1901 'the crowd . . . besides being *very selected* was very big, and prominent were the elegant women who lent a happy note to the festivities'. As for the players, mention was made of the Rio lads' 'correctness during the game . . . this was to be expected from boys who benefit from a polished and distinguished education'. After the first match we are told that 'the *captain* of the Paulista *team* gave the first *hurrah*, warmly reciprocated by the players and the numerous spectators'. The captain was Charles Miller.

Later, at an 'intimate banquet' offered by the hosts, Charles, for some reason absent from the proceedings, was the object of one of the toasts: 'the *best all-round sportsman*', proposed Rio skipper Oscar Cox. The raising of glasses was rounded off by Casemiro da Costa toasting the health of King Edward VII and the President of Brazil. In this overt show of symbiosis between Britain and Brazil, the other foreign nationals were patently ignored. We can wonder, for example, at Nobiling's reaction to the final toast – 'following an old English custom', as one newspaper put it.

Perhaps it was British hegemony on such occasions that might have provoked Nobiling's outspoken remarks on SPAC's exclusiveness, and the way it favoured an individual approach to the game over teamwork. But Miller admitted to Paulo Varzea that he preferred the 'dribbling game', and he didn't hide his distaste for 'the game played in the north of England' which he found 'less elaborate, uglier and contained too many passes'. After the second game of the historic Rio *v* São Paulo series an attempt was made, one of the first in Brazil, to describe a style of play. Significantly, the views of Nobiling and Miller are echoed:

> The *S. Paulo-teem* [*sic*] defended well in the two matches, but their attack suffered from their *forwards'* lack of *training* together. These

forwards are good players, make no mistake about it, but they are very selfish. They want to play alone and this is impossible. The other big defect of the *forwards* of the *S. Paulo-teem* was that they didn't keep their line. Many times we saw Miller and A. Costa alone in front of the enemy *Goal* [*sic*], without being able to do anything with the ball because they lacked the support of the other 3 *forwards*.

(*O Commercio de S. Paulo*, 21 October 1901)

It seems the observation was more of a reflection on the first game. For the second encounter Miller made changes, resulting in the Paulista attackers imitating the '*combination*' displayed by their opponents. Appropriately, in terms of results, there was parity: 2–2 and then 0–0. And folklore provides a delicious anecdote: did Oscar Cox, during preparations for the event, really enquire as to whether it was necessary to bring 'goal posts, nets and whitewash for marking the pitch' from Rio?

Charles Miller's reserved unassuming nature might explain why, in the view of Brazilian historians, he was not perceived as being a principal player in the founding of the 'Liga Paulista de Foot-ball' in December 1901. This impression is compounded by the fact that, for whatever reason, a SPAC delegation failed to turn up to the inaugural meeting at SC Internacional's headquarters. Five days later, on 18 December, representatives from the full complement of clubs assembled 'to deal with the revision of the statutes of the Liga Paulista de Foot-ball'. We are told that SPAC was 'represented by its captain, Mr Charles Muller [*sic*]' – the periodic corruption of his surname was something he would have to live with.

The Liga Paulista's first board of directors included da Costa and Nobiling – but not Miller. Again, ostensibly, it was a sign that Charles was content to take a back seat in the running of the new body. The only indication of a much greater involvement is in a letter to his school. The reference is succinct – but sadly oversimplified: '. . . a Brazilian by the name of Antonio Casimiro da Costa [*sic*], educated in Switzerland, and myself formed a League. He gave a silver cup. Five clubs entered . . .'

In May 1902 SC Germânia, CA Paulistano, AA Mackenzie College, SC Internacional and São Paulo Athletic Club commenced competition for Brazil's first football championship.

The fixture list dictated that Charles and his SPAC side kick off their campaign against Paulistano on 8 May. According to *O Estado de São Paulo*: 'The most distinguished families of our society and lovers of this interesting type of sport' were present at the Velódromo. An early goal from Charles set SPAC on course for a 4–0 victory – 'very uneven' was *O Estado*'s verdict on the game. At the end of the report, praise was heaped on the visitors' captain: 'It is undeniable that the honours of the day go to Mr Charles Muller [*sic*], who made passes and other plays of an admirable steadiness and mastery.'

Casemiro da Costa was in charge of that game, and at the succeeding fixture Charles began official refereeing duties. Even in these early days the performance of the match official was scrutinised. But correspondents did their best to be diplomatic. Concerning SPAC's opening home fixture, *O Estado* wrote of Mr Lamont: 'As a referee he delighted some and displeased others; however, it appeared that if his decisions were not fair, they were sincere.' One year later, a Portuguese version of the 'Referee's Chart' appeared in the *Guia Esportiva* in São Paulo. Charles Miller had given a copy of the 1902 edition to *O Estado* correspondent Mário Cardim for him to translate.

Throughout the first decade of this century – and on until the First World War – Brazilians would gauge their footballing ability by how well they performed against the British. In the first weeks of the fledgling Paulista league, SPAC may have enjoyed three comfortable wins – but they were not invincible. Towards the end of June 1902, two Brazilian teams greatly boosted interest in the game by upsetting the 'Inglezes'. Firstly, a combined Brazilian XI beat an 'English' side 3–0. It's worth noting that for games with a national flavour, Charles Miller always turned out for the British community, although he would later insist that he was first and foremost a Paulista. In contrast, Anglo-Brazilian Oscar Cox saw himself as a Brazilian player.

The second triumph was far more satisfying, provoking a spontaneous demonstration of feeling. Paulistano had the temerity to come away from São Paulo Athletic with a 1–0 win. In terms of competitive football, as Mazzoni points out, 'this was the first victory by a Brazilian side against the English'. At the final whistle there was a pitch invasion, and afterwards the crowd took the celebration to the streets. Later that day both teams and club members went to the theatre. Reportedly, in the middle of the show, a group of fans started up the Paulistano chant, making 'an infernal din'. A security guard intervened and threatened to make arrests. It was to the demonstrators' good fortune that the guard was a 'fervent Paulistano supporter', for, on learning of the reason for the disturbance, he proceeded to join in. The day after, *O Estado* dared to suggest that Paulistano 'promises to be São Paulo's *team*'.

A fortnight later, Paulistano's ascendance was evinced in the line-up chosen for the second visit of a team from Rio. Five of their players were included to SPAC's three, Miller being joined by Boyes and Jeffery. No doubt there were eyebrows raised in some quarters concerning the absence of a Germânia player in the XI. Two Internacional members, including da Costa, were picked, and a Mackenzie half-back. In the event, 'the great Rio–S. Paulo meeting' never took place – firstly because the visitors were unable to play on the proposed Saturday; and secondly because Miller and Boyes were required to play cricket in Santos, the match having been 'rigidly fixed since the beginning of the year'. This delightful example of British intransigence shows Charles in the Corinthian mould of all-round sportsman, and, further, suggests that his presence was a prerequisite for an important football game to take place.

Nevertheless, on the Sunday, 13 July 1902, as a compromise, a Rio XI met Paulistano at the Velódromo; and a day later SC Internacional took on the Cariocas. At the first match a card was distributed, giving the players' names, definitions in Portuguese of some English football terms and a diagram of the field of play. The list of terms bears a striking resemblance to the one published in the 1893–94 Hampshire FA handbook – another indication of Miller's pivotal role. As with the names of the British players, reproduction of English terms inevitably posed problems. In this instance, 'tripping' became 'hipping', a 'kick' a 'hick'. It was not until 1918 that an attempt was made to create a list of Portuguese equivalents to describe, as one Brazilian writer puts it, 'imported football, *made in England*'.

But the card was certainly a useful aid in the familiarisation process, *O Commercio de S. Paulo* describing it as 'greatly contributing to the perfect appreciation of the game'. Perhaps it was wise to leave the finer points of the off-side rule to knowledgeable officials such as da Costa or Miller. On Paulistano's card: 'OFF-SIDE – it is when a player is momentarily prevented from kicking the ball.' It was a brave attempt at simplification; but would it, one wonders, have been endorsed by Miller?

Paradoxically, the two losses incurred by the Rio team in São Paulo were the prelude to the founding of the capital's first football club. One week after the trip to São Paulo, 22-year-old Oscar Cox and 19 others from the upper echelons of Carioca society met to establish Fluminense Football Club. The fact that most of their names were Brazilian belied the club's strong British character. One of Fluminense's first initiatives was to promote a visit to Rio by the Paulistas.

Through a memorandum in English, members were called on to finance the event:

> As a Foot-Ball [*sic*] Team will arrive from S. Paulo on 4th October, and as the two Rio teams that have gone to S. Paulo have always been well received, a subscription is hereby opened to defray their expenses here in Rio. It should be clearly understood that, in case a big dinner is given, only the Paulistas' share will be paid for out of the proceeds of this subscription.

Of those that signed, the Robinsons and C.H. Pullen were hints of two famous Carioca footballing families. They belonged to Paysandu Cricket Club on whose ground Rio's first inter-state matches were played. Rio recorded its first victories – but the Paulistas had travelled without the Paulistano contingent. The trip clashed with the penultimate Liga Paulista fixture. By beating Mackenzie, Paulistano finished their season on the same number of points as SPAC. With goal difference not counted, Brazil's first championship would be decided by a play-off.

It was eight years, almost to the day, since Charles disembarked in Santos. Returning in his mind to the kick-abouts on the Várzea do Carmo, he'd have smiled wryly: then football was a private pastime, now it was a public passion. Sunday, 26 October 1902. In the eight preceding competitive games Charles had scored eight goals – a clear leader in the table of goalscorers. The events of that historic Sunday afternoon were recorded in detail by *O Estado de São Paulo*. In the translation which follows, the italicised words are identical to the ones in the original article:

FOOT-BALL
1902 CHAMPIONSHIP
Winner: *S. Paulo Athletic Club*

Yesterday, at 4 p.m., the final *foot-ball match*, organised by the *Liga Paulista de Foot-ball*, to decide the winner of this year's league, took place at the ex-Velódromo Paulista, today Club Athletico Paulistano's ground. *São Paulo Athletic Club* won by two *gools* to one.

As we were predicting, the attendance was extraordinary, about four thousand people continuously applauding the formidable players with enthusiasm.

The elegant young ladies, who lent the utmost charm to this festive occasion, were visibly agitated whenever the ball went near either goal, agitation that transformed itself into loud cheers when the ball was cleared.

The elegant stands trembled with noise made by the numerous spectators.

From the start, the game was extremely vigorous and heavy on both sides.

Unfortunately, this *match* did not finish as they wanted it to. Early in the game, Mr João da Costa Marques, a Paulistano *forward*, fell over and one of his opponents by mistake stepped on his arm, dislocating it. He was unable to continue. If it was not for this sad incident, everything would have run in perfect harmony.

At the end of the game, Mr Antônio C. da Costa, president of the *Liga Paulista de Foot-ball*, presented the cup to Mr Charles Miller, the honourable *captain* of the winning *team*.

After filling the cup with *champagne* Mr Charles Miller offered it to Mr Antônio C. Costa [*sic*] who, after drinking the winners' health, gave it back to Mr Miller. He in turn passed it to Mr Olavo de Barros, the honourable Paulistano *captain*.

He, after toasting the health of the opposition, returned it to Mr Charles Miller who congratulated the opposing *team* and then poured the rest of the *champagne* over the match ball. After this ceremony, the members of both teams received small bouquets of freshly cut flowers.

A group of admirers gave a crown of laurels to Mr Olavo de Barros, the Paulistano *captain*.

It is impossible to write about the game, for it was one of the most lively and exciting ones we have ever seen.

The formidable teams that played yesterday lined up as follows:

CLUB ATHLETICO PAULISTANO
Jorge de Miranda Filho
Thiers – Rubião
E.Barros, Olavo, Renato
B. Cerqueira, J. Marques, A. Rocha, Ibanez, O. Marques

Blacklock, Montandon, Muller [*sic*], Brough, Boyes
Heyeock [*sic*], Wucherer, Biddell
A. Kenworthy – G. Kenworthy
W. Jeffery
S. PAULO ATHLETIC CLUB

When the teams were in position, Mr Rocio Egydio de Souza Aranha blew his whistle, giving the ball to Paulistano whose fortune it was to *kick*-off.

However, they did not have much luck for they soon conceded a *corner-kick*.

After this the Athletic Club forwards won the ball and took it to the *11 yards* line where Paulistano full-back Mr G. Rubião brilliantly kicked it away. [Almost certainly 12 not 11 yards was intended. It appears that the old 12 yards line marked the limit of the penalty area.]

On one of these attempts the ball was taken up by Athletic Club *forward* Mr Boyes beyond the *11 yards* line. There he gave a brilliant *passe* to his team-mate Charles Muller [*sic*] who with a magnificent *shoot* scored the first *goal* for his club.

After this *goal* the São Paulo Athletic Club lads put together a vigorous attack, but the Paulistano defence left nothing to be desired.

The contest that was now going on was indescribable, during the short time that the ball stayed in the centre of the field. Sometimes it was won by Paulistano, at other times by Athletic Club.

One of the Paulistano players kicked the ball out, over the touch-line, so it was a throw-in for the Athletic *team*. Mr Biddell took the throw-in and skilfully managed to find his colleague Mr Blacklock. He advanced a little before sending a well-judged pass to Mr Montandon. He in turn laid it off to Mr Charles Miller who, with a fine low *shoot*, scored the second *goal* for S. Paulo Athletic Club.

Just minutes after this *goal* the *half time* whistle was blown.

The crowd which filled the elegant stands broke into a noisy clapping and cheering of both *teams*.

The interval lasted only ten minutes, at the end of which these glorious and formidable *teams* returned to the field of play.

At this stage of the game, Paulistano *forwards* Messrs A. Rocha and B. Cerqueira had already picked up injuries to add to the ones they'd started the match with. But despite this, their *team* mounted a masterly attack, several times managing to take the ball up to their opponents' *full-backs*. Brilliant *shoots*, however, were fruitless, as they were courageously stopped by S. Paulo Athletic Club *gool-keeper* Mr W. Jeffery who then threw the ball out to his forwards. They, once in possession, energetically took the ball up to the opposition's *gool* where countless *shoots* were saved by *gool-keeper* Mr Jorge de Miranda.

After a hard-fought battle, the Paulistano *forwards* gained possession and with some fine passes took the ball up to the *11 yards* line. When Paulistano forward Mr Alvaro Rocha received the ball he found the Athletic Club's net with a powerful *shoot*, thus scoring Paulistano's first *goal*.

The enthusiasm of the spectators after this *goal* bordered on the delirious. The elegant stands trembled and it seemed they would fall apart. The distinguished families waved their hands and cheered the Paulistano players.

When order was restored, the spectators' attention returned to focusing on the game where a truly emotional battle was developing.

It was, therefore, two *goals* to one when the *referee* blew the final whistle.

The enthusiastic clapping increased.

As a whole, the S. Paulo Athletic Club team played excellently. We would single out Messrs Jeffery who showed himself to be a true *goal-keeper*; Charles Miller, the glorious *captain*, who once again showed his skill in this game; A. Kenworthy, a good *full-back*; Heycock and Wucherer excellent *half-backs*; and Broyes [*sic*], an untiring *forward*.

The Paulistano players, on the whole, did very well; however, we can single out Mr Olavo de Barros, the honourable *captain* of his *team*, tenacious and untiring; A. Rocha and Ibanez, admirable *forwards*. Renato was a splendid *half-back*, Rubião and Thiers two resistant and firm *full-backs*, and Jorge Miranda Filho, despite letting in two *goals*, played admirably, a number of times saving difficult and strong *shoots* on his *goal*.

On receiving the cup, Mr Charles Miller invited the Paulistano *team* and several members of other clubs to São Paulo Athletic Club's ground where *champagne* was offered to the guests from the league championship trophy. There were a number of speeches and much cheering.

We offer our congratulations to the São Paulo Athletic Club *team*, as personified by their honourable *captain*, for yesterday's victory, and to Paulistano for the extraordinary courage with which they kept going in spite of the trying circumstances.

Probably penned by Mário Cardim, the account, pompous on the face of it, convincingly depicts the loftiness of the occasion. The modern reader is transported to a scene whose atmosphere is not far removed from a medieval pageant: description of the game is eclipsed by references to the chivalry of the protagonists, while 'elegant young ladies' are fully absorbed by the spectacle. It is not the fact of SPAC's victory that is important, it is the manner in which it was achieved; afterwards, Charles Miller's actions are the focus for comment.

The pouring of champagne on the ball is a powerful image, heartbreaking, though, if in the 1880s you had committed yourself to the rules of Temperance, one of Southampton's first clubs. Charles may have first seen this done in the company of Corinthians players. Perhaps the footballs he brought back with him from England had been similarly consecrated. It would enhance the legend to say they were.

Back in the old country, the Corinthians, in October 1902, could have done with Charles Miller's well-preserved predatory instinct in front of goal. A bleak period in their history was beginning – made bleaker by G.O. Smith's retirement, and aggravated in 1907 by a rift with the FA. At the end of the first decade of the century, short of decent opposition, the club still managed to maintain a decent standard of play – as Brazilians would discover for themselves. But even before that, Paulistas and Cariocas had been given opportunities to demonstrate their skills against more modest foreign opponents.

FOUR
Consular Support

Charles was no more than 1m 65 tall. 67 at the most. But what agility, what skill! And do you know what? I've followed football right up to today and I haven't seen better. Not even this Pelé who you're talking so much about.

One of Miller's team-mates, Rangel Viotti,
interviewed by João Saldanha. Published in
Manchete, 6 August 1967

Charles – Skill in which the player bends his leg back and kicks the ball with his heel [later corrupted to chaleira, *the Portuguese for 'kettle'].*

One of the entries in a dictionary of football terms
drawn up by the São Paulo Sports Writers'
Association in 1918. Quoted in Tomás Mazzoni's
História do Futebol no Brasil (1950), p.121

You will be surprised to hear that football is the game here. We have no less than sixty or seventy clubs in S. Paul's [sic] city alone . . . We always get two or three thousand people to a League match, but for the final we had 6,000 . . . A week ago I was asked to referee in a match of small boys, twenty a side. I told them that it was absurd them playing twenty a side; but no, they wanted it. I thought, of course, the whole thing would be a muddle, but I found I was very much mistaken. They played two half-hours, and I only had to give two hands. The youngsters hardly spoke a word during the game, kept their places and played well; even for this match about 1,500 people turned up.

An Entirely Different Game

No less than 2,000 footballs have been sold here within the last twelve months; nearly every village has a club now.

From Charles Miller's letter published in the
Banister Court School Magazine, March 1904

'The microbe of football is more virulent and more persistent than any other of its kind' – so wrote William Pickford in 1906. Had he wished to include a foreign illustration of this point, he would not have found a better example than the wildfire spread of the sport in São Paulo. It is possible that it had come to his notice that one of the instigators was a former Hampshire player. But if news had reached him by way of Banister Court's Headmaster, Christopher Ellaby, then Pickford remains silent on the subject.

Nevertheless, Charles Miller's letter to his old school provides unique and eloquent testimony as to how enthralled Brazilians had become by, in Pickford's words, 'the big bounding ball'. In the above extract, figures for the number of clubs, attendances and the sale of footballs show an increasing level of interest. But it is Charles's account of a refereeing experience that is particularly revealing. He describes how he, one of the founders of the Liga Paulista, is wrong-footed by a group of 'small boys'. How, he had reasoned, could 40 youngsters possibly have a serious game of football? Half a century on, Tom Finney would be left equally spellbound at the seemingly effortless way in which young Brazilians take to the game.

But it is not as if conveying the news about football was the central topic of Charles's dispatch. He starts out by depicting the 'English' railway and his home town with its 'European appearance' and changeable climate, 'very much as in England'. Then, when he comes to sport, it is cricket that he mentions first. Since the revelations of Mr A. Richards of Santos in 1894 not a lot had changed. Those outside the British community still viewed the game with indifference, and the difficulty in arranging fixtures persisted. One bright spot was the series of matches against an XI from the Argentine.

For Brazilian football, this sporting link proved vital. It would have put Charles in touch with the men who played for and managed Alumni, far and away the foremost football club in Buenos Aires. Alumni had started out as the English High School Athletic Club. It is not inconceivable that, when a squad of Argentinian fooballers first visited Brazil in 1908, one or two of the players were old cricket adversaries of Charles Miller.

Readers of Charles's letter are given an overview of the British sports being played in Brazil – golf and tennis are also named. As a result, there is little information regarding personal sporting achievement. Charles does find it genuinely difficult to believe that he was elected to captain the 1902 cricket team to Argentina – given that eight of the players were from Rio.

And there is passing reference to his and da Costa's combined effort in setting up the Liga Paulista. São Paulo Athletic Club (SPAC) had latterly repeated their victory in the 1902 championship. But Charles offers no indication as to his contribution to these successes. Of the 1903 final he writes: 'The Brazilians scored the first goal, and you never heard such a row as the spectators kicked up; we scored twice in the second half.'

Once again, SPAC's play-off opponents were Paulistano. The opening goal is related with feeling, and then immediately there is a clinical ending to the report. Perhaps this is Charles's way of bottling up the details of Paulistano's post-match protests. The Liga Paulista had thrown out claims that a penalty should have been given for hands against SPAC full-back Jeffery and that the second half had finished six minutes early. Afterwards, some Paulistano officials felt aggrieved that the session had been presided over by Charles Miller – supposedly as acting president and with an interest in the case he should have vacated the chair. Paulistano then called a general assembly and when the meeting decided not to pursue the matter, the club president and fellow board members resigned *en masse*. Now, this was passion, but perhaps not the sort to which Charles subscribed.

The 1903 championship had also thrown up an incident which, on the surface, showed that not everyone was gripped by football fever. It happened before one of the SPAC *v* Paulistano encounters. A SPAC player, wearing his kit, was making his way to the Velódromo, when he was stopped by a policeman:

> As the Englishman didn't speak much Portuguese he ended up being detained for 'being dressed for carnival, out of season, offensively showing his legs in public in the centre of the city'. Worried by the delay of the athlete, the directors of the two clubs telephoned the police and located him at the main police station. The misunderstanding was explained and the player released.

As a reason for having a match put back half an hour it is probably unique. But one wonders whether, behind the policeman's uniform, there lurked a Paulistano supporter. Shenanigans or not, for the next pre-season 'international', Charles and the team of 'Extrangeiros' were taken to the venue in a 'special tram' laid on by the Light and Power Company.

The destination of the Light's tram was Germânia's home ground, the Parque Antarctica. It was there, on that Sunday, 20 March 1904, that an XI made up of German and British players beat the 'Brasileiros' 3–2, Charles scoring two of the goals. Inscribed on the winners' medal is the word 'kermesse', confirming that this was a charity event. One of Miller's team-mates that afternoon was Hermann Friese who, according to one contemporary columnist, was 'the most extraordinary sportsman that São Paulo has ever seen'. Friese's other gift was for middle-distance running, the source of his supreme stamina on the football field. In the SPAC *v* Germânia game in June 1904:

> Friese played in attack and in defence, shining as always. Now and then he set off with the ball from one side of the field to the other, giving it to whichever of his *forwards* was best placed. In defence, several times we saw him protect the Germânia *goal*.

It was SPAC's first competitive match of the year in a Liga Paulista that now comprised six clubs, AA das Palmeiras the new member. In light of SPAC's supposed superiority, the journalist considered the 1–0 victory 'the equivalent of a defeat'. Charles scored the goal which separated the teams:

> Miller takes the ball forward. Pudney goes to meet him. Riether runs to help him; both collide, stare at each other and argue instead of giving chase to Miller who calmly reaches the Germânia goal area where he *schoota* [*sic*]. The ball enters the right of the *goal*, right in the corner. The *goal keeper* [*sic*] was at the far left of the *goal*.

The word *schoot* was now being conjugated in Portuguese. In this report, there are nine other instances where Miller and a variation of *schoot* are linked. Also, the word 'penalty-kick' receives an ample airing. Not content to simply relate the incident in which one of the Germânia forwards is upended inside the SPAC penalty area, the reporter includes a paraphrase of the relevant section from the rule book. The hapless match official is then further taken to task for 'forgetting to discount the two minutes during which the game was suspended after Jeffery had dislocated his arm'. We are not told whether it was Jeffery, back on the pitch with his arm in a sling, who had come close to conceding the spot-kick. Today, the lengthy report from *O Estado de São Paulo* is among the handful of Charles's cutttings that are known to exist

On and off the sports field, 1904 was, for Charles Miller, a watershed year. In April, at the age of 29, he had been appointed Acting British Vice-Consul in São Paulo, standing in for Percy Lupton, his uncle, who was ostensibly off to England on leave. Charles held this unsalaried post for ten years. Not only that, he took over the running of his uncle's travel business, becoming the Royal Mail's agent. It was probably through the channels that accompanied these positions that Charles received details of the first visit by a British football club to South America.

It so happened that the group of British players who arrived in Rio in June 1904 belonged to Miller's former club, Southampton. In the ten years since Charles left England, Saints had won the Southern League six times and had twice been losing finalists in the prestigious English Cup – prompting calls from high quarters for this 'influential' club to be integrated into the Football League. Rio was only a stop-off for them; journey's end was Buenos Aires. In another letter published in the *Banister Court School Magazine*, Charles explains how every effort was made to bring the Saints to São Paulo:

> We did our best to have the Southampton team up here, but they could not come. I went down to Rio specially to see them. I think we could have given them a pretty good game.

In fact several matches were arranged, only to be cancelled when acceptable alterations to the tourists' 'boat arrangements' proved elusive. In the Saints party was Fred Mouncher whose photograph, originally destined for São Paulo, is now in the possession of the Hampshire FA.

While in Rio, as a matter of course, there was a game for Charles to referee. It was part of the Rio Cricket and Athletic Association's 'Annual Athletic Sports'. Had Charles also visited Rio's newest club, Bangu, and a training session been scheduled, it is likely he would have been roped into playing.

Like Rio Cricket and Paysandu, Bangu Athletic Club owed its

existence to the desire of a group of British immigrants to create a leisure facility for themselves – but two things set it very much apart. The first was its location, in a northern suburb, 'in those days . . . very far from the centre of the city'. In fact, it still is an interminable distance by bus from Rio's central Praça Tiradentes. British players, therefore, were at a premium.

The second thing which made Bangu different was its direct link to a textile firm, Companhia Progresso Industrial do Brasil. The foundation document, dated 17 April 1904, spelt out the aims of the 'club': to organise games of 'Football', 'Cricket' and 'Lawn Tennis'. There were some other English words in the Portuguese text – 'meeting', 'captain' and 'match'. Founder member and football captain John Stark was 'invited to speak to the director of the company in order to arrange the necessary cloth for the club's strip'. The club colours, it was agreed, would be white and red; and membership rates were set.

Curiously, there were several important absentees from the founding session. Of these, Thomas Donohoe, appointed vice-president, is the one who is credited with bringing the first football to Bangu in the late-1890s. And doubtless it was he who had a provisional pitch laid out. What was unique in the case of Bangu was that, due to the insufficient number of British foremen to make up 22 players, Donohoe and his fellow directors had no option but to pick members of the Brazilian workforce. Hence, the birth of what sociologist Waldenyr Caldas has termed 'football's working-class élite'.

It did not take long for the football club to become more prominent than the factory. A successful team was thus seen as enhancing the image of the company. For Caldas, it was when Brazilian workers were preferred, by necessity, to British players that 'the democratisation of our football truly began'. In stark contrast, for clubs such as Fluminense – or Botafogo, founded four months after Bangu – to field an XI containing players of mixed class and colour was unthinkable. 'Only respectable people,' wrote Mário Filho. Men of means:

> In order to join Fluminense the player had to live the same life as an Oscar Cox, Félix Frias or Horácio da Costa Santos, a Waterman, a Francis Walter, or an Etchegary, all established men, chiefs of firms, first-rate employees of big companies, sons of rich fathers, educated in Europe, used to spending money. It was a hard life. Those who did not have access to a constant supply of ready money couldn't stand the strain.

At the same time as the Bangu British started to show a disregard for Carioca football's social and racial barriers, a leading article in a São Paulo newspaper was happily predicting that *'foot-ball'* was 'just another fad'. It came the day after Paulistano and SPAC had drawn 0–0 at the Velódromo – the second time in the 1904 season that honours between the two clubs had been shared. In the 'enormous crowd' there was 'an invigorating hint of joviality'. That there were no goals, however, had no bearing on the outspoken attack that followed.

As played by Brazilians, the sport was described as 'the blind and barmy battle of physical force without the intervention of our superior faculties'. The bodily dangers of the game were emphasised – in the extreme: 'There's nothing like this [brutal] exercise to turn a healthy and happy boy into a wretched cardiac case.' There may have been calls for 'the modification of the way we play [so as to] restore to *foot-ball* the reasonable physiognomy that came from England', but this was flatly rejected, for the journalist concluded that Brazilians would never be able to tone down their style of play. 'Football,' he wrote, 'is an English game and should only be played by the English.'

Some Paulistano supporters might have nodded their heads in agreement after their team, once again, lost narrowly to São Paulo Athletic in the championship play-off. In a novel form of advertising, a different football was used in each half – each supplied by a local sports firm. For Paulistano, misery was compounded by the fact that the only goal of the game – scored by Charles Miller – was the result of a mistake by their keeper. Charles, therefore, collected the Casemiro da Costa trophy, which was now SPAC's for keeps; and he and one of his team-mates, Herbert Boyes, topped the league's scoring list with nine goals. The stalwart defender Walter Jeffery completed a trio of SPAC players, the only ones present on all three play-off occasions.

At this point in time, October 1904, the fact that Charles held the post of Vice-Consul served to underscore Britain's influence in Paulista football, while defeat for Paulistano merely hardened the resolve of the club's directorate. No sooner had the champagne corks been gathered than work began on improving the facilities and fittings at the Velódromo. As a report in the Paulistano archives attests, no expense was spared to create a club equal to the best in Europe. The football field was 'entirely redone', and four tennis courts and a swimming-pool were constructed. English and French names were *de rigueur*, so it was 'Twiford [*sic*] Sanitary Company' in the changing-rooms, and copies of *The Graphic* and *Vie au grand air* in the members' lounge. Tennis nets and posts were supplied by the London firm of M. Ayres – 'through the good offices of Mr Charles Miller'. CA Paulistano was now, at least in appearance, more European than its British neighbour. It would not be too long before the same could be said of its football.

★ ★ ★

The ceremonial sword from Charles's time as a consular official lies today on the hall table in Helena Miller's apartment. The painting of young Charles wearing a kilt hangs near by. Here a collection of silver, there a favourite chair. The character of Brazil's most famous football pioneer is indelibly stamped on this intimate space. Outside, on higher ground, massive hoardings on the Rua Paulista cast a shadow over the street; down the adjacent Rua Augusta, São Paulo Athletic Club is a brisk ten-minute walk away. When I visited Helena for the first time, towards the end of 1994, I was as ignorant of her father's achievements as many of the other journalists she had agreed to meet.

My questions were mostly perfunctory – eliciting a brief family history, the story of the legendary footballs and a version of how the game was organised. We spoke in Portuguese over a ritual afternoon-tea. I concluded by asking Helena what Brazil's football centenary meant for her:

> To remember my father, all our friends, the Hollands, the Boyes, so many of my father's friends who took part in those first games. I'm still in touch with the children of some of those pioneers of football in Brazil. I'm 85 years old and these friends of mine are more or less the same age. From time to time I receive a letter from one of them: 'I saw the photographs, I read your interview.' So all this is still very much alive.

It seems the São Paulo British community is as closely knit now as it was in the early years of this century. During a subsequent meeting, Helena provided a glimpse of her father's courtship of her mother, bound then by strict moral constraints. The object of Charles's affections was a talented pianist, ten years his junior:

> My father used to go over to my grandparents' place because he was my mother's second cousin. He brought with him two friends who began to court mother's two sisters. It was all one happy family. The

funny thing was they used to stay there in the evening and when ten
o'clock struck my grandfather would get up out of his chair, shut
the window and say: 'It's ten o'clock and it's not raining.'

One of Charles's companions was SPAC team-mate Frank
Robinson. In January 1906 Charles married Antonietta Rudge, a
bond which brought together the worlds of sport and music, a bond
between two celebrities.

This was also the year in which SPAC purchased the land on which
it stands today. Prominent SPAC member William Rule was asked by
Dona Veridiana Prado to assist her son Eduardo who was about to be
arrested for some political offence. Charles Rule, Helena's cousin,
takes up the story:

> Next day my father was seen walking down the Rua São Bento
> talking French to a padre. And took him down to the station and
> shipped him up country to some place where he had friends. And, of
> course, the lad was not arrested . . . In due course, when the trouble
> had calmed down, my father and Charlie Miller arranged to ship him
> on the Royal Mail to Europe . . . He didn't require a passport or
> anything – some document or other was sufficient . . . Charlie Miller
> and my dad enjoyed the fun they had with this business. And Dona
> Veridiana wanted to recompense both of them, and they wouldn't
> have anything to do with it. They said: 'You give us the ground and
> we'll give you so much.' And they paid so much for the ground.

In histories of football in Brazil, SPAC's success is invariably put
down to the efforts and achievements of Charles Miller. And, as is
often the case, behind-the-scenes contributions are forgotten. Clearly,
when football was being organised in São Paulo, Charles and his
cousin Willie Rule were working in tandem. As Rule's son explained:
'Charles looked after the sport, my father looked after the playing-
fields, and arranging the necessary areas to play soccer.' In 1938
SPAC's jubilee publication paid tribute to the work of William Fox
Rule, affirming that he was indeed 'for many years the moving spirit
of the Club'.

★   ★   ★

When SPAC's slide from the top began it was Germânia who
delivered the blow that sent shockwaves through Paulista football

circles. After the 6–0 victory over the British at the Velódromo, Friese and his colleagues ran Paulistano close in the race for the title, Friese finishing with the unparalleled scoring record of 14 goals in ten games. SPAC lost six of their games in the 1905 championship – and in the following season results went from bad to worse. Indeed, with half the fixtures played, there were signs that SPAC were struggling to put out a team.

On 7 July 1906, the day before the SPAC *v* Germânia game, the *Correio Paulistano* reported that the British Club's first team included 'elements which had not yet appeared on a pitch this year'. SPAC lost 3–1 and there were suggestions that they were 'unprepared and lacked combination in every department'. Matters came to a head when, a month later, the club suffered what would be its heaviest ever defeat, 9–1 against SC Internacional. It must have been particularly galling for Charles Miller. He had chosen to play in goal. *O Estado*'s verdict was that SPAC's forwards and defenders were 'so weak and indecisive that all Miller's efforts to defend his goal were rendered useless'.

Stung by the result, and with playing resources that were patently limited, SPAC pulled out of the league with three matches remaining and Miller felt obliged to tender his resignation from the league's directorate. 'Imperious motives' were given by *O Estado* as the reason for SPAC's unexpected decision. Not long after, tensions were further exacerbated when AA das Palmeiras were thrown out of the league over gate-money irregularities. Withdrawals from competition would soon be replicated in Rio where a first championship was being played out. Ironically, on the day SPAC were being thrashed by Internacional, 5 August, the 11 Britons of Paysandu were defeating Fluminense 3–1 in Rio. This avenged a 7–1 loss in the season-opener but turned out to be the only points conceded by the eventual champions.

From now on, in both major football centres, the local British teams were there to be beaten, and the Brazilians more often than not did just that. But it was true that most Brazilian clubs could count on the services of a handful of players of British origin – like Fluminense, who fielded Salmond, Buchan, Waterman and Edwin Cox. In São Paulo, the only reminder of SPAC's heyday was the occasional performance by Charles Miller as a forward in a representative side. His playing days were numbered, but, as an administrator, he would continue to hold a key role.

It was as a result of negotiations led by Miller that Brazilians would be able to measure their progress against foreign opposition. Attempts to bring Southampton to São Paulo had been ill-starred, and there was similar frustration when Nottingham Forest visited Argentina in 1905. Finally, in July 1906, a team from South Africa – guests of the Argentine FA – agreed to play a match in São Paulo. In front of a packed Velódromo the British expatriates from the Cape 'punished the footballers of our land', Miller included, in scoring six goals without reply. Expert coaching, some felt, was what was needed.

Ambitious CA Paulistano – who else? – appear to be the first Brazilian club to officially engage the services of a 'trainer' from Britain. In February 1907 the club were able to announce that Jock Hamilton of Fulham FC would be arriving in April 'to oversee the preparation of its football teams'. FA chief Frederick Wall was involved in the 'careful and prolonged negotiations' in bringing Hamilton out. Also, there were hopes that Fulham could be persuaded to visit São Paulo. Paulistano president Antônio Prado Júnior, during a trip to Europe, would supposedly contact Fulham while in London to watch the Cup final. But this was the last to be heard of the proposed tour. Fulham secured the Southern League title while their trainer was just beginning his work in Brazil.

Fittingly, Paulistano's first competitive game under Hamilton was against SPAC, back in the league and, unlike the previous season, with a purely British look to their line-up. Two former SPAC players, Jeffery and Robottom, were in the Paulistano XI. On May 30 the British offered a peek of times past with a 3–1 win, and Miller, between the sticks, was mentioned with obligatory reverence. 'It is true,' wrote *O Estado*, 'that the skill of this player was once more demonstrated, for every ball that was sent towards his goal was returned immediately.' Hamilton later turned out for Paulistano in most of their friendlies and did a lot of refereeing, and before he left, in early July, a benefit 'sports festival' was held for him at the Velódromo. Paulistano's championship win in the following season was held up as proof that the venture had been beneficial.

Hamilton's recruitment is significant for a number of reasons. The fact that the Fulham man was a professional sportsman was not seen as tainting Paulista football's amateur aura. Brazilians took advantage of his presence by planning for the future, for not only was he given the Paulistano club's first team to coach: every morning from eight till nine Jock put the members' sons through their paces. So they too learnt the latest training methods and how to apply the laws of the game to the letter. This was the beginning of formal football contacts between Britain and Brazil.

On his return to London, Hamilton let it be known that the standard of football in Brazil was fast improving. 'In fact, I was very much surprised to find the game so advanced,' he said, 'and their combination is really clever.' In the same interview, Jock related that despite the players' keenness, a hectic lifestyle meant that they needed 'a lot of coaxing to train properly'. According to him, the players 'are about equal to our second strength amateurs at the game'. He also noticed a curious custom: 'to have goal judges as well as "ref" and linesmen.' But, he found, the goal judges 'were absent . . . when I whistled'. Later, a translated version of these comments appeared in the São Paulo press, 'second strength' becoming 'second division'. It may have been a slip, but it was wishful thinking.

Charles Miller chose the English summer of 1907 to return to the land where he had spent the greater part of his childhood. No matter that SPAC was only halfway through its fixture list, or that the first competitive games between Rio and São Paulo had been scheduled. It was an opportunity to escape the many social, sporting and business commitments in Brazil, and it would enable his wife to advance her career as a concert pianist. Of course there was a visit to Banister Court. The *School Magazine* later recorded that 'a few minutes after he arrived he was playing in a match . . . and showed glimpses of his old form by scoring two goals'. Somehow in the midst of their varied and colourful lives the Millers started a family. Carlos was born several months before the trip to England, Helena in 1909.

While in London Charles most likely had a meeting with Frederick Wall and perhaps looked up Jock Hamilton. It's an intriguing fact that Miller's friend Fred Mouncher was transferred from Southampton to Fulham in November 1907, a coincidence that prompts speculation. But what is certain is that the following April the Liga Paulista received an invitation from the English FA to send a team to London. 'Excellent terms' were offered, a reason why, one newspaper report opined, 'the trip of the Paulista footballers will certainly go ahead'. There was then a caveat:

> Everyone knows what English football is, even the amateur game. Because of this it is hoped that our footballers are already preparing themselves . . . for a defeat in honourable conditions.

It would take 50 years for Brazilians to finally rid themselves of such deference and self-denigration. Needless to say, the 1908 tour never took place. Instead, football relations were established with Argentina.

As with the visit of the South Africans, it was Charles who made the initial enquiry. In fact *The Standard*, a Buenos Aires English-language newspaper, mentions him as having made requests for a tour 'during several years'. The article went on to say that 'Mr Miller has taken much trouble in teaching Brazilians and was chiefly instrumental in bringing out two trainers from England during the past season'. The identity of Hamilton's associate, if indeed there were two trainers, remains a mystery. But what is important is the indication that Charles, besides being a dedicated football instructor, had a crucial role in contracting coaches from Britain. In Brazil his influence on the game, after SPAC's third Liga Paulista title, has been largely overlooked.

The squad of players from Buenos Aires arrived in São Paulo at the end of June. Built around a group of Brown brothers from Alumni, the team of amateurs representing the Argentine Football Association was far superior to anything the Brazilian associations could muster. The only home side to avoid defeat was the Paulista Foreigners XI. In the second half of a 2–2 draw Charles Miller, 'although a veteran, showed his old class in scoring two goals'. In Rio, the Brasileiros went down narrowly, 3–2. But in the five other games the visitors won with something to spare.

Later, a view of Brazilian football was given by an AFA member who had toured. Of the four players singled out as 'first class', just one, the ex-Germânia defender Tommy Ritcher, was from São Paulo. Two played for Rio Cricket – Mutzembecker and Hawkey, 'the best player Brazil showed up'; and the fourth was Fluminense's Edwin Cox. Contrary to what Hamilton had found, the Brazilians' combination was described as 'poor', but the AFA member did have effective teamwork to compare it to, and, certainly in São Paulo, preparation for the matches was half-hearted. If Hawkey was indeed the Argentinians' most impressive opponent, here was an indication that Britons could still be just as influential on Brazilian pitches as off them.

We have seen how SPAC were involved in an ugly dispute over the refereeing of their 1903 play-off match against Paulistano. Hans Nobiling was one of the match officials on that day. As the decade drew to a close, referees were still subjected to torrid outbursts from club directors, players and supporters – and British officials were not exempt. In July 1909 Frank Robinson, 'a veteran who knows all the rules', was called to account for failing to punish violent conduct. But worse still, soon afterwards, Alex Hutchison, a recent arrival from Britain, became embroiled in controversy with his own club, SC

Americano. It did not matter that he had reportedly officiated in the Scottish First Division. The problem arose over his interpretation of the offside rule. A player, it was generally felt, could not be offside if he hadn't touched the ball. Americano took their protest to the Liga Paulista and it was ruled that the match in question had to be replayed.

In the following season Hutchison again found himself in hot water. This time it was Paulistano who were incensed. In a letter to the governing body they complained that their keeper had had a penalty awarded against him for breaking the steps rule and that one of their players had been dismissed 'for a simple foul'. The Paulistano president defended the action of the club captain in taking his players off the field in protest at 'the incompetence of a partial referee who never again should be allowed to undertake this difficult mission'. What Paulistano wanted was a change to an article in the League's statutes: the creation of a body that would have powers to 'reform' the existing laws of the game and investigate refereeing complaints.

On 25 July 1910 at an extraordinary general meeting of the Liga Paulista there was heated discussion and Paulistano's proposal was unanimously rejected. The threat to the referee's autonomy had been thwarted, and the only sanction meted out to Paulistano was the docking of two points for the histrionics of its players. The heavy-handed comments aimed at Hutchison were not addressed. The Liga Paulista did come up with an ingenious way of dealing with Paulistano's intransigence, however. Just over a month later a group of Corinthians from England would be arriving in São Paulo. The Paulistano skipper was given the task of selecting a Paulistas XI, and for their game against the famous amateurs Hutchison was chosen to take charge.

FIVE

Corinthians

. . . Your past is a flag
Your present a lesson
You figure among the leaders
Of our British sport . . .

From the club song of Sport Club
Corinthians Paulista

The great professional clubs like Aston Villa, Preston North End
and Sunderland of the past, and Everton, Sheffield Wednesday
and Manchester United of the most recent times, and the
brilliant Scottish amateurs of Queen's Park, [all had] their great
years, but they never won such general and lasting affection as
the Corinthians. Their football, though of a different type, may
have been equally fine, but underlying it has been the thought
that it had been a business first and pleasure second. But
Corinthians football has always been a pleasure and nothing
else. They gained nothing by their skill but the satisfaction which
the exercise [of] such skill could give.

The Times, circa 1908, quoted by David Miller in
an article in John Mills's *Corinthian Casuals Football*
Club: Brazil Tour 1988, SPAC, São Paulo, 1989

When the Brazilian football magazine *Placar* set about compiling a
special edition to celebrate Brazilian football's 100 Years in 1994 it was
decided to include a section on 'The Great Teams'. Corinthians
Paulista was chosen to symbolise the period from 1950 to 1955. Their
captain, the right-wing in the 'attack with a hunger for goals', was

Cláudio Christóvam de Pinho. Cláudio has fond memories of that period – although his omission from Brazil's 1950 World Cup team still rankles. One anecdote stands out and serves to illustrate the brilliance of that Corinthians side and the uniqueness of Brazil's brand of football.

It was during a tour of Scandinavia in 1952. Cláudio recalls a moment from Corinthians' game against a Gothenburg XI: '[While] me and Luisinho, who was my inside-right, were exchanging headed passes, without letting the ball touch the ground, the Gothenburg centre-half stood in between us clapping.' Later, another Swedish crowd were reportedly amazed at Corinthians'' electrifying game, full of filigree, with a juggling display . . . This was no football team, it was a group of artists.'

But they weren't the first Corinthians side to make their mark in northern Europe. Forty-eight years before, the English Corinthians chalked up five comfortable wins in five games, despite having to play on gravel pitches. 'They are somewhat dangerous to fall on, and the Corinthian players wore woollen kneecaps,' wrote one historian. Conditions had improved in Cláudio's day.

This chapter is concerned with how Corinthians Paulista, the club at which Cláudio spent 15 seasons, came to be formed – the run-up to the birth of what today is arguably Brazil's most popular club. It was, of course, a direct result of a fortnight's 'missionary work' by their famous forebears from England. The Corinthians had been forced to intensify their touring activity simply because, following the 'split' with the FA in 1907, there was a lack of credible opposition at home. Clubs affiliated to the renegade Amateur Football Association were barred from competing against FA members. Almost immediately, the Corinthians made a third visit to South Africa, then there were short tours to Paris and Prague and finally, in 1910, to Brazil.

On 6 August *The Times* announced that 'a Corinthian football team' had departed for Rio de Janeiro by the SS *Amazon*. The brief item added that 'they are going out at the request of the Fluminense Club of Rio'. Oscar Cox had his connections in England just as Antônio Prado did. But Cox's enterprising invitation to the Corinthians would not have gone down well in FA circles. By negotiating with the ostracised club, Brazilian football chiefs risked damaging their relations with the FA. It was perhaps a reason why a São Paulo bid to bring out the Corinthians, supported by Charles Miller, did not materialise.

We have seen how the FA acted as an intermediary in Paulistano's contracting of Jock Hamilton, and later, Fulham may have been close to making a trip to Brazil. But then in 1909 two other professional clubs, Everton and Tottenham Hotspur, passed tantalisingly by Rio. Could it be that football politics contributed to the fact that neither club was persuaded to break its journey? There seems little doubt that if sides had had to be taken, Charles Miller would have favoured the Corinthians' position. He was probably grateful, therefore, that the Cariocas were the ones to make the contentious move.

Not surprisingly, when news of the Corinthians' impending arrival reached São Paulo, the Liga Paulista lost no time in contacting the tour sponsors with a view to adding their city to the itinerary. Soon, Charles was being asked to pick one of the three Paulista teams that would meet the English amateurs and to travel to Rio to represent the Liga Paulista. They arrived – 15 players and Mr H. Hughes-Onslow, Secretary of the Amateur FA – on 22 August and were conveniently lodged at the Metropole Hotel in the Laranjeiras area of the city. It couldn't have been far from their hosts' headquarters, the venue for the exhibition matches. It fell to the hosts themselves to take a brave step into the unknown as the first Brazilian club to take on a recognised team from Britain.

24 August

Corinthians 10 Fluminense 1

Given the fact that it was a working day, the atmosphere inside the Guanabara stadium remained vibrant throughout the game. *O Paiz's* report tells us that at precisely 4 p.m. the teams came out accompanied by referee W.U. Timmis, an experienced Corinthian and the only member of the party to have been on the Scandinavian tour in 1904.

Fluminense kicked off and, catching their opponents unawares, remarkably opened the scoring with less than two minutes gone. 'The ball was taken to within twelve yards of the goal without any member of the opposing side touching it, from where Gomes netted firmly.' The Corinthians' response was to put together a series of attacks, one of these allowing Day to bring the scores level. Then, shortly afterwards, left-winger Coleby beat Waterman in the Fluminense goal to put the visitors ahead.

The Brazilians were shaken by the sudden reverse in fortunes, the threat from their attack all but drying up. We are told that 'their forwards, timid and indecisive, rarely crossed the halfway line; and when one of them did manage to break clear he lost the ball because he had no one to pass it to.' With play rooted in the hosts' half it was only a matter of time before the Corinthians increased their lead. Day made it 3–1, and from a corner centre-forward Vidal added a fourth. Ten minutes before the break Day completed his hat-trick, and as the Fluminense players were sensing the sanctuary of the dressing-room goals by Day and Coleby compounded their misery.

In the second half, a reorganised Fluminense attack created chances only to be let down by poor finishing. Meanwhile, the Corinthians 'calmly' went about their work, and in the 57th minute Day increased their lead, taking his personal tally to five. Right-wing Thew netted the visitors' ninth, and then the Rio side made one last effort to salvage some pride with a mixture of 'strong attacks and daring defending'. However, before the end the masters' score reached double figures courtesy of a goal from Vidal. *O Paiz*'s report ended with the words 'let's hope this serves as a lesson not only for the Fluminense lads but for all those footballers who were present at yesterday's game'. One thing that particularly impressed the locals was the visitors' accurate passing, sometimes covering the width of the pitch.

On 26 August the Corinthians continued where they had left off, disposing of a team representing Rio 8–1, A.T. Coleby contributing six goals to the total. Nevertheless, there were those who thought that the difference between the sides was not as great as the scorelines suggested. The *Folha do Dia*, for example, referred to the Corinthians' 'teamwork and assured and solid play', but noted 'passes that were too high, defenders slipping up, shots off target'. With their reputation at stake, world champions would not do these things on purpose, the paper concluded. 'Compared to our players they play very well,' opined the *Folha*, 'but they would come unstuck against some of the teams in England.' The message was that the tourists were not invincible.

The stay in Rio was slightly longer than the usual whistle-stop proportions, giving an opportunity, therefore, to enjoy sights such as the Corcovado mountain and the Jardim Botânico. In addition there were outings to the theatre, a banquet and, of course, a game of cricket. The tour was to prove as beneficial to the sporting endeavours of British expatriates as it was to Brazilians.

28 August
Corinthians 5   Brasileiros 2
For the tourists' last exhibition in Rio, on a Sunday, the atmosphere at Fluminense's stadium by far surpassed that of the previous games.

O Paiz would write 'there was excitement, madness, patriotic fever'. The match kicked off shortly after 4 p.m.

For twenty minutes both teams had an equal share of the play, and then, in the space of three minutes, goals by Day and Brisley put the visitors in command. The Brazilians, however, stuck to their attacking game and Edwin Cox reduced the arrears, taking advantage of Abelardo's flooring of keeper Rogers. Reaction was swift, the Corinthians restoring their two-goal lead, and despite an animated end to the half there was no more scoring.

After the interval, it was almost half an hour before the next goal arrived, Brisley converting a breakaway opportunity to make it 4–1. Far from dying, the game continued to be hotly contested, and two minutes from time Abelardo hammered in a long-range shot for the Brazilians' second goal. After scoring, the home side's vulnerability was again apparent, resulting in Morgan-Owen notching the Corinthians' fifth. *O Paiz* concluded that they had been right to predict that the Brazilians' performance would improve – the match had been 'one single sensation without interruption'.

Charles Miller would have attended this match, and no doubt, at some point, he discussed his own Corinthians credentials with the visitors, several of whom had been, like him, team-mates of G.O. Smith and C. Wreford-Brown. For Charles, time with the Corinthians party might have served to sharpen in his mind the images of his school days. Just as he had taken the train from Bournemouth to Southampton following the 1894 Hampshire *v* Corinthians fixture, so now he returned to São Paulo bringing with him the current Corinthians.

At the Luz station in São Paulo, the party was greeted by 'members of the League directorate and affiliated clubs, and a large number of footballers', and taken to the Hotel Majestic 'in cars artistically decorated with flowers'. Had Edward VII visited São Paulo he would not have received a grander welcome. Later, a tour of the city included visits to the Palmeiras and Paulistano grounds, and in the evening the tourists went to the Casino-Theatre.

For the first exhibition, the Corinthians would face the reigning São Paulo champions, AA das Palmeiras. The *Correio Paulistano* was certain that if the latter played 'only a passing game, making an intelligent combination, the defeat will be by a minimal goal difference'. Conversely, if the 'detested individual game' were employed, the Brazilians would be crushed. What would Charles have made of such open disdain for the dribbling game he had done much to popularise?

31 August
Corinthians 2   Palmeiras 0

The Velódromo ground was the venue for the English amateurs' first exhibition in São Paulo, and with the city's high society well represented the event was more akin to a 'social happening'. Indeed, several local newspapers began their reports with references to the number of beautiful women in the main stand – 'very selected, wearing the latest fashions', according to one; 'a human wave, like a waterfall, rippling and luminous', the view of another. It bore out Jock Hamilton's comment that it was 'astonishing the number of ladies you see at the matches'. At 4.15 p.m. referee Hermann Friese led the teams out, and the visitors, on winning the toss, elected to play with a strong wind behind them.

The Palmeiras defence soon found themselves with a struggle on their hands, and, while appearing to have the situation under control, they were unable to prevent Day from opening the scoring in the fifth minute. The Corinthians now mounted a series of attacks, pegging their opponents back in their own half. In a rare moment, pressure was relieved and the ball threaded intelligently through to the Palmeiras front-runners by Rubens Salles; however, the move ended with a shot into the hands of Rogers in the Corinthians goal. Straightaway, in their enthusiasm to seize on a possible slip, Irineu and Eurico Mendes ran into the keeper and were then 'violently charged by Page and thrown to the ground'. The crowd were in uproar, but the defender's challenge was adjudged to have been legal.

The Corinthians renewed their assault on the Palmeiras goal and had their finishing been better there would have been more scoring. As the game went on, the home side's attack became increasingly more active. Left-winger Godinho twice wasted promising positions, shooting when a pass would have been better; and then, for once, Page was beaten and a shot sent in which Rogers did well to keep out. Nevertheless, the visitors' pressing finally told and in the last quarter of the half a second goal was scored through Day. The Corinthians' inside-right had kept possession despite the attentions of one of the Palmeiras backs and although his first effort was saved he made no mistake with the rebound. At half-time the 2–0 scoreline prevailed.

After the interval the game continued in the same vein with the Corinthians dominating the exchanges, keeping their opponents on the defensive. However, the English side came up against stubborn resistance and not even Day could find a way to increase their advantage. At the other end, chances were few and far between, and whenever the Palmeiras forwards had the ball a shot or a pass was hurried and the move broke down. Just before the end, haste again was the home side's undoing when Eurico and Godinho, having combined to dispossess the Corinthians' keeper, failed to spot several colleagues unmarked in front of goal, and instead attempted unsuccessfully a more direct route to goal. Thus, the score remained unaltered.

At the final whistle there was enthusiastic applause for both sides and Rubens Salles, noted the correspondent for *O Estado de São Paulo*, was 'carried off in triumph'. So impressive had he been that a group of admirers presented him with a gold chronometer. Indeed, the Corinthians were rumoured to have suggested to Rubens that he return to England with them – but he rejected the offer. Years later, Charles Miller referred to him as 'the most complete centre-half' that he had known.

The next day the *Correio Paulistano* produced a detailed analysis of the Corinthians' style of play, underlining the importance of team-work and good passing:

> A pass, a run or a header by one of the Corinthians' players is understood by every one of his team-mates, and is performed with intuition that is intelligent, certain and fatal. If in any phase of the game the defence clears the ball to any area of the field, it is mathematically calculated the way in which the ball takes the direction it takes, falls where it falls, has someone waiting for it, well-placed, ready to make good use of it.

Brazilians certainly marvelled at the effortless way in which the Corinthians were able to keep possession. In fact it was suggested that the preoccupation of the English with passing was to the detriment of their shooting which was described as 'very poor'. Nevertheless, waiting for an opportunity to shoot near the target rather than attempting a long-range effort was seen as a quality.

As regards individual performances, the *Correio* singled out the work of the visitors' leading striker, inside-right Day, his principal skill being an intelligent positional sense while waiting for the ball or after releasing it. *O Estado* agreed that Day was the pick of the forwards, but for this newspaper it was centre-half Morgan-Owen who particularly caught the eye: 'When he is running he is not a man, he is a deer; with incredible flexibility he squeezes between opponents like a cobra; there is no opening that he cannot slip through, chasing after the ball until he can give it to a better-placed colleague.'

As for the home XI, José Rubião was praised for his inspired team selection, choosing most of the players from one of São Paulo's best club sides, Palmeiras, as opposed to the policy, previously used against foreign teams, of bringing together players from a number of clubs. Not surprisingly, comment about Palmeiras's display centred on the heroics of their back division 'whose soul was made up of Rubens Salles, full-back Urbano and keeper Orlando'. Opinion was divided as to the merits of the hosts' attack.

2 September
Corinthians 5   Paulistas 0
For the second exhibition at the Velódromo the Corinthians made three changes to their side, Morgan-Owen, Vidal and Brisley giving way to Snell, Coleby and Tetley. In organising the Paulista XI, Fernando de Macedo Soares of CA Paulistano typically had summoned players from several clubs; and as usual no training session was held beforehand. At 4.15 p.m. Alex Hutchison led out the teams, and before another capacity crowd the Paulistas kicked off.

In the opening ten minutes the home side, with the forwards linking well, came close to taking the lead. But the English full-backs, Page and Timmis, each had an opportunity to show their skill, and the danger was averted. In contrast, the visitors' first attack stemmed from a fine breakaway by Thew in which he took on and beat the defence only to see his shot stopped by Orlando. More Paulista attacks followed; however, as in the previous game, there was a lack of calm in the final third of the pitch, and instead of turning pressure into goals the Brazilians eventually found themselves a goal down. After half an hour's play Day took a corner and Snell headed the ball powerfully into the net. Soon after, play was held up for five minutes when a challenge from Snell left Menezes concussed. The full-back was taken off and by the time he returned his team had lost their momentum.

After the interval, the visitors took the initiative and with the Paulistas' defence losing its shape it was not long before they went further ahead. First, a shot by Snell was adjudged to have crossed the line after it had bounced down off the crossbar, it being just as well for the hapless Hutchison that there were no league points at stake. Then Snell completed his hat-trick converting a pass from Coleby. Corinthians' fourth goal came from the boot of Day, and this prompted the home side to alter their formation, Rubens resorting to a forward role. Shortly afterwards, Octavio was upended inside the area by Timmis, but Ritcher's spot-kick was saved by Rogers. To add insult to injury, Snell netted the visitors' fifth.

The São Paulo Saturday papers offered different perspectives on this latest defeat suffered by a local selection. According to the *Correio Paulistano* the Paulista front-runners had performed 'brilliantly' and had been unfortunate to come up against a goalkeeper at the top of his game; also, they could have done with more help from the half-backs. Moreover, there was only one explicable reason for the loss: 'The defective defence which absolutely did not live up to general expectations, in terms of play and effort.' As for *O Estado de São Paulo* it was the Corinthians players' use of their weight that was the deciding factor in the second half, resulting in a number of 'violent challenges' which stirred the passions of the crowd. But *O Estado* strongly objected to the behaviour of some of the spectators whose whistling, booing and shouting would have served to intensify the visitors' resolve.

Also on the Saturday, the Corinthians party were taken by train to Jundiaí where they spent the day as guests of the Count of Prates at his Santa Gertrudes ranch. They were accompanied by Liga Paulista officials and members of the press. As in Rio, along with the theatre visits and official dinners, there was plenty to keep the visitors occupied.

4 September
Corinthians 8   Extrangeiros 2
To round off the exhibition series it was the turn of Charles Miller's Foreigners XI to take on the visitors. *O Estado* had called for the inclusion of Hermann Friese at centre-forward, but when the team came out neither Friese nor any other of his Germânia colleagues were present. Miller had chosen an almost exclusively 'British' XI, Paulistano's Tommy Ritcher being the exception. Later *O Estado* would lament that it was not the strongest side that could have been put out. As for the Corinthians line-up, skipper Morgan-Owen was included, along with Vidal and Brisley. The number of spectators at the Velódromo was 'colossal', and the presence of state president Dr Albuquerque Lins and members of his government lent importance to the occasion. At precisely 4.15 p.m. referee Octávio Bicudo gave the signal for the match to start.

After a brief sortie by the São Paulo forwards in which keeper Rogers was tested, the visitors gradually found their rhythm and drew first blood when Brisley went round Ritcher and scored. Then, with Ritcher and Astbury looking decidedly insecure, Snell set up Coleby for Corinthians' second goal. The Extrangeiros retaliated and centre-forward Hamilton wasted two good opportunities, misses that were soon punished when Snell capped a fine move by making it 3–0. Morrow, guarding the home side's net, kept out a number of well-placed shots, but he was powerless to prevent Snell from notching the Corinthians' fourth and fifth goals. Towards the end of the half, Day added two goals to the visitors' tally, the second a shot from 30 yards that went in off the crossbar.

After the break, the complexion of the game changed completely, the Extrangeiros doing most of the attacking, the Corinthians being content to sit back on their lead. Eventually, Steward put the ball past Rogers, only for Snell to restore his side's seven-goal advantage with a powerful shot. Now the home side intensified their attacks, and Miller, having moved to the wing, netted the São Paulo team's second goal. He might have had another had he converted a penalty-kick awarded for a foul by Page. After that, despite more pressure from the Extrangeiros, there was no more scoring. Boyes, Charles's attacking partner of old, had been a 'hero' in defence.

Later the same day, the Corinthians were guests of honour at a banquet hosted by the Liga Paulista in the Majestic Hotel. The press described the farewell party in detail, listing the names of the guests, the menu which included '*Coeur de filet de boeuf à la Corinthian*', the pieces played by the sextet, the valuable gifts presented to the tourists and the various toasts and speeches. Walter Jeffery spoke on behalf of the Liga Paulista, after which Morgan-Owen replied. Referring to the exhibition matches, the Corinthian skipper admitted that he and his colleagues had found the grounds to be too small (the Argentinians were of a similar view), but it had given him pleasure to discover that there were naturally gifted players in São Paulo and that football in the city was progressing well. In the words of one writer 'it was the first medal to be pinned on the chest of football in São Paulo and Brazil'.

As the proceedings drew to a close a representative of the Paulista press extended 'an honourable greeting' to England, inviting everyone to join in singing 'God save the King'. His Majesty's consular official, Charles Miller, then gave a toast to the President of Brazil. It was September 1910. Nothing, it seemed, had changed since that evening some nine years before when, with Paulistas and Cariocas together, Britain was shown to have a central place in Brazilian football.

The following morning a sizeable group representing football in

São Paulo gathered at the Luz station for the Corinthians' departure. There were further expressions of gratitude by the Englishmen for the welcome they had received, and the Liga Paulista's directors gave them a set of photographs of the final game of the tour. *O Estado* caught the mood of this gentlemanly occasion: 'When the train was about to leave the most cordial good wishes were exchanged, and three cheers were given for the Corinthians, for Fluminense and for the Liga Paulista.' It was rituals such as this that reinforced the loftiness of football's place in Brazilian society.

★ ★ ★

Stories abound about the precise nature of the events which led to the founding of Sport Club Corinthians Paulista. The bare facts are that a group of Brazilians, in the main São Paulo Railway employees, were inspired to form a club after watching the English Corinthians – either at the Velódromo or on film of the games screened at the Radium cinema in São Paulo. The first meeting is said to have taken place on the evening of 1 September under a street-lamp in the Bom Retiro district. Miguel Bataglia was elected president. Four days later, at a subsequent gathering, the name Corinthians was adopted. Most Corintianos may not know it, but according to Charles Miller's cousin, Charles Rule, it was Miller who suggested the name to Bataglia.

Charles, his 36th birthday approaching, had decided that the Extrangeiros *v* Corinthians fixture would be his last official game. Perhaps this had influenced his decision to choose a scratch XI that was virtually the SPAC first team – with the obvious benefit the experience would bring to the younger players – for the match. Whatever Miller's reasons for excluding some of the best German players (the exception being Ritcher), an English-language newspaper in Rio, the *Brazilian Review*, used the 'Englishness' of the Extrangeiros as a prong in an unsavoury attack on what it believed were the inadequacies of the Brazilian sides.

For the *Review*, in the final match of the tour, the intention had been 'to show the Corinthians a game of clean English football as opposed to the exotic variety that they were given in some of the preceding matches'. As for the other exhibitions, the visitors had 'run circles round the best Brazilian sides', slacking through tiredness in the opening games in São Paulo. There was also reference to the atmosphere at one of the matches: 'the continuous roar of taunts, jeers and hisses directed by the crowd against the visiting team.' Leading Rio and São Paulo dailies were up in arms.

The insinuation was that the Corinthians had been subjected to the 'coarseness' of the Brazilian players. In a strong rebuttal *O Estado* reproduced in its entirety the English text of a letter sent by the Corinthians to the Liga Paulista, giving emphasis to the phrase 'no one could have shown greater hospitality than you did to us'. The Corinthians' excessive use of their weight, although acknowledged to be legitimate, was frowned upon, forcing the 'one-sided English referee' to give 'innumerous free-kicks and even a penalty' against them. Alex Hutchison was becoming used to being a target for abuse. Indeed, *O Estado* argued that some of the aggressive chanting had been aimed at the referee, and that, besides, the 'guests' would have distinguished between the booing and the applause that they had received.

There is no knowing why the *Review* should have decided to publish such a provocative piece. Some of the allegations do seem far-fetched. What the episode reveals is that for Brazilians, football, while firmly in the hands of the élite, occupied an important position in Brazilian society. The *Review*'s comments may well have been sensationalist, but they had touched a nerve. The riposte in the press underlined the positive aspects of the Brazilian game and made it plain that the Corinthians were not above criticism themselves. One of the things that had been learnt was the effective use of 'charges', the *Jornal do Commercio* insisting that 'we were not used to them, neither did we expect the Corinthian players to use them so much'.

Three years later, the Corinthians were back and the physical play of one of their Rio opponents would lead to their undoing. It would have surprised them to discover that the player in question was an amateur from Liverpool.

SIX

The Anfield Amateur

Welfare is an excellent type of the amateur player, and he has shaped very creditably whenever drafted into the league team at Anfield. We would there were more men of the same calibre forthcoming, for they exercise a beneficial leavening on the cause of football in this city.

Everton and Liverpool Official Football Programme,
12 April 1913

Combining the characteristics of a bustling leader with a commendable control of the ball, and the exercise of judgment in passing to his comrades, Welfare kept the Wednesday defence in a state of continual anxiety.

Athletic News, 17 February 1913

Mr T.H. Jackson, the indefatigable secretary to the famous amateur organisation, is proud of his team, and has reason to be. The Nomads, when at full strength, are the finest exponents of amateur football in the kingdom.

Chester AFC Programme, quoted in the *Birkenhead and Cheshire Advertiser*, 21 October 1911

At Hoylake, on the tip of the Wirral, they called him 'The Mad Horse'. In the *Liverpool Echo* his surname was preceded by the initials J.H. until an item, shortly after his full Liverpool début, set the record straight. For a leading writer in Rio de Janeiro, he was 'a kind of yankee in the Court of King Arthur', a sobriquet which was intended to express the player's unique contribution to his club: 'It was as if Fluminense were using an illicit weapon.' The variety of names for Harry Welfare adds to the mystery surrounding his remarkable journey from top amateur footballer on Merseyside to foremost player, coach and administrator of the game in Brazil.

But what was the basis for Welfare's success in the four decades leading up to the 1950 World Cup tournament? How had he risen to prominence before his departure for Rio in 1913? What follows will be an attempt to provide a background to the life in Brazil of one of football's forgotten mavericks.

Harry was born on 20 August 1888 in the Wavertree district of Liverpool, the year in which Charles Miller was poised to break into the Banister Court XI. Just as Charles's father had sought work abroad, Harry's was allegedly prospecting for gold in Australia before settling in England. Clearly, in Harry's case, the taste for adventure passed from father to son – and daughter. One of Harry's sisters was to emigrate to Canada, another, a popular schoolteacher, would become the first woman in Liverpool to ride the prestigious Douglas motorcycle.

Early signs of ability on the football field might have been shown when Harry was playing for Sefton Park School and later Oulton Secondary School in the Second Division of the South Lancashire Amateur Combination. It was through Merseyside's mazy system of leagues that Welfare progressed, representing such clubs as the Liverpool Caledonians and Sandown. The big two, Liverpool and Everton, spent the period following the former's promotion to the First Division in 1905 until Harry's leaving for Brazil leap-frogging over one another in the table. Tranmere Rovers were not yet a part of the League fold.

With a proven record as a goal-getter, the first challenge of note arrived at the beginning of the 1909–10 season when 21-year-old Harry was signed by St Helens Recreation. In a practice match on 21 August he netted for the blue-shirted second-teamers as they defeated the senior side. He was being earmarked to replace a local favourite.

> In the Reds section the familiar figure of Juddy Roberts was missing. Wellfare [*sic*], who is meant to take his place, is a much more sturdy-looking man. Wellfare is much taller and more powerful looking than Roberts and he showed signs of being a most useful

player. If he fulfils expectations the loss of the evergreen Juddy will
not be so severely felt.

The Recs were members of the Lancashire Combination Division
1, a competition which included the reserve teams of several First
Division clubs. A couple of games into the new season and the
qualities that were to have such an impact on football in Brazil were
already evident in Welfare's game. Allied to the powerful physique was
a fleet-footedness that took even his fellow forwards by surprise. A
reporter on the *St Helens Newspaper & Advertiser* liked what he saw:

> He is very fast, and it is rather a novelty for the Recs to have a fast
> centre-forward. In the past the trouble has always been that the
> wings were too quick for the centre – now they are scarcely fast
> enough. Welfare's dribbles down the centre were a treat to witness,
> for he went at top speed and tricked man after man, only to be
> defeated many times by sheer hard luck. When he had once got past
> a man, that man was finished with, for Welfare went too quick to be
> caught again. The centre-forward position is one of the strongest
> points of the team, judging from last night's play.

The praise seemed well founded as, a fortnight later, Harry scored
twice in a 6–0 win against Southport Central. It was the Recs' first
win of the campaign. But then, suddenly, triggered by a loss to
neighbours St Helens Town, the new centre-forward was inexplicably
demoted to the A team, a rare trough in an otherwise ascendant
career. In November his absence from the senior side was bemoaned
in the local press, but it wasn't until January that he was reinstated.
Included for the Recs' game against Everton Reserves at Goodison
Park, Welfare led the attack for the rest of the season.

Transience, though, was to be Harry's trademark, and in the
summer of 1910 he returned to Sandown. But he remained registered
to St Helens, for this was the reason why Southport, another Lancashire Combination club, were prevented from signing him. Sandown
must have thought highly of Welfare for they made him their player-
secretary. For a while, at least, there would be no more visits to the
glamour grounds of the north – but this would not have bothered
Harry. He seemed content to play his football at a lower level and to
play for the fun of it. It was a philosophy that would have struck a
chord with Charles Miller.

Indeed, on the very same weekend that Charles bowed out of

representative football in Brazil in the presence of the English Corinthians, Harry was playing for Sandown against a team from the Central Gasworks. Experiences close in spirit if not in distance or relevance.

Not long afterwards, the honourable attitude of the Sandown players was confirmed in the wake of a heavy defeat. Of their opponents, West Toxteth, the *Liverpool Football Echo* wrote that the 6–2 scoreline 'was not their only satisfaction, for we have received a sporting testimonial of the Sandowners' idea of sportsmanship, which clearly proves that games can be enjoyed, though lost'.

Quite how Harry Welfare became associated with the Northern Nomads AFC remains unclear, but the itinerant nature of the amateur club clearly suited him. During the 1910–11 season the Nomads were tenants at Tranmere's Prenton Park ground. As with the Corinthians, with whom they were compared, the Nomads' fixture list consisted mainly of friendlies. Unlike the Londoners, however, they had not subscribed to the breakaway Amateur Football Association. They were therefore entitled to arrange games with the second strings of League clubs and to compete in cup competitions. They even took the Corinthians' place for the traditional New Year's match against Queen's Park.

It may be that Harry had already begun work as a schoolmaster in Liverpool, his background chiming therefore with the Nomads' policy of attracting players from northern colleges and universities. If indeed he had applied to join the club then it is likely that he was first introduced into the side when several regulars were called up for an amateur international trial at the end of January 1911. Other absences ensued and after Harry's Prenton Park début the *Birkenhead and Cheshire Advertiser* correspondent admitted that he liked the new inside-right, 'as besides being a good shot he has plenty of dash and he made a most capable partner to Barlow', England amateur international G.H. Barlow no less.

But Welfare did not abandon Sandown, turning out for them in between games for the Nomads. Not only that, as the season drew to a close, he helped Hoylake carry off the Cheshire League Shield and several local trophies. Team-mates must never have known when they were next going to see him. In March and April Harry notched goals for each of these clubs, the best, possibly, in the Nomads' last home game, against Amateur Alliance champions South Nottingham. This strike, we are told, 'was worth going some distance to see. Welfare secured about 30 yards from the visiting goal, and tricking four opponents very cleverly he planted the ball past Daft.' Stamina, skill and a nose for goal – these were elements around which his reputation was being made.

Touring, while not on the same scale as that of the Corinthians, was an integral part of the Nomads' activities. But when a group set off for the Low Countries and Germany in May 1911, Harry, possibly due to his teaching commitments, stayed behind. Although the Nomads returned unbeaten, at the AGM in July Honorary Secretary Thomas Jackson 'reminded members that Continental clubs were fast approaching the best standard of British football'. Perhaps if those governing the British game had taken notice of and acted on pronouncements such as this, Britain's aloofness with regard to foreign football might not have been so intractable. The irony was that, as part of Brazil's preparations for the 1950 World Cup, it was an Englishman who was dispatched to London to recruit referees for Rio and São Paulo. That Englishman was Harry Welfare.

Much of what Harry knew about football administration had been learnt on Merseyside. Not long after the spell as Sandown's secretary he was elected onto the Nomads' management committee, in August 1911. An influential figure was Thomas 'Pa' Jackson who, like the Corinthians' N.L. Jackson, was the leading spirit of his club. The fixtures he had arranged with Lancashire's professional clubs brought in a large portion of the Nomads' revenue. A Liverpool solicitor, Jackson later assisted the first directors of Tranmere Rovers AFC Ltd in the legalities of changing to a limited company. Welfare, therefore, like Miller, would arrive in Brazil with practical knowledge of how the game was run – to add to adroitness on the pitch.

But if his involvement in committee work implied a serious, disciplined attitude to football, Harry, in his early 20s, was also undoubtedly a free spirit. Unorthodox and unpredictable, this was reflected in the way he played the game and why he kept clubs on tenterhooks over his availability. An example of an engagement which backfired occurred at the start of the 1911–12 season.

Southport Central, a club on a par with St Helens Recs, had for some time been interested in signing Welfare. In July 1911, finally, it was announced that the player's signature had been secured. Ten days after becoming a Nomads' committee member, Harry took part in one of Southport's practice games. But on the following Saturday, for a similar match, he failed to put in an appearance. Harry, it transpired, had been competing at an athletics meeting – 'Footballer as prize winner' ran the headline of this report:

> At the Moreton sports on Saturday last Mr H. Welfare, the Northern
> Nomad and Hoylake forward, accomplished a fine feat by winning
> the 100, 220 and 440 yards handicaps and so taking home three
> valuable prizes. We congratulate this energetic athlete on his signal
> success, which is rather unique.
>
> *Birkenhead and Cheshire Advertiser*, 30 August 1911

Despite the absence of their new player, Southport expected
Welfare to be playing for them against Manchester City Reserves in
the season-opener. Harry, however, once more absented himself,
turning out instead for the Nomads. One game later the *Southport
Guardian* wrote that Central were 'still unable to command the
services of Welfare . . .' It is not clear how the episode ended. But had
Harry stayed at Southport he would have risked causing further
irritation. Several weeks later he was off on a camp organised by the
Territorial Army. The drilling and field training he underwent were
probably viewed by the Southport board as a form of rightful
retribution.

By early October 1911 Harry was back playing for the Nomads.
During the next six months he consolidated his place in their forward
line and went on two tours – the New Year's excursion to Scotland
and the trip to the Low Countries at Easter. One of the leading goalscorers on the Wirral, he was particularly prolific over the Christmas
period, finding the net 14 times in five games. It was typical of his
enthusiasm and sense of abandon that, having guested for Hoylake on
Christmas Day morning, he had another game for them 24 hours later
and then donned a Nomads' shirt later the same day. Around this time
he received a worthy and insightful accolade from a columnist who
went by the name of 'The Man in the Moon'. Harry had just bagged
four of the Nomads' seven goals in a cup semi-final:

> I was particularly struck by the play of Welfare, the Nomads' centre-
> forward, who as a worker in the position must stand unrivalled in
> the district. True, at times he is risky, to say nothing of being 'most
> pushing', but he never once will adopt foul tactics. Although on
> occasions [he has] been knocked and kicked about in a manner most
> shameful, I have yet to await the day – which I hope will never come
> – when he descends even so low as to retaliate. This abstention from
> treachery is the secret of his success, and I hope his nobility of
> character will earn for him the popularity he deserves.

Such 'nobility' was part and parcel of the Nomads' ethos and precisely why they were portrayed as 'a fine lot of sports' and 'pure amateurs'. It is hard to think that four years later Harry Welfare was required to provide proof of his amateur credentials by the footballing authorities in Rio. The confusion arose over Harry's previous attachment to a Football League club.

In August 1912 Harry followed in the footsteps of several other Nomads when he signed an amateur form for a professional club. His 'aptitude for goals' – 35 in the Nomads' last campaign – had persuaded First Division Liverpool to take a closer look at him. Welfare was given a run-out in one of the Reds' warm-up games. His contribution was tentative; however, the *Liverpool Echo*'s reporter gave him the benefit of the doubt:

> Welfare flattered but to deceive. Still he is the right type of player for the centre position, big and bustling. There is method in his dash and force and direction in his shooting, and if it was rather superficial, I think he is a player who will improve.

After that, as the season drew nearer, the only references to him in the *Echo* were illustrations of the punning possibilities of his name – 'Is the name Welfare a good omen for the Reds?' and 'Everyone is anxious for Liverpool's Welfare and Everton's, too!'. The first of these proved fateful, for, when Liverpool Reserves began their Central League fixtures, we are told that 'the forward line was rearranged owing to the inability of Welfare to appear'. Fickle as ever, he was, of course, still drawn to the Nomads.

Some form of compromise must have been reached, for Harry was allowed to stay with the Nomads, returning to Anfield when the amateurs were knocked out of the English Cup. He made his début for Liverpool Reserves away to Blackburn Rovers in mid-October and was on the scoresheet one month later at Crewe. But initially he found goals hard to come by – just the one in a dozen Central League starts before the year was out. In December, Liverpool released Harry for a North *v* South amateur international trial match at York. He is listed in the *Yorkshire Herald* of 7 December 1912 as a North reserve; however, there is no conclusive proof that he played.

What we do know is that he had impressed the Liverpool directors sufficiently to be given his League début for the visit of Sheffield Wednesday on 15 February 1913. With the regular number 9 injured, the other option of shuffling the forward line was rejected. A fortnight before, Harry had scored against Everton Reserves, a game watched by a crowd of 20,000, and his 'forcefulness' was especially noted. Indeed, the *Echo*'s 'Anfielder' had high hopes that Welfare would be promoted, even before the decision was made public. 'With experience in better-class company he has every appearance of developing into a really capable centre-forward; and Central League football is not likely to improve him – he is a bit too classy.' Now 'their' man was in the team, the *Echo*, on the eve of the game, appealed for patience. 'Spectators must not expect him to be a G.O. Smith at his first appearance . . . let them give him a fair chance to settle down.' In the event, the cautionary words were unwarranted.

League leaders Sheffield Wednesday were seen off 2–1, Harry having a hand in both goals and seeing two of his shots hit the woodwork. On the following Monday he was singled out in the *Echo*'s sports column. In an analysis of his performance he was likened to a former Reds forward, a player who had had a fleeting association with the club. It was a prescient comparison:

> He resembles Blanthorne in that he is of big height, can head a ball, and has a cramped run. He worked like a 'brick' all through the game, and his dash, tired as he was from the three-quarters stage, was ever to be feared. Three times a Wednesday full-back tried to clear and the ball cannoned against Welfare. I like the centre that follows up. Welfare used his weight fairly and with good result, and it was delicious to see him bowl over one of the Wednesday defenders. It is easy to get a man down if he is unbalanced or is on one leg, but Welfare got his man straight on the shoulder, and though the resistance was great, Welfare put his man down. I was sorry the Northern Nomad amateur didn't get a goal, for he deserved one. His inward pass and his care for the wings were judicious and timed to the right fraction of a minute . . .

The *Echo* wasn't the only Liverpool newspaper to sing Harry's praises. The *Courier* described him as a 'fearless amateur, who not only plays with mature judgment, but is as formidable as a stone wall when it comes to charging'. For the *Post*, he 'made a reputation for himself, and his future career will be followed with much interest'. No one knew it, but four months later Harry Welfare would be packing his bags, preparing to sail for Rio.

Although ineligible for Liverpool's English Cup tie against Newcastle, Harry kept his place for the next two League games. His solitary goal in League football arrived on 1 March – Anfield the venue, Derby County the visitors. A week later he led the Liverpool attack at White Hart Lane. Perhaps Harry was one of the small group of players who, prior to the match, were involved in a road accident. The *Echo* prefaced its match report with the details: 'The journey from Euston Square to Tottenham was made through a snowstorm, and one of the taxi-cabs containing four of the players came into violent collision with an electric tramcar.' The fortunate four, unhurt, were safely delivered to the ground.

The London game might have been Harry's last in the League, had some Liverpool first-teamers not been accused of 'throwing' a subsequent home fixture. By the time Chelsea visited Anfield on Easter Monday, 24 March, the amateur was playing once more for the reserves, Liverpool's first-choice centre-forward having returned from injury. What happened during the Chelsea game incensed the Liverpool supporters and provoked accusatory remarks from Football League official H.G. Norris. The Lancashire press report cited by Mr Norris was quoted in the *Echo*:

> Liverpool never appeared desirous of obtaining goals, whereas they allowed their opponents every opportunity of so doing. Never in their career have they given a worse exhibition, and few of the team will emerge from the contest with added reputation. Genuine performers on the Liverpool side could be numbered on the fingers of one hand. Their opponents were feeble in the extreme, yet they won.

The Liverpool directors responded by dropping four forwards for the visit of Manchester United on the following Saturday, and Welfare was one of those who were drafted in. Before an 'unusually small' attendance, the Reds were beaten 2–0, and the word on Welfare was that he was 'lame almost throughout'. The four absentees were restored for the remaining matches.

If, around this time, Harry had become aware of the offer of a teaching post in Rio, he probably would have had no qualms about leaving the Reds given the insidious behaviour of some of his teammates and the murky motives behind his brief recall. A Football League enquiry may have exonerated both sets of players, but the 'grave charges' left a bitter mark on the season. Worse, of course, was to come two years later when four Liverpool players received suspensions for their involvement in football betting's *cause célèbre*.

The first inkling that Harry was on the move came on the last Saturday of the season. Instead of turning out for Liverpool Reserves, he elected to play for Tranmere Rovers, adding a goal to his hat-trick for them five weeks earlier. The following Wednesday his name was not on the list of those players being retained by Liverpool – and yet on the same day, 30 April, he participated in the final of the Liverpool Cup, scoring for the Reds in a 3–1 win over Everton. This was Harry's last game for Liverpool. A timely comment in the *Echo* reflected perhaps the opinion of those running the club: 'Welfare may be all right, but yet an amateur, and we want wholehoggers.'

But for the Liverpool directors, firm commitment was something that had to be bought. They clearly wanted Welfare to stay and apparently placed two offers before him – '£3 a week if he wished to continue his teaching pursuits, or the maximum wage if he could see his way to "wed" himself to the club altogether'. Harry's refusal to go down the professional route was to be expected and most likely came after arrangements for his departure had been set in motion. His decision to leave probably had less to do with football; it was rather a response to a craving for adventure.

News that Harry might be leaving was first reported in the *Echo* on 23 May under the heading 'Blow for the Reds'. A week later there was confirmation. The supporters were sorry to see him go:

> Welfare's severance from Liverpool occasioned surprise and regret among the club's following. The amateur centre-forward has secured an appointment as gymnastic instructor in the Argentine. His going will prove something of a loss to the 'Livers', as he has proved himself a most promising player.

If it is not a journalist's mistake, the reference to Harry's destination is puzzling. It would certainly have been in character for him to have interrupted his voyage in Rio. But the inference in an essay by Mário Filho on Welfare's arrival in Rio is that the Ginásio Anglo-Brasileiro, a boys' boarding school run on English lines, had appointed him based on information received from England. Mário Filho had obviously talked to Welfare about this, which makes it all the more frustrating to read his version of the teacher's first meeting with his new employers – a colourful mixture of fact and concocted dialogue. How tempting it is to believe the suggestion that even before Harry had arrived in Rio, plans were being made for him to join Fluminense Football Club.

SEVEN

A Début in Rio

It was a successful shoot [sic], from close range, which came from dribling [sic] which veteran Fluminense's excellent new center-forward [sic] uses and abuses. We'd like to believe that this one defect noted in Fluminense's new 'player' is due to lack of confidence in his new team-mates. We don't doubt that he himself will recognise – good player that he is – that excessive 'dribling' is merely a show for the spectators.

From a report in the *Jornal do Commercio*,
22 August 1913

His inclusion in the Rio teams marked, without doubt, an epoch in the national sport. Welfare's epoch must be common knowledge in Rio and in the various states – in São Paulo stories about the exploits of the great center [sic] spread quickly – and it must be left to posterity as one of the symptoms of the progress of 'football' among us.

From a pen picture in the *Correio da Manhã*,
3 October 1915

There can be few sports organisations in the world that can boast archives as extensive as Fluminense's. The fact that it is so well preserved is due to the devotion and resourcefulness of curator José Borges Júnior (Zezinho). The notebooks and bound volumes of cuttings that chart the development of the club in the first quarter of the twentieth century are kept in a cubbyhole at one end of the main stand. This is Flumemória. Here, an entry in a Members' Register throws light on the events leading to Harry Welfare's joining the club.

It is recorded that Welfare's Fluminense membership was proposed by the club's vice-president, Félix Frias, and accepted at a directors' meeting on 8 July 1913. Ten days later, Harry boarded the Royal Mail's SS *Amazon* in Southampton. It would appear, indeed, that, having learnt that the Anglo-Brasileiro's new teacher had played First Division football in England, Fluminense lost no time in ensuring that the player – subject of course to his approval – would be wearing their colours rather than those of a rival. The school's PE teacher, J.A. Quincey-Taylor, happened to be Fluminense's coach, and it was most likely he who introduced Harry to the club.

For Fluminense, the city's oldest and most successful club, Welfare could not have come to Rio at a better time. The club had been rebuilding its team since the end of the 1911 season when nine players left to form a football section at Flamengo. That season, by a curious coincidence, the club had broken new ground in Rio by employing a British coach, Charlie Williams. Before coming to Brazil, Williams had held coaching positions in Denmark and in France; while as a player, keeping goal for Manchester City, he had once scored famously with a wind-assisted goal-kick. As from March 1911, in what amounted to a blatant contravention of the amateur rules of the Rio league, Williams received a salary of £18 a month and had all his expenses paid. It is not clear the extent to which he was involved in the controversy that led to the discontent within the ranks. The players stuck it out to see the championship secured – and then departed.

Harry's arrival also coincided with a brief peak in the fortunes of one of the capital's two British clubs. A founder member of the Rio league, Paysandu had won the title in 1912. It was a team based around members of two families, the Pullens and the Robinsons. Two players stood out – inside-forward Sidney Pullen and centre-forward Harry Robinson. In 1912 Robinson had netted half the club's colossal goals total of 64 in 14 games, including eight in a game against Mangueira. In the following season, however, in a manner reminiscent of Charles Miller, Harry Robinson switched to playing in goal. If Fluminense hadn't swooped to enlist Welfare he may well have been persuaded by Paysandu to fill the vacant spot in their forward line. Soon, mockingly, the fixture list provided everyone with a sight of what might have been.

For his début in Rio, the last thing Harry would have expected was to come up against opposition from England. As in 1910, it was Fluminense who invited the Corinthians to tour. It did not matter that Harry had not played competitively since his arrival, his *curriculum vitae* alone would have ensured that he was selected to represent the Brazilian capital in the opening encounter. One of his striking partners was Sidney Pullen. Two other members of the Rio British community were included in the side, Harry Robinson and Flamengo's Lawrence Andrews. In 1913, British involvement in Brazilian football was far greater in Rio than it was in São Paulo.

The Corinthians had set out for Brazil on 1 August, a party of 15, several of whom had toured in 1910. A prominent member of the team told *The Sportsman* that 'they had a good side, which included several first-class cricketers, and they would probably vary the programme arranged by taking part in cricket matches'. For this self-assured Corinthian, football – bearing in mind the comfortable victories of the previous tour – was not the only purpose of this visit. It was perhaps such an attitude that led to two of the senior tourists, Morgan-Owen and Day, sitting out the first match. Brazilians, on the other hand, prepared for the worst; Woosnam, for instance, was described as 'the best centre-half in the world'.

The account which follows, written by one of the Corinthians, was reproduced a month later on the front page of *The Sportsman*. It was accompanied by short sketches of the two other games in Rio. If the London readership was in doubt, the Rio forward whose name looked familiar was indeed the same player who had appeared at White Hart Lane for Liverpool earlier in the year.

CORINTHIANS *v* RIO DE JANEIRO

Played on August 21. A slight wind blew down the ground, which is narrow and rather short, and this, coupled with the intense hardness of the surface, made the ball exceedingly difficult to control. The Corinthians won the toss, and played with the wind. After fast play, during which both sides attacked, Woosnam scored with a good shot from 20 yards out three minutes from the start. The home team showed no sign of demoralisation, and the game continued even, both sides attacking in turn, but the Corinthian attack looked the more dangerous, and the Rio goalkeeper received several powerful shots from Sloley, Foster and Thompson. Turner had decidedly less to do. Towards the end of the first half the Rio forwards forced several corners, and in clearing from one of them Vidal and an opponent together attempted to head the ball. Vidal succeeded, but the referee awarded a penalty, which made the score one-all two minutes before half-time.

On changing ends Snell went centre-forward and Sloley inside-right, Thompson taking Snell's place at full-back. Woosnam made another good but ineffective shot with his left off a full pitch, after which the home forwards pressed for some time. But there was little to choose between the sides, although the Corinthians' shots were better directed. Ten minutes from time the Rio right-wing attacked, and as the result of an unfortunate misunderstanding between Thompson and Turner, Welfare scored an easy goal, making the score 2–1 in favour of the home side. Snell and Thompson then changed places again, and Foster and Sloley both nearly equalised, but nothing further was scored.

The home side, apart from weak shooting, were always able to hold their own. The Corinthians were considerably heavier, but their opponents were quite equal to them in speed, and were, if anything, quicker on the ball at close quarters. The home team played better and the Corinthians worse than in the corresponding match of 1910. The most conspicuous contributors to the victory were the goalkeeper, both full-backs, the centre-forward and inside-right.

RIO DE JANEIRO: H. Robinson; Píndaro and Nery; Lawrence, Mutz and Rolando; Oswaldo, Sidney, H. Welfare, Mimi and Lauro.

CORINTHIANS: N.V.C. Turner; I.E. Snell and H.V. Bury; L.A. Vidal, M. Woosnam and J.C. Gow; R.C. Cutter, R.G. Thompson, R. Sloley, A.W. Foster and R.C. Maples.

(18 September 1913)

In Rio, the result and the way the home team had played were greeted with 'general surprise'. According to the *Jornal do Commercio*, 'we have never seen a carioca team, a scratch XI representing our nationality, so well organised as the one which played yesterday'. It was hailed as a victory of Brazil over England. At the same time, previous suggestions that the visitors were world-beaters were hastily revised, the report stating that the 1910 Corinthians were far superior. But what impression, apart from the 'easy' winning goal, did Harry Welfare make?

The effusive tone of the *Jornal do Commercio*'s opening remarks extended to the appraisal of the players. But no one was singled out. At the heart of the Rio front line 'Mimi, Welfare and Sidney exceeded all expectations . . . whether combined or individual their industry was fully evident.' Ironically, the one critical point was Harry's perceived tendency to hold on to the ball too long. His supporters on Merseyside would have chuckled at that. Some Brazilians were clearly expecting the new man to exemplify the finer points of the revered passing game.

But the Corinthians saw it differently. Their reaction, for game two of the tour, against a Foreigners XI, was to give special attention to the former Northern Nomad. The visitors won 4–0 and, for *The Sportsman*'s correspondent, 'Welfare, who was always dangerous in the first match, seemed perfectly harmless when opposed by Morgan-Owen.'

Revealing a Brazilian line-up above makes it necessary to comment on some of the names. In this 1913 Rio side for one of the full-backs, Píndaro, a first name is used, for the other, Nery, a surname. Mutz is short for Mutzembecker. Use of the first name for Lawrence Andrews and Sidney Pullen appears to be a way of indicating that they are Brazilian-born. The one nickname, Mimi, for Benjamin Sodré, is a foretaste in a process that culminated in the creation of the names Pelé and Garrincha. Today, as in 1913, it is first names that predominate.

It was Mimi who was one of the heroes of the Corinthians' last game in Rio. The same newspaper which had cautioned Welfare about dribbling too much was now referring to Mimi's 'unsurpassed' performance – 'in driblings [*sic*], in rushes, in passes and in breakaways, ultimately reproduced in every form'. The tourists squeezed home 2–1, but it was Mimi's individual effort for the Brazilians' goal which stole the show. For Welfare, almost certainly watching from the stand, any doubts he had about the quality of football in Rio were considerably lessened. One week later, Mimi's Botafogo inflicted a 3–0 defeat on Fluminense in Welfare's first game for his new club.

The exhibition series involving the Corinthians would also have demonstrated to Harry the popularity of the game among Brazilians, as well as its élitist character. There were gates of six to ten thousand at Fluminense's stadium, and the final match was watched by several members of the Brazilian Cabinet and by the British and American ambassadors. But whereas in Rio football had one governing body, in São Paulo there were now two. It was the breakaway Associação Paulista dos Esportes Atléticos, led by Paulistano, that hosted the second leg of the Corinthians' tour.

In his second report, *The Sportsman*'s correspondent again took pains to emphasise that playing conditions left much to be desired. But this could not hide the fact that in São Paulo, just as in Rio, the standard of football had 'substantially improved'. An XI organised by Paulistano led the way.

CORINTHIANS v PAULISTA [*sic*]

Played at São Paolo [*sic*] on Thursday, August 28. The ground was still as narrow as in 1910 — 65 yards or thereabouts — but it was not nearly so difficult to control the ball here as in Rio, the grass, or rather the kind of spreading plantain, being reasonably thick and soft. There were, however, patches all down the centre, and particularly in front of goal, where the ground was perfectly bare, and as fast as a ground could be. The Corinthian side . . . pressed from the start, and after five minutes' play Woosnam scored from 20 yards out. Two minutes later some good passing between Snell and Day ended in the latter scoring. The Corinthians had decidedly the best of the game, but did not score again. At half-time Vidal took Snell's place at centre-forward, Bury going right-half and Snell full-back. The change strengthened the defence at the expense of the attack. The home side forced their only corner, and their outside-right headed a goal. The Corinthians won by 2–1. Mr Miller, the British vice-consul, proved an efficient referee.

(24 September 1913)

Charles Miller may have refereed the opening game, but in terms of British involvement in Paulista football it was merely symbolic. On the eve of the Corinthians' arrival in São Paulo, Charles was evidently preparing the São Paulo Athletic cricket team for a match against the gentleman amateurs. As that prominent Corinthian had intimated in London, the tour programme was indeed altered and a day was spent playing cricket and tennis at SPAC. Also, as if to underline that an era had ended, there were local press references to Charles's consular activities — an official reception and a meeting with a state secretary — alongside football comment. The plain fact was that SPAC no longer had a football team.

It seems there were two main reasons why the British Club pulled out of the Liga Paulista at the end of the 1912 season — this time for good. First, the club had won the League in 1911, but never received the silver prize. Previous winners AA das Palmeiras had fallen out with the governing body and refused to hand over the trophy. Secondly, there was Americano's flagrant breaking of the rules by signing two Uruguayans. 'False amateurism', it was euphemistically called. SPAC councillor and historian John Mills believes it was other clubs' violation of the amateur ethos — the very principles on which SPAC was formed — that forced his predecessors to act.

By the time the Corinthians arrived, several former SPAC players were representing Brazilian clubs – among them, one of the most conspicuous was Jack Astbury. A full-back for Paulistano in their 2–1 defeat by the visitors, Astbury was appointed to take charge of the next exhibition. The encounter produced a glut of goals, but also a glimpse of the unsavoury side of football.

Mackenzie, perceived to be APEA's best prepared side, received an 8–2 drubbing. But more serious and surprising than the scoreline was the behaviour in the second half of some of the home players. According to the *Correio Paulistano*, 'Mackenzie completely lost their cool, playing as if they were blind, behaving with brutality and managing to injure several of the opposing forwards and half-backs.' The offenders, it was felt, should have been dismissed. One was promptly given a suspension. The Corinthian reporter referred to an 'unsportsmanlike display . . . confined to some four or five players'. Poor Astbury must have been relieved to resume full-back duties for the final match.

To everyone's relief this fixture was played in an 'exemplary spirit' and appropriately honours between the visitors and AA das Palmeiras were shared. Rubens Salles had impressed the Corinthians in 1910, and now one of their number described him as 'a player of rare talent'. It was a goal by Rubens that brought the sides level at 1–1. But although, again, they had avoided defeat, a view from their opponents was that the Brazilians would be hard pushed 'to make an even game against an average English University side playing under English conditions'. It seems a harsh statement and it may have been different had the Corinthians come up against the nascent talent of Friedenreich and Formiga. They were helping Americano defeat an Argentine XI in Buenos Aires – Brazil's first success away from home.

As Tomás Mazzoni points out in his *História do Futebol no Brasil*, 1913 was the year in which Brazilian football entered its 'adolescent phase'. Apart from the wins against the Corinthians and the Argentinos, teams representing the principal football centres of Rio and São Paulo recorded home victories over sides from Portugal and Chile. It is an indication of the strides made by the Brazilian game since 1910 that during the Corinthians' second visit post-match reports were markedly less enthusiastic in their comment on the tourists. There was a predictability to the Corinthians' football – 'the way they play is always the same', *O Estado* noted. One year later, the Corinthians were probably spared further embarrassment when a third tour to South America was cancelled due to the outbreak of war in Europe.

Another important feature of the 1913 season was the resumption of matches between Rio and São Paulo. A cup was offered for competition by the Rio *Correio da Manhã*. The first encounter took place in November at Fluminense. It was another first for Welfare. He was joined in the Rio side by Harry Robinson and Sidney Pullen. In contrast, the team mustered by the Liga Paulista contained just one man of British origin. He was Archibald McLean. Like Welfare, McLean had arrived in Brazil as a national football style was emerging. Perhaps he didn't have as big an impact as Welfare on the Brazilian game, but he did help to ensure that in São Paulo there was a lifeline for British football after SPAC's demise.

A painting of Charles Miller by F. Pierech, *c*.1878; and Charles (left) and John Miller at Banister Court School in the 1880s (courtesy Helena Miller)

The victorious Banister Court sixes team, April 1892 (from left): W. Hartley, J.P. Galloway, C. Miller, L.H. Gay, A.W. Denning and R.V.L. Dashwood (courtesy Hampshire FA)

Southampton St Mary's, 1893–94 season
(front row from left): C. Miller, G. Nineham,
E.J. Nicholls, W. Stride, G.W. Verney,
J. Dollin, G. Marshall; (back): V. Barton, Dr
R. Bencraft, R. Ruffell, E.J. Taylor, G. Carter,
G. Price, J. Dorkin, C. Knight (secretary),
H. Johns (treasurer)
INSET: Charles's first medal for St Mary's

The Hampshire side that faced the Corinthians, March 1894 (standing):
W. Pickford, J. Nethercote, J.W. Dorkin, W. Reynolds, T.H. Stokes,
H. Ward, Dr R. Bencraft; (on chairs): F.M. Walker, D.C. Stewart,
A. Denning, J. George, C. Miller; (on ground): G. Ridges, H. Dawson
(courtesy Hampshire FA)

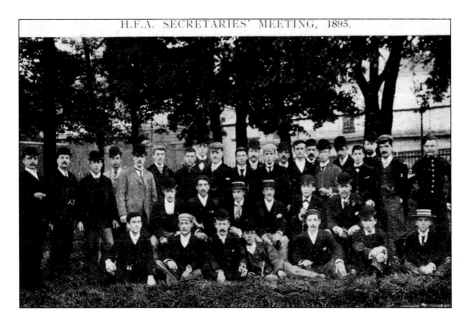

ABOVE: The presence of Charles Miller (on ground, far right) indicates that the date of this photo, in William Pickford's *Golden Jubilee Book*, is incorrect. This group of Hampshire secretaries was taken on 12 May 1894 in Southampton. Pickford is in the middle row (fourth left), and at the back (seventh right) is Banister's headmaster Christopher Ellaby (courtesy Hampshire FA)

BELOW: Back in Brazil: for Charles (extreme right), initially, wickets and runs take precedence over goals

São Paulo *v* Rio, October 1901: ABOVE: Miller holds off a challenge in the first game; BELOW: Farewell to the Carioca players at the Luz station, São Paulo. Charles Miller is at the front, fourth from right

TOP: São Paulo Athletic Club's third successive championship. Miller and club president William Rule (at top) are featured; MIDDLE: the main stand at the Velódromo. The notice at the back reads: 'Booing is expressly forbidden'; BOTTOM: Paulistano players, in the white shirts, on their way to defeating SPAC at the Velódromo in 1905

Pioneers in Rio: LEFT: Oscar Cox (Fluminense); RIGHT: Thomas Donohoe (Bangu)

Brazil's first professional coaches: pictured in the 1906–7 season are LEFT: Fulham's
Jock Hamilton; and RIGHT: Charlie Williams of Brentford

Northern Nomads AFC, 1911–12 season (courtesy Wirral Library and Information Services). Harry Welfare is in the back row (far right); INSET: Harry pictured in the *Everton and Liverpool Official Football Programme*, 12 April 1913

Scottish Wanderers, São Paulo, 1912. Archie McLean is in the front row (far right); INSET: Archie during his spell with Ayr FC, 1909–10 season

The Corinthians in Rio, 1913: TOP: Welfare takes aim for the Rio Foreigners
XI; MIDDLE: the obligatory banquet – and INSET: two of the returning
tourists: LEFT: M.M. Morgan-Owen (photo: Swaine); RIGHT: S.H. Day; and
BOTTOM: the Rio side that won 2–1 – Harry Robinson (back row, centre),
Lawrence Andrews (on the left in the middle row), and in the front row
Sidney Pullen (second left) and Harry Welfare (centre)

EIGHT

Wandered from Scotland

He is combative, impatient of discipline, often bearing the seeds of self-destruction. For him, the bravura individual performance will always come more easily than the methodical subordination to a plan devised by others. His gifts are those of the improviser . . . He is quite simply the Scottish Footballer.

The Scottish Footballer, Bob Crampsey (1978), p.76

The Brazilians play a happy game of football because when they learn the game on the beaches, as Scots used to do in the street, their great joy is in beating a man and scoring a goal. In that way naturalness comes through. Their game remains attractive because they recognise that at some stage a chance must be taken in trying to beat a man or making a chancy pass. They are not slaves to safety.

John Rafferty in 'When Will We See Your Like Again?',
The Changing Face of Scottish Football, edited by
Mike Aitken (1977)

. . . Mac Lean [sic] was an artist, a worthy exponent of the Scottish school. His scientific football became more prominent when he formed a partnership on the left wing with another of his compatriots Hopkins. That left wing was a machine.

História do Futebol no Brasil 1894–1950,
Tomás Mazzoni (1950), p.89

Saturday, 18 May 1912. 'Football Smoker', announced the *Paisley and Renfrewshire Gazette.* 'Tonight a smoking concert under the auspices of Johnstone FC will be held in the Liberal Club Hall. The main feature of the evening will be the presentation of the Consolation Cup and badges, also the Victoria Cup and badges, won by the team in a season which, as a whole, was successful for the Newfielders, from a playing point of view.' At the smoker, the value of that success was soon made apparent.

Johnstone's vice-president revealed that during the 1911–12 season the club had come perilously close to insolvency. It was the revenue from the run in the Consolation Cup that had saved the directors from having to 'close the gates at Newfield about February'. Now, membership of the Scottish Second League was being sought, and there were words of support from several of the guests, including the president of the Renfrewshire FA and an SFA representative. But for one of the players present, consolation, that year, was about more than a trophy and badges.

Several weeks later Archie McLean, his first season with the club just completed, was as the local press put it 'called to Brazil on business'. In São Paulo he would have been relieved to discover that a decent standard of football was being played by clubs in the Consolação area of the city. Not only did a British club there belong to a local league, there was also a sufficient number of Scots at his workplace to form a team. If McLean had ever written down the details of his football career, for the year 1912 there would have been a ready-made heading. 'From Consolation Cup to Consolação', he could have called it.

At Johnstone's end of season gathering Archie, we are told, was one of three players who contributed to 'an entertaining programme of songs and readings'. But in Brazil it was entertainment of a different kind for which he became known. Nicknamed 'The Little Deer' by Paulistas on account of his speed, McLean demonstrated the points of combination between a winger and an inside-forward. For Mazzoni, he and another Scot, Hopkins, were 'the inventors of the *tabelinha*' (literally meaning 'little chart' in Portuguese) – an interpassing move involving two players. In Scottish senior football, though, it took time for Archie's game to reach the level of consistency that so readily won him admirers in Brazil.

★ ★ ★

A summer evening in Paisley in 1908 and there was a knock on the door of the McLean household. Archie had already gone to bed. 'I was wakened up,' he recalled, 'and told that a director of Ayr FC was waiting for me. Out I went to the door, and there I was signed on.' Archie McLean's entry into senior football may have been unorthodox, but it was unsurprising. He might easily have taken the same road south of the border as Main, the player he'd been brought in to replace.

Earlier that year, during Woolwich Arsenal's whistle-stop tour of Scotland, Archie had been invited to join the Londoners' squad. However, after two brief appearances, no offer was made. He had probably been spotted playing for Perthshire in the Glasgow Junior League. It was as a junior that he'd narrowly missed out on international honours; as he later explained, 'I had won my cap in the trials between Renfrewshire and Ayrshire, but through some misunderstanding my junior international cap went elsewhere.' Perhaps it is this that led one biographer to believe that Archie had represented his country.

McLean's two seasons with Ayr in the Scottish League Second Division are characterised by fluctuations in his form on the right wing. In January 1909, an instant in Ayr's Scottish Cup tie against Hibernian at Easter Road is a perfect illustration of this. The *Ayr Observer* notes that 'a run by McLean looked brilliant, but ended in the ball soaring high over the cross-bar'. He would score goals and have a hand in creating goals, but then he would provoke an adverse comment from the Ayr correspondent.

At the start of the 1909–10 season he was 'convincing'. But three weeks later, included in a report of a defeat by the Vale of Leven, were the lines: 'McLean failed ignominiously on several occasions when good chances came his way. He was not the clever winger we know him to be.' If his individual displays were erratic so too was Archie's combination with his inside-right. This is implied after a loss to Leith at Somerset Park – even though the two men were on song. We learn that, for the right wing, 'it was undoubtedly one of their good days, when they were in great form for doing things'. A prelude, this, to McLean's future partnership with Hopkins.

By the time Ayr amalgamated with neighbours Parkhouse midway through 1910 it is likely that Archie, in his early 20s, was already working or about to take up employment at one of the Paisley thread mills. For him to stay on in Ayr, it would require concessions from the directors of the newly formed Ayr United. The *Ayr Observer* tells us that the club had been unable to reach agreement with their preferred outside-right. It was most probably Archie who 'held out for terms which they were not prepared to accede to'. The player's subsequent signing for Galston meant a step down to the Scottish Union League, but at least it took him closer to Paisley.

At Galston, Archie made an immediate impact, scoring in each of his first three games. Personal high spots for the season included a 3–0 victory over Ayr United in the Ayrshire League and a trip to Celtic where Galston's exit from the Scottish Cup was by a solitary goal. But by the start of the following campaign he was on the move again. It was reported that he had joined Paisley club Abercorn; however, in September, he was turning out for local rivals Johnstone in the Union League. In one early-season report McLean was 'smart and cute with the ball, and took some holding'. Brazilians would have loved that.

Indeed, in December 1911, Archie was depicted by the *Paisley and Renfrewshire Gazette* in the vein in which he would grace Paulista football. Peebles Rovers had lost to Johnstone by the odd goal in five and the headline ran: 'McLean cleverly scores winning goal'. The report which followed emphasised what a valuable asset he was:

> His manipulation of the ball and speed were features of his play, and judging by Saturday's exhibition he can adapt himself to outside-left as well as outside-right. His splendid goal was a worthy finish to a fine afternoon's work, and the second goal by McInnes was chiefly attributable to the outside-left's smart play.

For the rest of the season Archie maintained this high standard, and in the Consolation Cup final he had the satisfaction of scoring against his former Galston team-mates. He appeared to have recaptured the form which had earlier attracted interest from England. But just as he was set to return to Scottish League competition, it was his job as a machine mechanic, not football, that caused him to be prised away from Paisley. His contract at J. & P. Coats' São Paulo mill was for three months – and, expecting him to return, Johnstone registered him for another season. But Archie stayed on in Brazil . . . for almost forty years.

★　★　★

Construction of Coats' São Paulo factory began in 1907 – the year after Charles Miller had pulled SPAC's disheartened football team from the Liga Paulista. If indeed the British Club were short of players, there were men among the new arrivals from Paisley who could be called on to make up the XI. That SPAC rejoined the League so swiftly can.be attributed in no small part to the sudden influx of Coats' managers and technicians. Their number had grown by the time Archie McLean arrived.

The first mention of 'Scottish Wanderers' in the São Paulo press was an announcement of their game against SC Internacional's 'Extra Team' on 11 August 1912. The team, drawn from the British staff of the Coats thread mill, lined up as follows:

Gardner
Clark Hutchison
Parker Richardson Kennedy
Woolley Wright McLean Simpson Hamilton

It seems hardly coincidental that barely had Archie been given his instructions by his new employers than a works football club was formed. In galvanising his fellow Scots, Archie received support from two men with experience in Brazilian football – Hutchison, better known for his refereeing, and Hamilton who had twice faced the English Corinthians in 1910. Significantly, both had connections with SC Americano.

It is curious that the formation of the Scottish Wanderers predates by just several months SPAC's final participation in official competition. Perhaps by August 1912 Athletic's fate had already been decided, thus triggering the action of the Coats members of the club. But it wasn't surprising that soon, having helped his new club get off the ground, Archie was included in SPAC's league side. Ironically his début, on 1 September, was against CA Ipiranga, a club from the district of São Paulo where Coats' Linhas Corrente operation was based.

Running in seven goals against Ipiranga, the SPAC side, in its twilight, recorded one of the most convincing victories in its history. *O Estado de São Paulo* does not tell us if McLean was one of the scorers. What it does do, at length, is to underline his impact on the match and to establish him as a presence in Paulista football:

> He showed that he is perfectly aware of his ability – revealing that he'd not been plucked from the reserves but is a forward with ample experience of first-class championships. This new component has

incontestably come to reinforce the forward line of the English team, whose weak point was precisely the left wing. It is even regrettable that only now, when the championship is almost over, could this footballer help Athletic out. For, by his display – his command of the ball, the judgment of his passes and the sureness of his kick – it was soon obvious that Mr McLean is a forward of indisputable merit. Moreover, a prominent place is reserved for him in this team.

Not since the peak of Miller's career had a SPAC player caught the imagination in such a way. But it didn't guarantee a place for Archie in the Paulista team. A few days later the Argentinos were in São Paulo, and, although three SPAC players were selected, the left-wing position went to Artur Friedenreich, a young and promising Brazilian. Whereas the Paulistas registered a first-ever win by a Brazilian side against Argentine opposition, Archie and a Foreigners XI were humbled by the same opponents 6–3.

During those first months in Brazil much of McLean's football took the form of friendlies, punctuated by competitive games for SPAC. The Scottish Wanderers, most of whom were natives of Paisley and the surrounding area, took their new venture seriously. Some would have said their approach was professional. They were kitted out in royal-blue shirts, with lion rampant badge, and white shorts – made with Coats thread presumably – and soon had fixed up a playing area where spectators paid to watch.

According to one of the Wanderers, the club needed all the money it could get: 'Expenses are very high, a ball itself costing £1 7s. 6d.' But he stopped short of revealing whether the players were being paid. The comment was part of a letter published in the *Paisley and Renfrewshire Gazette* on 9 November 1912. Sunday early-morning kick-offs were alluded to. But if this was intended to shock it was nothing compared to the account of a game played six weeks earlier. The Wanderers were supposed to have been inaugurating their new ground – 'presented to us by a Syrian gentleman'. Opponents Orient FC, easy prey for the Scots, had a novel way of letting off steam:

> It was rather an auspicious opening, as, near the end of the game, when we were leading by 12 to 2, the Orient players were getting annoyed at our passing game and started to hustle a bit. One of their players made straight for our outside-left with the intention of laying him low, but he came off second best. Instead of taking it and

saying nothing, he made off for our pavilion, returning with a knife. In a few minutes there were five or six knives on the job, but before they knew where they were a few Scotch fists were being put hard on their faces.

That timely action had effect, and in a minute there was a hasty retreat of the blood-seekers, they having had quite enough, as they say here, of the 'Systema Ingleza', and we left the field victors in the football by 12 to 2, also in the 'open events'.

The winger who was the object of the initial assault was of course Archie McLean. Amazingly, in the free-for-all that ensued, there appear to have been no serious casualties. And to reassure relatives and friends in Scotland, the writer went on to emphasise the 'sportsman-like' nature of the Wanderers' other encounters. How did the São Paulo press treat the incident? *O Estado*, having publicised the match, gave no indication as to its outcome – as was customary for the Scots' fixtures.

With SPAC about to retire from official competition, British involvement at the heart of Paulista football looked to be on the wane. But the above reference to the 'Systema Ingleza' suggests that a lasting mark had been made. Moreover, this particular playing style would be carried on, thanks largely to McLean, for the better part of the decade.

The Wanderers' correspondent also mentioned some of his team-mates. Three players stood out – centre-forward J.G. Hamilton, 'his dividing of the play and his shooting being excellent', goalkeeper A. Hutchison, 'very safe and bringing off saves of the miraculous order', and A. McLean, 'very clever on the ball, his play greatly pleasing the Brazilians'. No wonder the 1912 champions SC Americano persuaded Archie to join them. But paradoxically, when it came to Americano's pioneering trip to Argentina in August 1913, it was Alex Hutchison's refereeing skills that the Brazilians elected to take with them, not Archie's wizardry on the wing.

All the same, McLean helped Americano to retain the Liga Paulista trophy and was a member of the side that achieved a notable draw against a visiting XI from Chile. Meanwhile, in the rival league, set up by the Associação Paulista de Esportes Atléticos (APEA) to safeguard social distinctions in sport, three other ex-SPAC players won championship medals with Paulistano. At this point the directors of the APEA élite sought to strengthen their position. What better than to encourage the leading British footballers in São Paulo to join the APEA league with a team of their own? At the same time, it may be that Archie and his British colleagues were thinking along similar lines.

Perhaps it was to oil the wheels that a match took place in October 1913 between Paulistano and a team composed of former SPAC players. Along with McLean, the conveniently named Scottish Wanderers could count on the Paulistano trio of Astbury, Bradshaw and Banks: a year after its formation the Coats club was expanding. If there were doubts about the prospect of league competition the 4–0 victory over Paulistano, featuring a hat-trick by McLean, put paid to them. *O Estado* devoted its match report to introducing SPAC's reincarnated XI – and casting an eye into the future. 'With a little training, this team will be a tough opponent, in the event that it is affiliated next year, which is probable, to the Associação Paulista de Esportes Atléticos.' A fortnight later the Wanderers' membership of APEA was confirmed.

Around the time of the announcement most of the original team of Coats employees were listed in the press. But when the 1914 matches began it was clear that, on the playing front, changes were afoot. Two founder members, Frank Woolley and John Simpson, had represented the club at APEA's eve-of-season meeting to draw up fixtures. Yet on the Scottish Wanderers' first official team sheet, in April, Archie's was the only recognisable surname from the side of August 1912. Several ex-SPAC players were included and alongside Archie there was a winger who seems to have appeared out of nowhere, his name . . . Hopkins.

Of course, it was a tall order to expect the new partners to manufacture results on their own, and for all Archie's efforts – 'untiring', 'the soul of the attack' were typical of the reporting – just five points were garnered by the Scottish Wanderers from their ten games. The score-lines, though, tell a different story. Several losses by a single goal reveal that had the Wanderers not been overly reliant on the usual clutch of players, they would have been challenging the top team São Bento. According to Mazzoni, it was 'perhaps the most sensational championship to date'. But for the high-minded APEA officials and their allies it did not run as smoothly as they were hoping.

For example, the *Correio Paulistano* disapproved of 'the wide-scale use of rough play' and 'the most violent charges' during the Wanderers *v* AA das Palmeiras encounter at the end of May; and following the first match between 'Scottish' and Paulistano the governing body was called on to act to prevent a repeat of the uncouth barracking of the referee. 'The APEA directors should proceed with the utmost vigour to rigorously bar from entering the ground people who are not part of the distinguished and educated society that with praiseworthy diligence frequents the Velódromo.'

The problem for APEA hard-liners was that try as they might to preserve football as a game played by and for a social élite, very much with the early days of the Velódromo in mind, they were powerless to prevent the 'growing popularity' and 'democratisation' of the sport. 'Football,' wrote Mazzoni, 'was evolving, it was conquering the masses, it was ridding itself of its earlier élite outlook.' How ironic that the most prominent of the working-class clubs from which APEA dissociated itself was the one named after the archetypal aristocrats, the English Corinthians.

So where did Charles Miller and Archie McLean stand in this dispute? On the face of it, their positions were the opposite of what one might have expected. On the one hand, Charles, a living symbol of the good old days, remained loyal to the Liga Paulista by being on its referees list; on the other, Archie, a product of the working-class game from the West of Scotland, was seen to be endorsing a league whose principles were based on social exclusion. Both men probably had as little to do with the political infighting as possible – although it wasn't long before Archie's club found itself in hot water over the way in which it was being run.

To offset the Scottish Wanderers' modest league form, Archie could point to successes in representative matches. He had already been picked for a Paulista XI against the Cariocas; in 1914, with Hopkins and full-back O'May, he helped this team to a draw and a win against the cream of the Rio league. The same trio also contributed to APEA triumphs in a series with a visiting Italian side. All these fixtures were important marks in the progress of Brazilian football. But the event which generated most interest took place in Rio: the first exhibitions in Brazil by a group of professionals. Who would have imagined the consequences for world football of the brief visit made by a team from the English Southern League.

NINE

Grecians' Adventures

By this deed – appearing without training, but with ardour and good will, with politeness and chivalry, without the crude tactics of the visiting team – we managed to put ourselves on the map in South America or in any other part of the world where good football is played. The words of Exeter City's respected chairman with regard to our progress in this sport must have made a deep impression on those who run football in Brazil.

O Jockey, July 1914

The second match the City lost was against the Brazilians and this was the last game of the tour. The tourists were then begin-. ning to feel the effects of their journey, but Pratt said had they showed their true form they would have won easily.

Devon and Exeter Gazette, 11 August 1914

On the front page of the *Exeter Football Express* for Saturday, 21 February 1914, a cartoon takes pride of place. It depicts a man dressed in a tunic in pensive pose, leaning against a collection of suitably labelled cabin trunks and a kitbag. On the wall behind him there is a map of South America and a list of sailings. The drawing is set above a caption entitled 'The Argentine Tour':

> The Grecian (misquoting Hamlet and murdering metre):
> *To go or not to go? That is the question.*
> *Whether 'tis better to endure the slings and arrows of damp England's clime,*
> *Or spend three months next summer on the spree in Argentine.*

Put simply, this was the decision that confronted the management of Exeter City, the club popularly known as The Grecians. As directors deliberated, the *Football Express* did some gentle prodding.

Chiefly, it was felt that the tour would be instrumental in keeping the players together. Supporters were reminded that 'the City might now have had a Championship side if the manager had been able to retain the best of material his judgment has brought west'. A second consideration was the potential for profit – 'something in the club's coffers during a period when, in past seasons, it has been all paying out and nothing coming in'.

But worries were expressed. Not every player would benefit from 'a surfeit of summer football', and besides, there would most likely be bad pitches and the unpredictable playing methods of the hosts to contend with. 'Football,' wrote the aptly named 'Rover', 'on Continental and foreign tours is not all parlour billiards, as many a professional team has learnt from experience.' The ill health of manager Arthur Chadwick and the conflicting commitments of certain players were further reasons why the Exeter City board should be represented in Hamlet mode.

What swayed the Grecians' committee was, of course, the financial implications of the tour: Swindon Town's trip to Argentina two years earlier was known to have been a money-spinner. In Exeter's case the club's bank overdraft could be tackled, outstanding transfer fees met and players would be paid to stay put. But why the invitation to Exeter City, a club from the lower reaches of the Southern League? Although we can't be sure, the existence of a rapport between FA secretary Frederick Wall and Exeter chairman M.J. McGahey probably had a lot to do with it. Throughout the tour, it was McGahey's entertaining dispatches, reproduced in the *Express and Echo*, that kept Exeter followers *au courant*.

On the outward voyage there was plenty of sight-seeing and socialising. But for the players it wasn't all a case of all play and no work. The morning after leaving Madeira, the final shore stop before South America, a training programme began. McGahey provided an outline of the intended daily routine:

> Out of bed 6 a.m.; upper boat deck, skipping, punch-ball, dumb-bells, clubs, and general exercises, followed by short sprints. This for about an hour to 1½ hours. There is then rigged up on one of the upper decks a large sail full of sea water, into which they all have a plunge; a good rub down, and then to breakfast at 8.15. Throughout

the day there will be easy deck games. At 4.30, there will be another hour's work, mainly easy sprints and skipping, followed by a warm bath and a change for dinner.

With the assortment of courses to get through at each meal it wasn't surprising the players were keen to work out. In fact, early on, McGahey had to warn them against heading practice – 'if they started now they would be sick at the sight of a ball at the end of three weeks'. Not until Rio did they have a proper session with a ball.

Whatever they had been led to believe about football in South America, the Exeter party were unprepared for the sight that greeted them in Rio. Having spotted a game in progress they couldn't get ashore quick enough, 'only to discover that the match was between junior teams of about 18 to 20 years of age. They were all niggers, as black as your hat, and most of them playing in bare feet.' The group from Devon had unwittingly stumbled on the seeds that would spark a revolution in Brazilian football. A subsequent visit to Fluminense's tiptop facility put the experience firmly into perspective.

It was Paysandu's Harry Robinson who was charged to open negotiations with McGahey over the possibility of Exeter playing several games in Rio on their return journey. Officials in Brazil had been trying for ten years to persuade a professional English club to make an unscheduled stop-off. In next to no time McGahey had shown a readiness to co-operate. He wrote of the good impression made by Robinson ('the idol of the local sports, and a most charming fellow'), the fortunate coincidence of knowing one of his relatives in Devon and of the offer of satisfactory terms for the proposed matches. Further talks with co-promoters Fluminense were a formality.

At Fluminense the Exeter party could see for themselves the gulf between that dockland game and Rio's grandest club. 'Not only is there a good playing pitch . . . but they also have a small skating rink and any amount of tennis courts with asphalted floors.' While McGahey was shown round the premises his players had a useful kick-about on the 'fine turf', some of their shots causing a *Correio da Manhã* reporter to quiver. In a final comment on his visit to the club, McGahey left no doubt as to the huge gap in wealth between Brazilian football's haves and have-nots: 'The lowest price for admission to football matches here is about 4s. What would our spectators at home say to that?' It corroborates what the Scottish Wanderer had written about high costs.

Disparity in the quality of playing conditions was further

emphasised at Santos, the Grecians' next port of call. McGahey was in his element when describing the local club's pitch – and the drama that followed. 'If you imagine one of the worst junior grounds you know of, and then take it up and shake it like a carpet and plentifully besprinkle it with stones and pieces of bricks, and then bake the lot in a tropical sun, you will have some remote notion of the ground.' Thankfully, half a century on, Pelé had a smoother surface to play on . . . and so in 1914 did McGahey's men.

A suggestion that they should train on a nearby beach was taken up, the result being 'some very useful sprints' and 'a little ball practice'. It was then that the improvised plan backfired. After their workout the players went for a swim, unaware that a 'no bathing' policy was in force. A local resident made a complaint, a policeman went to investigate and as the *Express and Echo* headline deliciously stated: 'Whole Team Put Under Arrest.' If it wasn't for the lenience of the Santos Commissioner of Police, the Exeter players and chairman might have been forced to remain there.

By the time the Grecians' one-month stay in Argentina was over – their record showed one defeat in eight games – they had a fund of stories to add to the account of their brush with Brazilian law. In the last of his letters to be published in Exeter, McGahey relates how a game was almost abandoned when the club secretary of one of their opponents threatened to shoot the referee. In Rosario a consolation penalty to the home team was greeted by: 'Fireworks! Yells! Shrieks! and other excitement' – notably a brass band's continuous playing of the Argentine National Anthem. And later the game was interrupted by one of the police horses bolting across the pitch, having thrown its rider.

Away from the field of play the visitors could have done with a similar level of distraction. So incensed were they at being 'left to their own devices' that, before leaving Buenos Aires, they publicly criticised the tour organisers. It was a wonder Exeter didn't call off the Brazil leg of the trip and head straight home. That was certainly the feeling of those members of the party whose anger was vented in the *Buenos Aires Herald*. But that would have meant breaking the contract with the Rio clubs. If it was any consolation, there was the knowledge that McGahey had turned down a request for Exeter to visit São Paulo. That decision was to have repercussions in Rio.

For the three-match exhibition series Paysandu and Fluminense had received the backing of Rio's governing body, the Liga Metropolitana de Sports Athléticos. It was this organisation that took up suggestions in the Rio press that the Brasileiros team to face Exeter City should consist of players from Rio – and São Paulo. One of the originators of the idea, the *Correio da Manhã*, outlined why this made good sense: 'Not only can we demonstrate with greater precision the degree of development of Brazil's best-loved sport, represented by two of the top football-playing states, it will also serve as an experiment for the make-up of the Brazil XI which will go to Argentina in August or September to compete for the Julio Roca Cup.' One week before Exeter were due to return, the Liga Metropolitana contacted their allies in São Paulo, APEA.

Besides being asked to supply players for the Brasileiros XI, APEA were invited to participate in the scratch Inglezes team. Harry Robinson had selected the Scottish Wanderers trio of McLean, Hopkins and O'May. The arguments seemed convincing; Rio was confident the APEA committee would support the project. But it was not so simple – concurrence between Cariocas and Paulistas never is. With the first match less than 48 hours away it was reported in Rio that the Paulista players were having 'great difficulties' in taking part.

The problem was that the fixtures in question had been scheduled for a weekend. McLean and co had work commitments on the Saturday, while the Brazilians were needed by their clubs for a Sunday round of APEA league matches. For the players to be able to travel, APEA insisted that only a change of dates would do. This, however, was ruled out by the organising committee. The president of the Liga Metropolitana informed APEA of the decision – and made a final plea for the players to be sent.

18 July
Exeter City 3   Inglezes do Rio 0
With many potential spectators at work there was never going to be a large attendance at Fluminense's ground. Perhaps, too, word had got out that Harry Robinson's side, already depleted, would not be benefiting from the São Paulo Scots. Exeter, in contrast, were almost at full strength, Loram taking the place of the injured Pym in goal. They also had the vocal support of a large band of sailors from the SS *Glasgow*. The game kicked off at 3.30 p.m. with A. Taylor in charge.

The *Correio da Manhã*'s report makes it clear that the Exeter forwards laid 'uninterrupted siege' to Robinson's goal. But in the first half just the one goal was scored – and that the result of a mix-up between two defenders after half an hour's play. Hunter's strike from five yards no doubt provoked one of the 'fine and curious' chants from the watching sailors.

After the interval, more 'courageous defending' kept Exeter at bay until the 71st minute when Holt increased their lead, his cross from the right wing creeping into the net at the far post. Two minutes from time, inside-left Lovett notched the visitors' third with 'a powerful and calculated shot from about ten yards'. As for the Inglezes attack led by Harry Welfare, 'irregular and too hasty' was one verdict. The game had almost finished when Loram was finally tested.

The *Correio da Manhã* was quick to point out that this was not the Exeter that had been criticised by the Argentine press for using 'illegal methods'. Apart from Lagan's 'tendency to step on opponents' feet in the tackle', most of the players gave a 'perfect' exhibition. The *Correio* decided not to judge the professionals on one performance, especially as they had not been sufficently extended. However, several aspects of their play were emphasised. Particularly impressive was 'the intelligent and parallel positioning of the forwards and the half-backs', making it easier for Exeter to keep possession. And, when passing, short first-time balls on the ground were preferred.

Meanwhile, there was heartening news for those who were championing the formation of a Rio-São Paulo Brasileiros XI. With APEA having dispatched their treasurer to Rio to try to resolve the impasse, an agreement had been reached. The quid pro quo which guaranteed the sending of the Paulista players was the switching of the dates of the two remaining matches. The Exeter *v* Brasileiros encounter would now bring the series to a close.

19 July
Exeter City 5   Rio de Janeiro 3
For the second exhibition, crowd scenes at Fluminense's ground were 'extraordinary'. Once again SS *Glasgow* crew-members made their presence felt. The Rio side, similar to the one that had inflicted defeat on the Corinthians, included four of the Rio English XI – Welfare, Pullen, Brewerton and Robinson. The professionals made two changes to their line-up, Harding coming in for Smith at left-half and acting manager Pratt taking Holt's place in the forward line. The *Correio da Manhã* tells us that 'the match got under way at 3.36 p.m. under the direction of Bangu AC's Hugh Graham'.

Soon after kicking-off the home team produced an attack in which Harry Welfare shot powerfully over. A period of stalemate followed and then Exeter took the initiative with 'a series of excellent raids' spearheaded by Hunter and Lovett. This pressure led to the opening goal after ten minutes, Pratt collecting a poor clearance and beating Robinson with a low shot. Before the visitors could press home their advantage Rio pushed forward and five minutes later they drew level. Welfare, 'the soul of the Carioca front-line', received a pass from Pullen, broke clear and calmly placed a shot inside the right post.

Try as they might to regain the lead, Exeter were up against a stubborn defence. 'Full-backs Píndaro and Nery,' reported the *Correio*, 'served as an example to many a professional player who doesn't know the correct way to make use of his weight.' The same could have been said of Welfare. A tireless worker, he put his side ahead in the 25th minute: the centre-forward was again found in space and held off several challenges before shooting past Loram. After that, skilful defending kept the Exeter forwards in check.

Two minutes into the second half, Exeter fell further behind. It was a hat-trick for Welfare 'whose name was shouted repeatedly by the delirious spectators'. At this point the game deteriorated, the professionals' frustration translated into all manner of fouls. The Rio players stood their ground and Robinson made a string of fine saves, but eventually the opposition's superior strength told. Twenty minutes before the end Exeter centre-half Lagan headed in a corner and then Pratt netted the equaliser. Goodwin put the visitors in front and Hunter completed the scoring, another header from a corner.

The next day, the *Correio da Manhã*'s headline ran: 'Exeter City have serious difficulty in beating the Carioca eleven 5–3 – Welfare and Robinson the men of the match.' There was then disparaging commentary on Exeter's too-tough approach and unsportsmanlike behaviour. After the incident-free first game, Brazilians were now recalling the damning reports about Exeter that had been received from Argentina. 'It is a pity,' wrote the *Correio* with heavy understatement, 'that the group of masters sent out by the English FA do not want to participate in solely what is permitted in football.'

For the *Correio*, it was important to assert the moral superiority of amateur over professional football. Readers were reminded that the English Corinthians hadn't disgraced themselves in losing to the same Rio side; indeed, they remained paragons of how the game should be played. It was emphasised that 'victory is an accident of the game'. The behaviour of the Exeter players – appealing for fouls and questioning decisions – was therefore unwarranted. For the Rio XI, despite giving up a two-goal advantage, it had been worth losing, 'playing in a way that was always perfect, loyal and smooth'.

There were, nevertheless, points that had been learnt. The *Correio* noted Exeter's effective use of corner-kicks and, when going forward, their half-backs' 'perfect' positional sense, between both sets of forwards. Good teamwork had also been seen – 'until they began to intimidate their opponents'. Even where there was praise the context had to be reiterated. It appears that only one member of the Rio side came out of the match relatively unscathed – keeper Harry Robinson. It was he who had the decidedly difficult task of keeping order in the final exhibition.

21 July
Exeter City 0   Brasileiros 2

BRASILEIROS
Marcos [de Mendonça]
Píndaro Nery
Lagreca Rubens [Salles] Rolando
Oswaldo Abelardo Friedenreich Osman Formiga

v

Goodwin Lovett Hunter Whittaker Holt
Harding Lagan Rigby
Strettle Fort
Loram
EXETER CITY

From early in the afternoon, the main stand at Fluminense Football Club began to fill with numerous families belonging to high society, anxious to see the important football match announced for today. Surrounding the pitch a compact crowd was pressed up against the wire fence that protects the ground. At every moment dozens of spectators poured out of trams and cars. Soon there were no more seats to be had in the main stand, many going up onto the roof until that was full.

At 15.45 the English team came out and were greeted by a long round of applause. Soon after, the Brazilians appeared, the applause reaching ecstatic levels. Moments later the game began, arousing extraordinary interest in the spectators. The Brazilians soon mounted a series of attacks. With mastery and calm, the English backs prevented a score on several occasions. Feeling threatened, the English made several compact counter-attacks, but whenever the Brazilian goal was in danger Marcos, with great calm, kept out the violent shots.

There was a series of 'corners' and 'off-sides' for which the English appealed, referee Robinson acting with the maximum correctness. After 15 minutes of compact attacking the Brazilians skilfully managed to score the first goal through an accurate shot from Oswaldo. The spectators went wild, waving hats and walking sticks, and in the stand ladies and young girls waved handkerchiefs, shouting hurrahs to the Brazilian team.

When the game restarted the English tried to open their account with a violent attack which reached brutality. The Brazilians were already without Friedenreich who, as the first goal went in, received facial injuries after a fall provoked by a 'charge' from an English player. After receiving attention Friedenreich returned to the action, warmly applauded by the spectators.

Just under 15 minutes later, after pressing from both sides, the ball was taken up to the English goal. A well-constructed move ended with the ball coming to Osman who triumphantly scored the second goal for the national scratch eleven. Truly delirious applause broke out. The English tried again to reduce the arrears, but without success. There were no more goals. Friedenreich had to go off again with another head injury.

The crowd's enthusiasm was indescribable. The performance of Rubens, Píndaro and Oswaldo was celebrated and that of others who had distinguished themselves during the game. And there was praise for the correctness and mastery with which the Brazilians had rendered useless the efforts of the English professionals to beat them. Goal-keeper Marcos, helped by his backs, remained extremely calm, greatly contributing to his team's victory.

This is an English version of the telegram that appeared in the São Paulo press on 22 July. Sensing the significance of the news, *O Estado* made it a front-page feature. A day later, the same newspaper reproduced a match report and comments that had appeared in the Rio *Gazeta de Notícias*. There was special emphasis given to the contribution of the four Paulistas – 'the heroes of the day' – and there was even a reference to Píndaro's use of the 'charles'. It didn't seem all that long ago that Charles Miller had encountered a general lack of interest in football among Paulista editors, following competition between Rio and São Paulo.

Those pioneer games in which the spotlight was on Miller and Oscar Cox had helped football to consolidate. Now, as another landmark was passed, the euphoria of the Brazilian spectators spilled over into the columns of newspapers in the capital as well as in São Paulo. 'A Great Sporting Happening', proclaimed the *Correio da Manhã*: 'The national team played an extraordinary game. Above all expectations.' It was the first time that Brazil's yellow and green had been worn – a band of colour on white sleeves. But the *Correio* chose to highlight the blood-stains on Friedenreich's shirt.

On going a goal down the Exeter players had resorted again to 'a kind of game similar to "association", but in which "fouls" were common'. For Rio's reporters, at least, that was the consensus. Sadly there appears to be no surviving view from the Exeter camp. Certainly, on one occasion during the tour, McGahey had defended the actions of his players, in sharp contrast to local interpretation. 'Fouls there were in plenty. Our boys gave them what they asked for,' he wrote of the game with Racing Club. But in Rio, the Exeter chairman restricted his comments to showing his admiration at the way the Brazilians had played – 'guaranteeing sincerely that football in Brazil was more advanced than in Argentina'. Two months later, seven of the Rio-São Paulo side helped the first 'official' Brazil XI to defeat Argentina 1–0, the Roca Cup an added prize.

Sylvio Lagreca, one of the four Paulistas who faced Exeter, later recalled the match on 21 July 1914. The interview appeared in the *Gazeta Esportiva* in 1943 as part of a series entitled 'Remembering the greatest international feats of Brazilian sport'. He is asked to relate a particular moment of interest during the game. The one he selects is revealing:

> When the English were trailing, and up against our courage, four of them – the centre half, one of the full-backs and two forwards – just as the crowd were really getting worked up, left the pitch! I immediately drew this to the attention of Rubens and referee Robinson. Robinson stopped the game and we Paulistas went after the 'deserters'. 'Come back or the game will be abandoned,' we told them. Realising that their match fee might be affected, they returned.

Eye-witness reports do indeed confirm that a similar incident did take place. The point about Lagreca's seemingly embroidered anecdote is that it alludes starkly to the resistance in Brazil, in 1914, to professional sport. Here was a group of money-motivated sportsmen who thought nothing of leaving a game they were losing. A situation such as this would have been used by the men who ran the Liga

Metropolitana and its São Paulo equivalent APEA to justify and reinforce their lofty amateur stance. In July 1914 a lengthy and detailed article appeared in the Carioca and Paulista press on the finances of professional football in England. The 'violent play' and 'indiscipline' of the Exeter players was additional ammunition for the opponents of professionalism.

But clearly – as we have seen with the hiring of British coaches – there were double standards operating and a good deal of hypocrisy. Waldenyr Caldas, in his study of the democratisation of Brazilian football, notes that by 1914, as well as the collection of gate money, bonus payments were surreptitiously being made to players. He underlines that: 'It is a phase [up to 1933] in which our football really does oscillate between amateurism and a kind of semi-professionalism, practised but not assumed publicly by clubs and players.'

Conspicuous presences in Rio and São Paulo, both Harry Welfare and Archie McLean were to fall foul of their respective associations. In Welfare's case, it was an immediate consequence of the issues raised by the Grecians' visit.

TEN

Controversy

He's a Fluminense member
Known as 'the Englishman',
And when his team wins
'It was all his doing . . .'

Player by profession,
They only call him that through negligence
When he's given a strong performance,
Which only rarely does he fail to do.

When he plays in 'combination'
Urging on his fellow forwards,
He's almost a revered god:
Everything changes – it's different . . .

Let's hope Welfare doesn't stall
With all this incongruity . . .
Emperor in the attack
He has to be and . . . patience!

'Celebrity Gallery', *Sports*, ano 1 – no.1,
6 August 1915, Rio de Janeiro

As we see it, if, at the moment they were thrown out, the
Wanderers were in the same conditions in which for three years
they remained at the heart of APEA without ever stepping out of
line, they should not by a simple vote be excluded from the
association's list of clubs.

O Estado de São Paulo, 27 February 1916

In terms of amateurism, Fluminense Football Club liked to think of itself as the purest of the pure. As the club neared its fiftieth anniversary the in-house monthly (July 1948) reminded members of an episode in their organisation's history. It was held up as a 'perfect illustration' of the amateur concept – 'the secret of the moral greatness that trembles in the club's flag'.

In 1903 the club had sent a team to São Paulo for a three-game series. Finding themselves a man short for the final match, the Fluminense directors had approached Rio Cricket's R.H. Brooking who happened to be in São Paulo on cricketing duty. He agreed to help out and was given a membership form to complete. For Fluminense a signature sufficed. Brooking, however, insisted that only after he had paid the monthly tariff would he represent the club. This example of 'true amateurism' was also recounted by Paulista historian Paulo Varzea. But in 1910s Rio, a noble attitude was not the only prerequisite for participation in official amateur football.

After the début goal against the English Corinthians, Harry Welfare had quickly established himself as one of Rio's top players. In 1914 he led the Carioca League's scoring chart and was chosen again to represent Rio. Transition, though, from his sports schedule in Liverpool, had not been easy. As he later explained, commuting to Fluminense from his teaching post on the outskirts of Rio was where the problem lay:

> The school where I worked was situated next to the Vidigal beach, on the Gávea road. On match days I left at one in the afternoon, a brisk walk to Três Vendas (Jockey Club), took a tram to the Largo das Leões and then went by taxi to the club. When the game was over it was a rush to get back to the school where I put on a film for the students. It was tough!

Harry's success on the pitch made it tougher still. Questions began to be asked about his amateur status – culminating in an official inquiry by the Liga Metropolitana. The poem at the beginning of this chapter, published shortly before the Liga made known its findings, makes topical reference to Welfare's qualities as a player – as well as his predicament.

In its carefully worded response to the governing body, the Fluminense board reiterated that Welfare had played amateur football in England – 'if this were not the case, this club would not permit itself to ignore the League's rules and pick for its championship side a player who did not fit the official amateur model.' But, of course, it was Harry's spell with Liverpool that had roused suspicions, so to appease the Liga, Fluminense stated that the club were 'arranging for the necessary documents to be sent from England'. This bought time, ensuring that Harry, pending a ruling by the Liga, could continue to turn out for Fluminense.

By 1915 club rivalries had intensified – 'frighteningly so', is how a recent history of the Carioca championship puts it. The one surviving British club, Rio Cricket, were making the news – but for the wrong reasons. First, the club were penalised for fielding an ineligible player; then, a refereeing decision by one of their members, a W. Tulk, caused a match to be abandoned after a pitch invasion. The letter on which Harry's immediate future in the game seemed to hinge was dated 12 July 1915. Liverpool FC secretary George Patterson composed the reply that Fluminense were expecting:

> Mr Harry Welfare always played for us as an amateur. Prior to joining our club he played for several local clubs but always as an amateur and to our knowledge he was never a professional. I trust this will put the matter right.

By the time this testimonial found its way to Rio, Harry, almost defiantly, was in the process of netting 13 times in four games. It was a replica of one of his goal sprees on Merseyside.

Official vindication was not long in coming. But there was no apology, far from it. Just a formal affirmation of Harry's amateur past in a letter to Fluminense. In one long-winded sentence the Liga Metropolitana exhibited the kind of obstinacy that kept professionalism in Brazil underground for a further 18 years:

> ... Mr Harry Welfare, a player registered and accepted by the Liga, nothing having been discovered that might testify against his morals and there never having been any proofs that might lead the Liga not to recognise his amateur condition, continues to deserve from the Liga the necessary reputation and to have the required morals demanded by the Commission of Inquiry's rules, including the contractual agreement regarding his amateur status to be part of the Liga's pool of players, for which reason he was recently selected for the Liga's representative team ...
>
> *(13 September 1915)*

Although they'd been prepared to ban Welfare, the Liga must have been relieved that the player could take his place in the Rio XI for the forthcoming match against São Paulo. In a rare upset, Harry contributed two goals to the Cariocas' 5–2 victory. On the morning of the match, the *Correio da Manhã*, in its pen-picture of Welfare, made an exaggerated attempt to dispel any lingering doubts as to his bona fide amateur credentials. 'Besides being a distinguished sportsman, Welfare is a cultured soul, teaching several subjects at the Anglo-Brasileiro College where he is generally held in high esteem and respected by all members of staff.' As others would soon find out, a clean character was just one of a number of conditions which 'sportsmen' were obliged to fulfil.

★ ★ ★

In the São Paulo scratch XI the McLean–Hopkins partnership was continuing to prosper. As one contemporary biographer noted, it was the 'sensational' Rio–São Paulo games that made the duo famous. Archie, in fact, in competition for the cup put up by the *Correio da Manhã*, was the only Paulista not to miss a match. In November 1915 he was on the score-sheet as São Paulo took ultimate revenge for the unexpected defeat by Welfare and his team-mates. Eight goals were netted without reply, the *Correio Paulistano* remarking that 'Demósthenes, Friedenreich and McLean are a trinity in which 50 per cent of our team's chances of winning are based.'

In contrast, at club level, odds on a Wanderers win were still largely dependent on how well Archie and Hopkins were performing. For the 1915 season, faced just as SPAC had been with a shortage of playing members, the club had relaxed its selection policy. The 'Scottish' prefix was accordingly dropped and team lists included names such as Miguel, Rodella and Sant'Anna. Midway through the campaign there was talk of the Wanderers becoming 'a serious contender'. But although improving on their previous points tally, the club were unable to move into the top half of the six-team league.

Failure to outpoint the best sides was not the reason, however, why the Wanderers' APEA membership was suddenly rescinded early in 1916. It is clear that the governing body were looking for a way of bringing one of the newer clubs, Palestra Itália, into their organisation, guaranteeing in one stroke the support of São Paulo's burgeoning Italian colony. Certainly, there was an element of patronage involved, as intimated by Mazzoni when he wrote: 'Thanks to their good relations with the top officials at the Matarazzo firm, the Palestra directors succeeded in obtaining the desired place in APEA.' So Palestra came on board . . . but at the Wanderers' expense.

Mazzoni's version is that McLean's club 'were deemed no longer respectable enough'. And then he added: 'It was said that the Wanderers were not a properly organised club, but a group of British players who would meet in a bar . . . belonging to a member of the team and while they were there they would divide the gate money between them!' Since then the story, with its mythical overtones, has been used to level accusations of professionalism at the Wanderers (one of the latest mentions is in *A História do Campeonato Paulista*, 1997).

Press reports do confirm that the Wanderers held their meetings at the 'Bar Inglez'. In fact − a possible sign of impending trouble − members were summoned there to a general assembly in November 1915 'to discuss urgent business'. But it would also appear that in order to enlist Palestra, the APEA board were looking for a pretext.

It was at a meeting on 15 February 1916 that a decision was taken to revise APEA's list of clubs, 'a report to be presented, with some urgency, discussed and voted on at a specially convened assembly', this after a three-man commission had looked into 'the social and sporting situation' of member clubs and made recommendations. APEA, like its counterpart in Rio, was ostensibly purging its ranks − but just one club was being targeted. At that EGM the Wanderers, it appears, were not represented.

When the APEA directorate assembled again six days later the Wanderers' William Campbell need hardly have bothered to turn up let alone participate in the secret ballot that confirmed the fate of his club. Members voted unanimously to exclude the Wanderers 'for failing to produce the indispensable documents as evidence of the conditions required by the statutes'. What happened next revealed the true motives of the APEA chiefs:

> At a signal from the board, justifying its request, the filling of the vacancy left by the expulsion was put forward for discussion. Having examined the report and the general conditions of the different affiliates, in a special procedure it was unanimously decided to fill the vacancy immediately. It was proposed by Mr A. Rangel Christoffel of AA das Palmeiras, after a majority vote, that the place would be taken, under the conditions expressed in the statutes, by Palestra Itália.

The Wanderers may well have in some way stepped out of line, but *O Estado de São Paulo* was right to criticise the 'non-disciplinary' reasons for which the club were voted out – and to question whether the organisation of the other APEA clubs really was as flawless as it was made out to be.

If the charges against their club had been that serious then surely McLean and Hopkins would have been suspended. But the fact that within weeks they were free to join another APEA club made a mockery of the way in which the Wanderers had been treated. Archie was even included in the pool of referees announced by APEA in April 1916 – along with 41-year-old Charles Miller.

During the following season the McLean–Hopkins wing contributed to São Bento's finishing second in the league – and to the defeat of Carioca champions Flamengo. In a report of this game (in *O Correio Paulistano*, 30 June 1916) there is mention of 'the combined play that is peculiar to the two British players'. It is this interpassing that Brazilians refer to as *tabelinha* – 'little chart'.

★ ★ ★

Every year since the formation of the Liga Paulista in 1901 there had been at least one British team competing in the leagues of São Paulo and Rio. Every year, that is, until 1916. To add to the Wanderers' fall from grace, Rio Cricket closed its football section after finishing bottom and losing a play-off. As for Paysandu, the departure of Harry Robinson and others to enlist in the British army made it impossible for that club to continue to compete. In 1916 all that remained of a British presence in Brazilian football was a handful of individuals – among them Sidney Pullen.

Sidney was the son of the Rio British consul and his Brazilian wife, but, unlike Charles Miller, we should be wary of emphasising his Britishness. More often than not, it was his first name that appeared on team lists, emphasising the fact that he was Brazilian-born, and when war erupted in Europe he did not set out for the front until Brazil entered the conflict in October 1917. All the same, he'd been captain of Paysandu, and not long after joining Flamengo in 1915 he had shown solidarity with his former team-mates by persuading the club to change its colours to make them distinct from the German flag. The red and black, minus the white, are the current colours.

The question of nationality, however, became the subject of protest when Sidney was selected for Brazil in the unofficial South American championships of 1916. Up until then, in games against foreign opposition, he had represented Rio and the British community – but had never been chosen for a Brasileiros XI. 'The Argentines,' wrote Mário Filho, 'did not believe that a Brazilian could have such a typically English name, let alone have the appearance of an English-man. It was necessary to present a birth certificate and all the documents.'

Of course, the fuss would not have occurred had Rubens Salles been able to travel to Buenos Aires. The centre-half position that Sidney Pullen was eventually allowed to occupy was the property of the Paulistano player. Brazil finished third in the tournament, drawing with Argentina and Chile, and losing narrowly to Uruguay. Pullen, the only Anglo-Brazilian ever to turn out for Brazil, appeared in the three matches.

In the previous decade, if similar games involving Brazil had been played, it is doubtful whether Charles Miller would have participated. At that time, he probably saw himself as first and foremost a British subject, a feeling compounded by his consular appointment. Years later, however, when asked who he'd support if he had to choose between a Brazilian or a British team, it was Charles's Paulista roots that determined his response.

★ ★ ★

For Tomás Mazzoni, 1917 was the year Brazilian football 'came of age'. The game was being played throughout the whole republic, the rival governing bodies in São Paulo finally made their peace and a Confederação Brasileira de Desportos (CBD) was provisionally recognised by FIFA. But at the same time, the amateur rules were being increasingly flouted. In Rio, Fluminense were the team to beat, the majority of the players (including Welfare) living at the ground and encouraged to take part in daily training sessions. If there was a hint of professionalism here, the approach went unchallenged – at least by the Liga Metropolitana.

J.A. de Quincey-Taylor's *Diário do Trainer* is for the most part an attendance record. But observations, in English, reveal occasions when the Fluminense coach was hard pushed to implement his methods. During the 1918 season, training rarely started on time – if at all. Two days before a match with arch rivals Flamengo, the unfortunate Taylor made plain his growing frustration:

7 a.m. No work at this hour. The players would not get out of bed. At 8 a.m. the following did running exercises: Welfare, French, Vidal, Chico. The following slept in dormitory but did no work: Zezé, Machado, Mano, Fortes, Georges, Celso, Sylvio, Honório, Oswaldo, Baptista.

But as his players' domination of the Carioca championship continued, Taylor had to endure the unpredictable when it came to training. It would be interesting to know how Harry Welfare compared the set-up at Fluminense to that which he had experienced at Liverpool. The picture we get is that the facilities for football at Fluminense were equal to if not better than those offered by many of the top clubs in Britain. Harry and his Brazilian team-mates may not have received a salary from the club, but they were being lodged and fed.

Presumably, it was Harry's move to Fluminense's headquarters, around 1916, that resulted in him changing jobs: we have seen how isolated he was out at the Anglo-Brasileiro College. The change was as drastic as it was necessary. One of the firms he joined during the period to 1922 was the British steel importer P.S. Nicolson & Co. Ironically, change coincided with a period away from football. Several months after the Liga Metropolitana had ruled in his favour, Welfare sustained a knee injury that appears to have kept him out for almost two years.

In November 1917 Harry Welfare returned to action, with Fluminense on the verge of their first title since 1911 – the year nine of their players had defected to Flamengo. Taylor's diary records that Harry's training routine, in the week before his comeback, was made up of 'exercises, running and ball practice' . . . followed by a visit to the club's masseur. As well as the attention to physical preparation, the players, Mário Filho tells us, followed a special diet, which included tea on match-days ('Welfare's idea') to calm the players' nerves. Nothing, it seemed, was left to chance. In Fluminense's five remaining games Harry helped himself to eleven goals – including six against Bangu which remains a club record.

In his summary of the 1917 domestic season, Mazzoni notes the 'super-team' that Fluminense had assembled, a mixture of youth and experience, players who were at the peak of their form, 'including Welfare, a master in the art of scoring goals, an able exponent of the English school who had nevertheless adapted to our style of play'. Harry adapted, but in doing so he introduced specific skills to the Brazilian game. Max Valentim tells us, in his work *O Futebol e sua*

Técnica, that Welfare taught Fluminense's inside-forwards how to use the through ball. And he also identifies two of his dribbling techniques: 'This break or feint of the body which the English call "swerving" and the jump to one side while running with the ball ("side-stepping").' For Valentim, writing in 1941, Welfare was 'one of the greatest centre-forwards to have played in Brazil'.

Certainly, it was largely down to Harry's goals (48 in 40 games) that, beginning with the 1917 triumph, Fluminense carried off three league titles in as many years. Just how consistent he was can be seen in his scoring pattern during this period – and this is recorded later in an appendix. One match that stands out was the return fixture with Flamengo, towards the end of the 1919 season, in which the outcome of the championship was decided. Welfare was featured and so too was Sidney Pullen, back from serving in the British army. But it was Fluminense's legendary keeper, Marcos de Mendonça, who particularly caught the eye.

Writer Paulo Coelho Netto's brother, Emanuel (Mano), played in that Fla–Flu, and in *O Fluminense na Intimidade* (Volume 3) he describes, with characteristic fervour, unashamedly partisan, some of the excitement of what is today perhaps the most classic event in the Brazilian sporting calendar:

> When it was still 0–0 Zezé scored a goal but the referee disallowed it for an offside that didn't exist. Then he gave a penalty against Fluminense. Japonês took it and Marcos saved, but the ball came back to Japonês who hit another powerful shot. Marcos saved again and the ball fell to Sidney who did his best to make amends. But the remarkable keeper, the best in Brazil of his era, blocked this shot too. This time the ball spilled out to Junqueira. At that moment the unexpected occurred: the fourth save of the majestic series was greeted with a striking silence that was truly astonishing. Suddenly everyone stood up and deliriously cheered the phenomenal Marcos de Mendonça ...

Fluminense went on to win 4–0, Welfare scoring the second goal, and to honour the 'heroes' of the first 'tricampeonato' in Carioca football there was a fanfare – and a 21-gun salute, fired from a small cannon which today sits in the Fluminense Museum. The president of Brazil came down on to the pitch to present gold medals to the winners. For Harry, in terms of achievement, it was one better than his former Liverpool team-mates – runners-up, five years earlier, in the first English Cup final to be attended by a British monarch.

Back in 1913, one of the touring Corinthians had predicted 'a brilliant future' for Brazilian football. Brazil's victory in the 1919 South American championship bore this out, as well as providing evidence of the emergence of a Brazilian style of play – based less on the trademark teamwork of the English Corinthians, more on the 'individualist tendency'. The São Paulo magazine *Sports* made this the theme of an article in its first issue:

> As opposed to the British school which dictates that the ball be taken by all the forwards right up to the opposition's goal and put in from the closest possible range, the Brazilian school states that shots be taken from any distance, the precision of the shot being worth more than the fact that it is made close to the target. And it further states that the collective advance of the whole forward line is not necessary, it's enough for two or three players to break away with the ball, which, by its devastating speed, completely unexpected, disorientates the entire rival defence.
>
> *(November 1919)*

'Brazilian Innovation', the article was headed. Here is an early reference to the element of surprise and risk-taking which we have come to expect from Brazilian sides. And just when Brazilian football was being shown to be different from the British style, the São Paulo Sports Writers' Association brought out a dictionary of football terms in Portuguese. Only one item survived from the vocabulary of former times: '*Charles* – Skill in which the player bends his leg back and kicks the ball with his heel.'

Whereas Miller's heel trick anticipated the improvisational aspect of the Brazilian game, Harry Welfare was a model of aggression and athleticism; which was why at a track-and-field meeting (such as the one at Fluminense in 1921) Harry was equally at home throwing a discus or a javelin as running in the 100 metres. Zezé Moreira, coach in the 1950s of the Brazilian national side, recalls seeing him on a football pitch, providing an image of what it must have been like for a defender to have Harry bearing down on him. 'Welfare was a formidable player. He was robust. In those days you were allowed to bounce the keeper and the ball into the net. He was skilled at this. If the ball was in the goal area he'd come in like a tank – that's what they called him – and he'd play the keeper and the ball and the goal stood.'

But in one celebrated incident involving a full-back, The Tank overstepped the mark. At least that was how the referee saw it. It occurred during a Fluminense *v* Botafogo game in July 1921. As the *Correio da Manhã* explained, 'Welfare, who had already clashed with Palamone, in an effort to dispossess him, violently charged him, injuring him.' Palamone and Welfare were renowned for their intense rivalry; but on this occasion, before he knew it Harry, wearing the captain's armband, had received his marching orders.

The *Correio* thought it was a harsh decision, and the Fluminense directors were quick to comment. The following note was added to Harry's details in the Fluminense Members' Book: 'Praised at a board meeting on 25 July 1921 for the correct manner in which he behaved during the game against Botafogo FC on 24 July 1921.' What mattered to the board was the fact that Harry had accepted the decision without complaint.

As for the referee, R.L. Todd, like several of his British predecessors he was no stranger to controversy. In the 1919 South American championship he had reportedly disallowed a legitimate 'goal' by Argentina at a critical stage of their match with Brazil.

In a derisive postscript to the sending-off, thirty years later Harry was charged with the task of recruiting British referees for the Rio Federation.

★   ★   ★

If mystery surrounded Harry Welfare's leaving Liverpool, the same could be said of his farewell to Fluminense. During the three seasons following the *tricampeonato* he had been club captain. Perhaps he expected to be offered a coaching position when he finally stopped playing in 1924. On April 27 he appeared in the second of Fluminense's three games in the Torneio Initium, a pre-season competition, and scored his side's winning goal against Botafogo. Fluminense went on to lift the trophy. The fact that this, Welfare's last official game, was a pre-season fixture is in itself curious.

If Harry *did* have control of the team, it must have been for a limited period; for the squad of players that went on to win the 1924 Carioca championship was coached by Charlie Williams, back at Fluminense after a twelve-year absence. It is not clear why Williams returned to the club at that moment – and how this affected Welfare's involvement in the football section. What we do know is that Harry remained at Fluminense, apparently continuing to live on site and transferring his competitive appetite to the club's basketball courts; he was among the group that were Rio champions in 1924.

It was in 1926 that Harry, 37, finally transferred his allegiance to a rival football club. When it happened there was a brashness to it that mirrored his departure from Liverpool. Flávio Costa was in Rio at the time, just embarking on a successful playing career; he later was Brazil's coach in their traumatic World Cup of 1950. According to him, Welfare's move didn't go down well: 'It was very problematical . . . no one moved clubs. It wasn't the thing to do.' Especially when a paid coaching post was on offer, and the club making that offer was Vasco da Gama.

When Harry was persuaded to join Vasco, Rio's traditional clubs were still smarting from that organisation's outrageous and spectacular challenge to their authority. In 1923 newly promoted Vasco had won the Carioca league with a team that included four blacks or mulattos and four illiterate whites. Suddenly, the dockland players that had alerted the attention of the Exeter City party had a stage on which to perform, deserving of their talents. In fact in that glorious season Vasco, according to Mário Filho, made all their opponents look ordinary. A revolution had begun.

Not surprisingly, the élite fought back. Eight clubs, led by Fluminense, broke away to form the Associação Metropolitana de Esportes Athléticos (AMEA), leaving Vasco and the other minnows with their 'athletes of doubtful profession' to battle it out for an unofficial title. Even when Vasco were allowed to join AMEA a year later, desperate attempts were made to force the club to toe the amateur line – and that meant that racial and social discrimination persisted. Players were required to have a recognisable job and before taking part in a league game they had to show they could write their names. Vasco's coup in signing on Harry Welfare can be seen as another blow for their detractors.

But, of course, it was particularly galling for Fluminense. Whatever Harry's reasons were for leaving – and unfortunately these remain elusive – the club's official line appears to be that the main motive was money: 'The Englishman had fallen on hard times.' Better this than admit that his defection was principled. Perhaps. Though intriguingly – and counter to the suggestion that Harry was struggling to make ends meet – Flávio Costa recalls visiting a sports shop in the early 1920s that was owned by Welfare!

Two years later, in May 1928, Fluminense's in-house magazine *Tricolor* (Ano II, No.7) had a feature on Harry Welfare. It was made out to be a homage to an important member of the *tricampeonato* and was accompanied by an elegant photograph of the player. Tellingly, what followed was a bizarre rebuttal of rumours that the club had originally 'imported him from England' and that he had 'received payments'. All the texts relating to the saga recounted at the beginning of this chapter were fully reproduced as proof that '*under the Fluminense banner Harry Welfare was always an amateur*' (the original text was italicised at this point).

It does seem that Fluminense were conveniently distancing themselves from Welfare. Just as, with inevitable irony, one of Harry's teams was about to produce an important result: a combined Rio/São Paulo XI's convincing win over Motherwell in June 1928 was, according to Geraldo Romualdo da Silva, 'one of the most historic feats in Brazilian football of the period'. But even before that, other British sides – albeit lesser ones – had been put through the mill in Brazil.

ELEVEN

Blue in Brazil

The pioneers are no longer the masters; apt pupils amongst the Continental and South American republics field representative teams equal [to] if not better than Britain's best. The sooner that is recognised and frankly admitted by home associations and clubs the better. Even today, despite unsatisfactory results obtained abroad by leading League clubs, the insular prejudice which is unfortunately characteristic of the Britisher in politics and commerce and socially has its damaging effect also in the widely extending world of football.

From 'Our Football Prestige' by David Jack,
in *All Sports Weekly*, 8 June 1929

The visits of Motherwell and Chelsea did us a power of good. It was obvious that the change in the offside law, introduced in 1925, lured the British teams into a defensive formation – the third back – making them easy prey for South American sides in which the attacking qualities of the centre-halves were preserved.

Beginning and development of football in São Paulo,
Paulo Varzea (1954)

When Charles Rule described to me the role of his father and cousin Charles in promoting football in São Paulo, he alluded to an important influence – 'Sometimes a ship from Santos came up, sent a team and they used to play together.' British sailors had reportedly given demonstrations of the game on Brazilian beaches in the 1870s. And there were periodic reminders of this, long after Miller and his fellow pioneers had retired. By then, though, 'showing the flag' had become a humbling experience.

The visit to São Paulo of a scratch team from the battleships *Hood* and *Repulse* in September 1922 is a case in point. It says a lot for the continued standing of the British in Brazil that no sooner had this group of His Majesty's sailors breezed into Santos than they had managed to secure a game against League champions Paulistano. Presumably, it was São Paulo Athletic Club (SPAC) that made the arrangements – and it was they who provided the referee. What the sailors could have done with were several players to bolster their side.

For Paulistano, without their star forwards Friedenreich and Formiga, took the game seriously, scoring seven goals to the sailors' one. The skill displayed by Mário on completing his hat-trick gave a taste of what future British opponents could expect, the player 'dribbling through the entire defence, rounding the keeper and planting the ball in the net'. Such a match, with its predictable out-come, may seem inconsequential, but for Brazilians it clearly mattered. Mazzoni, most notably, includes it in his record of 'international games'.

Another heavy defeat was inflicted on a British XI in June 1925, but this time Paulistano's victims were Britannia AC, a club that had been set up by SPAC members. The fixture took place shortly after Paulistano had returned from their historic, hugely successful tour of Europe. (Of ten games in France, Switzerland and Portugal, just one was lost; the players were dubbed *Les Rois du Football*; and back home a monument was put up to commemorate Brazil's first sporting ambassadors.) And at the precise moment the club was contemplating withdrawal from the São Paulo Association. Britannia, therefore, soon found themselves in a similar position to that of the original Scottish Wanderers: encouraged to join an élite league that espoused social and racial selection.

The founding of the Liga de Amadores de Futebol (LAF) in December 1925 was a final attempt in São Paulo to 'develop football based on the most restricted amateurism'. Initially, Britannia probably saw it as their duty to be members of the new league, but following a winless 1926 season they gave up competitive football. During its brief LAF interlude, the Britannia side, like the Wanderers', was half-Brazilian in its make-up, and it contained Archie McLean alternating, as Charles Miller had done, between goalkeeper and a place in the forward line. Paulistano still have in their trophy cabinet a silver symbol of British backing for the LAF's conservatism and fight for amateur purity. In 1926 the Charles Miller Cup was competed for by teams in the LAF youth league.

★ ★ ★

Compared to São Paulo, British involvement in Carioca football was far more marked in the 1920s. For one thing, both Harry Welfare and Sidney Pullen (if we see him essentially as a product of the Rio British community: a one-time Paysandu/Estrangeiros player) were playing at the highest level until almost the midpoint of the decade – and connected with two of the most prominent clubs, Fluminense and Flamengo respectively. More significant, though, was the fact that these men, along with Charlie Williams, won six Carioca titles between them as team managers: Pullen for Flamengo as player–coach (1920, 1921, 1925), Williams with Fluminense (1924) and América (1928), and Welfare at Vasco (1929).

It was during Vasco's period of exclusion in 1924 that Cariocas had an opportunity to gauge Brazil's football progress against a group of British professionals. Plymouth Argyle's brief stop-off on the way to Argentina did not pass unnoticed, and the antics of one reporter served as a likely metaphor for the match that had been fixed for their return journey. 'Dribbling round Plymouth's footballers' was the headline for the *O Paiz* piece which described how referee F.W. Reeve, accompanying the tourists, had been tricked into divulging facts about the players.

Judging from one of the Plymouth manager's letters to the *Western Evening Herald*, it wasn't the only reason the press had for poking fun at the English visitors. Serious was not a word you could readily associate with the club's preparation for the games ahead. As Robert Jack admitted, the Rio nightlife was there to be sampled: 'Some of our party made a round of the cabarets, in many of which dancing is the main amusement, and everybody was aboard the *Avon* again by 4 a.m.'

If the management had been similarly indulgent on the way home, the players could have proceeded direct from the dance hall to the dressing-room. But then the match never did take place – more down to the impracticality of the scheduling rather than an inability to stay the course. Informed that the game would kick-off at eight in the morning, Plymouth's cabled response read: 'Fluminense FC – Rio – Regret. Impossible. Argyle.'

Back in Plymouth, Jack declared that the Argentines and the

Uruguayans 'could give any English League team a good game. The teams are strong in all departments, but shine particularly at forward. Their players are extremely quick in turning and twisting, and much quicker in passing than English teams.' He would have said the same of the Brazilians.

★　★　★

When the next British side of note ventured to South America there was no eleventh-hour effort to persuade them to exhibit their skills in Brazil. That wasn't necessary. In April 1928, as the Motherwell party were preparing to cross the Atlantic, it had already been decided that their itinerary would include two matches in Rio de Janeiro.

Motherwell's visit coincided with Brazil's emergence from a period of self-imposed isolation from the international game. Flávio Costa, who was playing for Flamengo at the time, recalls that 'our football was very raw because we didn't communicate with anyone. The Uruguayans and Argentines were more advanced than us because they kept up links with Europe' – a fact that was driven home when news of the Scots' three defeats in Argentina reached Rio. But were the side that had finished third in the Scottish First Division behind Rangers and Celtic really inferior to some of the previous visitors, as some reports were suggesting?

On the evening of 18 June coach John Hunter and his 16-man squad arrived back in the Brazilian capital and made a base at the Palace Hotel. With three days before the first game, there were the usual sights to see and a visit to Fluminense's stadium for the players to familiarise themselves with the floodlights. The first official match under lights in Brazil had taken place earlier in the year at Vasco's new stadium – a lead not followed in Britain until almost 25 years later.

While at Fluminense the Motherwell party had watched the Rio players train. Skipper Bobby Ferrier was quoted as saying that they weren't as good as the Argentines; and Hunter let it be known that due to the 'excellent preparation' of his players it was unlikely that they would be defeated. Fact or fiction, it was just the fillip the Brazilians needed.

21 June
Motherwell 1   Rio de Janeiro 1
The attendance at Fluminense's stadium was estimated to be in the region of 50,000 when, 'at precisely 10.20 p.m.', referee Affonso de

Castro gave the signal for the sides to come out. A preliminary game had been played between teams from the north and south of Rio.

From the outset the Scots put pressure on their opponents with a series of high balls into the Rio box. When Aguiar was dispossessed by Tennant, Ferrier had a long-range effort well-saved by Jaguaré. With most of the play in the Rio half, the game was 'monotonous, intense attacking being cancelled out by excellent defending'. Effective work on the right by Nascimento frustrated the efforts of Motherwell's renowned left flank of Ferrier and Stevenson. Eventually Scotland international Alex McClory had stops to make from Alfredo and Oswaldinho. At the interval it was goalless.

In the second half, the visitors took control, making their 'height advantage and better combination' count. Centre-forward Tennant eluded Pennaforte and with Jaguaré out of position a weak shot sufficed to open the scoring. It was now Rio's turn to press, and during a 'vigorous attack' the equaliser arrived. Oswaldinho, who had moved to centre-half in place of the injured Aguiar, received the ball near the halfway line. In a solo effort he proceeded to beat five Motherwell players before firing a shot into the net. Mazzoni describes it as 'one of the most sensational goals of all time scored in Brazil'.

Despite earning a draw, the Rio XI were criticised by the local press for a 'disjointed performance'. Consolation came in the form of praise from Motherwell, the Brazilians' agility and enthusiasm being particularly emphasised. If, by this point, John Hunter and Harry Welfare had met, they would have perhaps discovered the connection in their playing careers; for the *Folha da Manhã* (23 June 1928) informs us that Hunter had once been with Liverpool.

But that was probably as far as the fraternising went. Harry, it transpires, had been put in charge of Motherwell's other opponents, Brazil Select.

24 June
Motherwell 0   Rio/São Paulo XI 5

All seats were taken at Fluminense's Guanabara stadium. The prelude to the main event was a friendly between the weakest sides in the Carioca League, Syrio-Libanez and Vila Isabel. The national side was given a warm reception, in particular Paulistas Amilcar and Feitiço. At 2.35 p.m. Luiz Vinhaes's whistle was the signal for the Brazilians to kick off.

Most of the early play took place in midfield, and during a

Motherwell attack Helcio gave away a corner. The ball was cleared, but soon keeper Jaguaré was called on to make two saves. At the other end Petronilho shot wide following a good build-up. In the tenth minute the home side went into the lead, Feitiço beating his man and firing the ball into the net. The Brazilians took the game to their opponents, and the Scots responded with raids of their own. The encounter was evenly balanced. Vasco forward Paschoal missed an open goal – and then ten minutes before the break Feitiço put his side further ahead, beating McClory with a powerful shot.

After the restart the Scots tried hard to open their account, forcing Jaguaré to make three fine saves. 'Despite this offensive the Brazilians revealed a superior technique and were playing with assurance,' reported one commentator. Midway through the half a shot by Paschoal rebounded to De Maria and the Corinthians winger made it 3–0. The Motherwell players protested that De Maria was offside, but the goal stood. Ten minutes from time Feitiço converted a centre from Oswaldinho for the Brazilians' fourth goal and added a fifth a minute later. At the final whistle, notes Mazzoni, 'spectators rushed onto the pitch, carrying off our players in triumph'.

Hunter and Welfare would barely have had time for a handshake, for, as the *Motherwell Times* of 20 July 1928 reveals, the match 'was played so close to the Fir Parkers' sailing for home that they had to taxi to their boat in their football toggery'. If he was unable to hold a post-mortem in Rio, Hunter more than made up for it in Scotland. The Motherwell public were informed that 'the Brazilians played exceptionally fine football', and the coach left no doubt as to the strengths of the South American game: 'My word they can play football. We knew that before we took up the tour, but did not anticipate footcraft of such high order . . . Their ball control is simply magnificent, while their speed is a perfect revelation.'

But for one spectator, seventy years on, strange though it may seem, it's a Scottish lesson that has stuck in the memory. Flávio Costa vividly recalls the reaction to keeper McClory's goal-kicks: 'He placed the ball as the rule dictates, took several paces back – as keepers do today – and ran up and kicked the ball. The crowd had never seen anything like it – because we didn't do this. We didn't even observe the international rule – and so there was a "ceremony" inside the area, the ball was put on the ground, one of the backs passed it to the keeper and the keeper, with the ball in his hands, kicked it out.

'The Motherwell keeper did things according to the rule book and for our crowd that was unknown. They thought he was mad. When he ran up to kick the ball, the crowd' – Flávio Costa makes the crescendoing sound that keepers have become used to – 'made a racket. From then on the lesson that Motherwell left us was that we had to comply with the rule – kicking the ball out of the box in the proper way.' But conformity took time; and goal-kicks were apparently not the only aspect of the South American game that caused visitors to frown. One year later a Chelsea director informed the FA that: 'The non-observance of the laws of the game hindered real football. Charging of any form was strictly forbidden, and the goalkeeper was allowed to advance to the penalty area before kicking the ball when a goal-kick was being taken. Accidental hands was always penalised, and the "off-side" decisions on the whole were lamentably disheartening to the visiting side.'

★   ★   ★

São Paulo had never staged a match involving a British professional club, so the *Gazeta Esportiva*'s news of 8 April 1929 was particularly encouraging. Chelsea of the English Second Division had agreed to play two matches away from Rio, both in the first week of July – one in Santos against Santos FC, the other in São Paulo against Corinthians. Later, the Santos fixture would be replaced by a game between the tourists and a São Paulo XI.

While the sporting public in South America were eagerly anticipating matches between their best amateur sides and the professionals from London, serious reservations were being voiced in Britain over the very existence of close-season foreign tours. The Old Country's stature in terms of world football was not what it used to be and since the end of the war signs were that others were laying claim to Britain's previously unquestioned supremacy. In May the *All Sports Weekly* began a series of articles on 'The Continental Tours'. It was Arsenal's David Jack who presented the bleak picture: 'Even when imbued with the right spirit many of our touring teams find the unusual environment, hard grounds, poor refereeing, the heat, and the comparatively strong opposition too much for them after a strenuous season at home – and come away leaving anything but the best of impressions, which is a great pity.'

Moreover, Chelsea's task was starkly put: 'The Argentines and Uruguayans already have a worldwide reputation; they were the finalists in the last Olympic tournament, but, further than that, they both badly mangled Motherwell and Plymouth Argyle in recent years.

Chelsea's progress will be watched with deep interest, for their success is vitally necessary in Republics where British football has always gone through the melting pot.' Jack would have received a first-hand account of football in South America: his father had gone there in 1924 as Plymouth's manager.

The standard of football in Brazil may not have been considered on a par with that of its rivals to the south, but interest in the game was just as intense. Consequently, Chelsea's arrival in Rio on 16 May, *en route* for Buenos Aires, gave the press an opportunity to introduce the London club to the Brazilian sporting public. *O Estado de São Paulo*, for example, gave an outline of the tour, a list of all the members of the party, with a probable starting line-up, and facts about Chelsea's recent form in England.

Two weeks later, the recently lauched *Gazeta Esportiva* – Brazil's first sports daily – published a two-page pictorial presentation with photos of the players and action from cup and league matches. Naturally, the professionals' progress in Argentina was followed; and English football's latest novelty was revealed. On 10 June the *Gazeta* published a photo of the Chelsea players waving to the crowd in Buenos Aires, the novelty being the numbers on the backs of their shirts. 'Numbers were worn in the old Albion for the first time at the end of last year – and they say the idea met with success.' Maybe; but it was only an experiment. Ten years would pass before the Football League voted in favour of compulsory numbering of players.

Chelsea's return to Rio on 28 June was drawing near, and on 16 June *O Estado de São Paulo* provided detailed pen-pictures of the players, and the club's 'credentials'. It was pointed out that there were a number of internationals in the current side – and to increase expectation and to bolster Chelsea's image the paper resorted to hyperbole. Left-half Andrew Wilson was 'one of the best players in the world in recent years', Chelsea's Stamford Bridge stadium was, with the exception of Wembley, 'the biggest in the world' and the club was always seen in Britain as 'the one with the most internationals in its ranks'.

Back in England debate rumbled on over Britain's precarious position 'in the widely extending world of football'. According to David Jack, one of the causes of the failures abroad was the change in the offside rule, a change which had 'sacrificed natural craft and cleverness to speed' and this had 'played into the hands of the moderate type of player whose only assets are speed and dash, whose real football craft may be comparatively negligible'. Of course, what made the South Americans so potent was their combination of speed and cleverness; and it was acknowledged that their sides, along with several in Europe, now provided more than adequate competition: 'There is great improvement and development in the play of our foreign rivals – an improvement which has brought half a dozen Continental countries and the South Americans on a level with the best we can produce.' Chelsea were hardly the leading exponents of the British game – and, not surprisingly, during their current excursion, they were struggling.

Given the Pensioners' poor record in Argentina and Uruguay, the Cariocas must have fancied their chances of starting the four-match series with a victory. So far, of the twelve matches played, the tourists had won five, lost six and drawn one; but it had been a gruelling schedule with, on one occasion, two games being played on the same day in two different towns. In Brazil Chelsea would again come up against the South Americans' forte – 'the extreme rapidity of their game'. Even so, against a professional side, the Brazilians could take nothing for granted; and a split in the Rio camp over selection policy might well have had an adverse effect on the team.

On the morning of the game the *Folha da Manhã* attempted to analyse Chelsea's game based on material received from Argentina. In contrast to the South Americans' spontaneity, 'Chelsea play their football like a game of chess – slow and calculated, using their physical superiority to good advantage.' The English impress in 'the spectacular beauty of their game', more so than in their technique; and this is demonstrated in their heading, the way in which their backs clear the ball 'in any direction' and the static nature of the midfield. Further, 'unable to impress by the beauty of their technique, Chelsea had an attitude that was impressive'. The writer ended by suggesting that after the game opinions might well have to be revised.

28 June
Chelsea 1   Rio de Janeiro 1
The first fixture in the 'international season' sponsored by Fluminense took place at their Rua Guanabara stadium. New floodlights were inaugurated and the result was 'a great improvement in visibility'. A large crowd had assembled by the time Rio kicked off at 10.05 p.m. The match official was Arthur de Moraes e Castro.

In the opening quarter of an hour there were some lively exchanges with attacks at both ends; but the football lacked cohesion and skill, and several corners were squandered. For most of the first half the teams struggled to find any kind of rhythm. Millington in the Chelsea goal was the busier of the two keepers. With the interval approaching Rio produced their best spell – but the English countered and Jackson opened the scoring.

After the break the visitors attacked more and the route to goal was facilitated by an inert display from the Rio half-backs. The Cariocas came close to drawing level, but luck ran against them and too many mistakes were made. The equaliser finally arrived with nine minutes remaining, Ripper converting a centre from Nascimento. After that, Nilo missed an excellent chance to win the contest.

It had been a disappointing game. The *Folha da Manhã* correspondent described Chelsea as a team 'lacking in method, precision and above all loyalty' – loyalty to the principles of good-sportsmanship. The Londoners were fit, keen and they displayed good ball control. Typically their game ran like clockwork – 'cold and mathematical throughout'. As for Rio, besides the shortcomings in midfield, it was noted that they played 'without harmony and safety in defence', and their attacks were badly organised. Left-back Hespanhol was the star of the team, and up front Ripper and Lagarto made an impressive right flank.

As regards Chelsea's performance, *O Estado de São Paulo* came to similar conclusions – no player in the English side caught the eye, though they played well together as a team, especially the forwards. Inevitably, comparisons were made with Motherwell; and *O Estado* suggested that the Scots were 'much more impressive as they definitely displayed a quality of football that was more interesting, neater and more combined'.

30 June
Chelsea 1   Rio de Janeiro 2
For the second exhibition game staged by Fluminense FC there was a poor turn-out – testament to Chelsea's indifferent performance two days earlier. In the preliminary event the Vasco da Gama 2nd XI beat Fluminense Reserves 2–1. The tourists came out in their familiar blue shirts and black shorts, having made two changes to their line-up – Scotland international Tommy Law replacing Smith at right-back, and Chris Ferguson taking Crawford's place at inside-right. The Rio side was unchanged and on entering the field the players presented small English flags to the visitors. Affonso de Castro got the game under way at 3.38 p.m.

In the opening minutes both sides came close to scoring – the

Cariocas from an attack inspired by Luiz, the English taking advantage of Hespanhol's slackness. It was an early warning for the defences, for chances continued to come and go with regularity. Nilo shot poorly with Millington out of position, and a fine Chelsea move was 'very badly finished' by Weaver. Corners, too, were wasted. However, after the balanced beginning, the Cariocas appeared 'the masters of the situation – playing with true precision, particularly the left-sided forwards Nilo and Theophilo'. Still, another slip in the Rio rearguard put Pearson clear, but Hespanhol recovered well.

With half-time in sight Rio pounded away at the tourists' goal area. Hesitation cost Luiz an excellent opportunity to score, and then Millington stopped a long shot from Nilo. Lagarto went close and shots from Nilo and Luiz were well-saved by the Chelsea keeper. The pressure told in the 38th minute, Nilo heading Rio in front from Ripper's centre. But the visitors' reaction was swift and four minutes later it was all square again. Fortes and Fernando got in each other's way, Jackson broke away and his cross was converted by Chris Ferguson.

In the first minute of the second period Rio were ahead again, Theophilo outwitting the Chelsea backs before beating Millington. It was the sign for the Cariocas to start a fresh wave of attacking – and 'the English citadel was living dangerously'. Soon, the ball was in the net again, but there was no goal as Luiz had knocked it in with his hand. Also, the Rio forwards were being caught out by their opponents' use of the offside trap, 'a tactic which meant the game lost some of its brilliance'.

Right-wing Ripper set up chances for Lagarto and Nilo, but the one-goal difference prevailed. Now, as darkness fell, the floodlights were switched on. Chelsea were almost presented with an equaliser when Lagarto gave away a free-kick near the six-yard box. Pearson took the kick, but although Miller connected well he was adjudged offside. Near the end 'there was a small disagreement between Hespanhol and Jackson'; and Millington ensured that Chelsea did not concede a third goal.

Compared to Friday's game, the *Folha* correspondent thought Rio's forward-line had improved, and generally the team's play was 'relaxed'. However, again, the midfield gave a below-par performance. As regards Chelsea, opinion gleaned from their previous appearance was confirmed: the backs were slow and untidy, the attackers poor finishers. The only player to excel was keeper Millington. It was felt that 'Chelsea were indisputably much inferior to Motherwell', and that in São Paulo they would suffer heavy defeats.

Taking the night train from Rio, Chelsea arrived in São Paulo on the morning of 3 July – and already the Paulista press was looking for new angles on the Londoners' historic visit. How would Chelsea compare to other recent tourists – Rampla Juniors of Uruguay or the Hungarian side Ferencvaros? According to *O Estado de São Paulo*, there was much more interest generated prior to the visit of Ferencvaros, an unknown quantity who went on to prove their worth. But, for Chelsea's opener, it was hoped that Corinthians' wide support base would be mustered, despite 'the possible mediocrity of the English team' and the fact that the match was to be played on a week-day.

Another São Paulo daily, the *Folha da Manhã*, provided a more thorough preview of Chelsea *v* Corinthians. Full details of the tour were published and there were pen-pictures of the English players. Also, the comments of a *Diário Carioca* correspondent were cited in which Chelsea were considered a good side but lacking 'the spectacular element provided by a Ministrinho, running rings round a poor half-back'. Compared to the English, the Rio fans held a player like Vasco forward Paschoal in far greater esteem; yet, the correspondent insisted, 'we prefer Pearson or Crawford'. One 'strange' aspect of Chelsea's play was recounted: full-back Odell, under pressure, had sent a strong headed pass, followed by a warning shout, in the direction of his keeper, the ball being received 'with absolute safety'.

4 July
Chelsea 4   Corinthians 4
Chelsea's third game in Brazil was played at Palmeiras's Parque Antarctica stadium in front of an estimated attendance of 10,000. The Londoners made wholesale changes to the side that had lost 2–1 in Rio. A notable inclusion was star player Andy Wilson at inside-left. For the São Paulo champions, Guimarães made his début in the centre of midfield. In the preliminary game Corinthians' reserves drew 2–2 with Standard Oil FC, and then at 3.35 p.m. the main match began with Chelsea kicking off.

Early on, Corinthians centre-forward Gambinha broke through the middle only for his shot to be blocked by Law. Now it was the visitors' turn to attack. First, a move led by Elliott ended with Del Debbio intercepting Jackson's pass; and later Chelsea's front-runners combined well before setting up a chance for Jackson. The winger gathered the ball near the goal-line and his powerful shot passed narrowly over the bar. Corinthians were actually attacking more – but their finishing was poor. Peres went close, shooting over the bar after beating several opponents; and following a Corinthians corner Law it was again who cleared the danger.

Twenty minutes had gone, and then suddenly, in an eight-minute spell, Chelsea built a three-goal advantage. The first was a product of Bishop's run from midfield and pass to Elliott who set up Jackson for the score. Almost immediately Millington pulled off a fine save. But Wilson soon made it 2–0 direct from a free-kick after a foul by Nerino. A minute and a half later Elliott broke clear, got the better of Corinthians' backs and gave keeper Tuffy no chance. The Brazilians appeared disorganised, but they did not lose heart; and three minutes later Gambinha reduced the arrears with a shot that was deflected into the net off Law.

A brief period of stalemate ensued, the game being contested in the middle of the pitch. Then, in the 35th minute, Corinthians' Grané scored from a free-kick conceded by Law. At this point the English resorted to a more physical style of play and a number of fouls were committed. Gambinha's equaliser would not have helped matters, and the game continued to deteriorate – Corinthians showing a lack of understanding, Chelsea 'displaying inferior technique, in a sporting and social sense'.

After the interval it was not long before Chelsea resumed their strong-arm approach, and this and the behaviour of the crowd were deplored by the *Estado de São Paulo* correspondent. 'The shouting and booing of the spectators and the violence of the game made it look like a bullfight.'

De Maria missed a good opportunity in front of goal, but minutes later the Corinthians winger redeemed himself by putting his side ahead. Ten minutes later a long shot from Elliott brought the teams level again; and at the other end another chance was wasted, De Maria again the culprit. Now Guimarães produced a good run and shot, but Millington prevented a goal with 'the save of the day'.

Chelsea seemed content to soak up pressure, and their defence was backed up by a solid midfield. Corinthians' forwards were showing signs of nervousness. De Maria blasted over from two metres out, and then, from a similar position, Castelli hammered the ball against the bar and hit the rebound wide of the left post. The best counter the visitors had to offer was a move involving Elliott, Meredith and Jackson; but when Tuffy's goal was threatened, Del Debbio and Guimarães cleared the danger.

Despite the goals the match had left much to be desired, and many watching expressed their dissatisfaction by exiting before the end. Paulistas took their football seriously and *O Estado* was moved to remark: 'Those present were subjected to one of the greatest sporting deceptions in living memory in São Paulo.' Corinthians had given a weak display, in terms of teamwork and individual performance; and 'in their sporting apprenticeship this was an all-time low'. As for Chelsea, their reputation was further dented by 'a lack of technique and sporting education'; and while they had not played too badly, 'they could not be compared to São Paulo's stongest teams'.

7 July
Chelsea 1   São Paulo 3

For the final exhibition match of the series 'an enormous crowd' gathered at the Parque Antarctica ground. The *Times of Brazil* described the conditions: 'Rain had fallen in the early morning and it was hoped that this would make the Chelsea players feel more at home, but it proved insufficient to make the ball a little heavier, the ground too was treacherous ...' The tourists made three changes, Willie Ferguson (older brother of Chris) replacing Bishop in midfield, and Weaver and Pearson joining the forward-line. Once again they were led by 'the famous veteran', Andy Wilson. The Paulistas, looking to restore confidence after a rare defeat at the hands of Ferencvaros, came out with Argentino at centre-half and Petronilho filling the centre-forward spot. But these experiments were vociferously opposed by the local support, even before a ball was kicked. So, incredibly, with the teams in position, the Paulista selectors bowed at least in part to public pressure, pulling off Petronilho and sending on Araken of Santos. In a one-sided preliminary contest Portuguesa had beaten Ypiranga 5–2; and at 3.35 p.m. Francisco Cespede Guerra gave the signal for Chelsea to kick off.

'The first half of the game took place almost entirely in the Paulistas' half save for an occasional raid upon Chelsea territory which was usually successfully thwarted. Shot after shot was aimed at the Paulista goal but the custodian was exceedingly safe and many of the shots missed their mark.'

However, despite the number of wasted chances, Chelsea managed to take the lead after quarter of an hour. Wilson, running into the penalty area, received the ball from Elliott and sent a shot past keeper Athié.

The Paulistas' response was immediate, and from Ministrinho's high centre Feitiço headed in the equaliser. Now, the Brazilians' counter attacks were more frequent, and in the 34th minute Araken put them ahead after linking well with Santos colleague Feitiço. Nevertheless, according to the *Times of Brazil*, the Paulistas' goals should have been prevented and in both cases keeper Millington was at fault. 'He was never safe. He seemed to have a keen desire to play half-back and at the slightest approach of the opposing forwards went for a *passeio* ['walk'] and left his goal to "God and good neighbours".' Chelsea finished the half on top, but even though they had the advantage of a fairly strong breeze the Londoners were unable to draw level.

'The second half began at high speed which was kept up throughout, clearly showing that in spite of all rumours the Chelsea men were in very good training and if anything had the extra turn of speed for they almost invariably managed to be first on the ball.' However, the Pensioners' finishing continued to let them down; and their defence was put to the test more often. Still, the game remained open until the dying minutes when Law brought down Camarão inside the box. Feitiço's spot-kick put the result beyond doubt.

If the Paulista selectors' last-minute gamble – bringing in Araken and moving Feitiço to centre-forward – had paid off handsomely, the decision to persist with the latest centre-midfield recruit was not vindicated. Poor Argentino was not only booed throughout the match, his failing was also one of the main topics of press discussion. The search would therefore continue for someone to perform the centre-half duties, as the *Folha* put it, someone to be 'the axle, the soul, the spring, the life of the team'. Amilcar had been the principal playmaker – now his absence was being keenly felt. As for the other half-backs, Nerino and Serafini had shown why they were first-choice players. For the rest of the team there were varying amounts of praise, with a special mention for the captain Del Debbio.

As regards the English, the *Gazeta Esportiva* thought that they had given an excellent exhibition. 'Chelsea were defeated thanks to the solidity of our defence, chiefly in the second half, when the numbered shirts doubled their attacks in search of an equaliser.' Indeed, the *Gazeta* and the *Times of Brazil* agreed that the Londoners' display had surprised many of those present – the same people who, a few days earlier, had written them off. Chelsea's attacking qualities were particularly evident in the second half including, the *Gazeta* noted, 'all varieties of calculated passing, studied manoeuvres by the central trio, the wingers' centralised play, and all this happily neutralised and covered by the five-man Paulista defence'. Further, the Chelsea players had conducted themselves well: 'They did not resort to any form of brutality and left the referee in peace. Their sportsman-like spirit undid the bad impression that was left last Thursday.' Three members of the side stood out – Jackson, Wilson and Pearson. It is doubtful whether Chelsea were ever made aware of the favourable reaction provoked by their closing exhibition. But the team were given a big send-off at the Luz train station several hours after they had left the Parque Antarctica pitch. Later in the week they would board a steamship in Rio for the journey home.

Meanwhile, in England, there had been further calls for an end to continental touring, heightened by unsavoury incidents during Newcastle United's recent tour. In the *All Sports Weekly* former Manchester United stalwart Charlie Roberts had charted the decline of the British game in an article entitled 'Why I Condemn These Foreign Tours'. The deterioration in sporting relations with the Continent had reached a point where action should be taken: 'Our loss of prestige through results, and the charges laid against our sportsmanship, are matters which the Football Association cannot allow to go unchallenged.'

Clearly there was a contradiction to be addressed – on the one hand, tours were a means of raising revenue and an opportunity for a cheap holiday; on the other, it was imperative that during the exhibitions the standard of British League football should be upheld. As far as Roberts was concerned, too much was being asked of the players. He concluded: 'We cannot expect players to be at top playing pressure for half a dozen matches in the early summer, go into training at the beginning of August, and be at their best throughout a season. So the relaxation on the Continent. The fewer of these tours the better, for I cannot see how in a general way we can do ourselves and those before whom we play full justice.'

In Chelsea's case, the players had probably done as well as could be expected. They were, after all, an English Second Division side; and to make matters worse, they had been plagued by injuries. In Argentina, furthermore, they had on at least one occasion been subjected to disgraceful behaviour by local spectators and players. Impressions from one match were related in the *All Sports Weekly*: 'The referee was treated almost like a criminal by his own countrymen, and a Chelsea player was assaulted with a brutality that was the more regrettable because one of the principal assailants wore the uniform of a public service.'

Even if the Londoners were not entirely blameless, the consensus of opinion among the quality Buenos Aires papers was that 'the visitors were more sinned against than sinning'. Moreover, one critic in Buenos Aires wrote: 'We want to point out that Chelsea's record in

Argentina was one of keen, honest play, and that any difference of opinion has arisen as the result purely and simply of divergence in the interpretation of the rules that govern the British game of Soccer.'

But it was not only club sides who were finding it hard to hold their own in foreign lands. In 1929 British pride was further dented when England were beaten by Spain in Barcelona – their first ever reverse away from home. In the previous year the English FA had withdrawn from FIFA over the issue of 'broken time' payment for continental amateurs, and no team had been sent to the Olympic tournaments of 1924 and 1928. Now, with the inaugural World Cup in Montevideo just months away, there was speculation that England would not be taking part.

The *Gazeta Esportiva* discussed the topic of England's isolation from international competition, while at the same time underlining the progress made by South America's footballers. It was apparent that 'in their lofty disdain for everything that was not insular football, the British gave no importance to what was happening elsewhere'. So it was that Uruguay's Olympic triumphs were given scant coverage in the British press 'as if obeying a tacit accord not to disturb English public opinion and to make people believe piously that if England did not win these world championships it was because it did not deign to enter them'.

In football, as in other disciplines in which Britain had ruled supreme, the time had come for the country to make way for others. Failures abroad should have opened the eyes of British directors; and the *Gazeta* quoted comments by one of their number, Chelsea chairman W.C. Kirby. In an interview for the *Athletic News* Kirby had declared that 'the South Americans are true masters in tactical play', and that it was necessary to go back to England's heyday before the First World War to find anything that could compare. Also, the Chelsea players had marvelled at the style and ball control of the South Americans.

Certainly, Brazilians had every right to feel satisfied with their own contribution, with club and representative sides consistently achieving success against foreign opposition. In 1929 a total of 46 'international' matches had been played, the Brazilians winning 27 and the seven visiting clubs a mere seven between them. This summary gave encouragement for the future. But first, before progress in the international arena could be consolidated, the long-running dispute between the amateur and professional camps would have to be resolved. Predictably, Charles Miller and Harry Welfare had differing views on the issue.

TWELVE

Romance and Reality

The new generation salutes Charles Miller, the grandpa of our football

Banner shown by Corinthians supporters at
Pacaembú stadium, São Paulo, March 1944

[Welfare] was much more than a scorer of spectacular goals, for in the statistics he is up among the most efficient attack leaders of the continent, a true match-winner, as his countrymen say . . . The interval of 26 years has put an end to his fair hair and his youth, but not his passion for the game, set alight on the grounds of Great Britain, the great motherland.

O Futebol e sua Técnica, Max Valentim, 1941

It was billed as the 'Father *v* Son' reunion, a match at Pacaembú stadium between Corinthian Casuals and a 'Best-ever' Corinthians Paulista XI: on one team English amateurs descended from the Corinthian tourists of 1910, on the other a galaxy of former favourites – including Cláudio, Rivelino and Sócrates – representing the club that sprang from that 1910 visit. This was the cornerstone of São Paulo Athletic Club's centenary celebrations in 1988.

O *Estado de São Paulo* wrote of 'the Corinthian spirit of the English delegation' and the fact that for the 32-strong party 'results are not important, most important is being in contact with a football that they all admire'. Charles Miller, of course, would have approved of such sentiments; but for him, in the late-1920s, nostalgia was tinged with sorrow. At the same time, Harry Welfare, having shut out the past, was becoming dependent on results for his livelihood. The contrasting circumstances of the two men are the subject of this chapter.

Sixty years before SPAC's centenary, *O Estado* had tenuously taken the club's foundation to be the springboard for the evolution of Paulista football: it was these first members who were turned into footballers by Charles Miller. But that was not alluded to in Charles's *Estado* interview in the same year, 1928.

What *O Estado* sought from 'the introducer of football in São Paulo' was his opinion on the formation of a Liga Paulista de Profissionais de Futebol (LPPF) – the first attempt in Brazil, or in South America for that matter, to make professionalism official. The LPPF's aim was to contract individual players, put them into three groups based on ability, and create teams. Reaction to the initiative was polarised, and as a forum for discussion *O Estado* launched its own survey of public opinion. It was in this context that Charles Miller, in a rare return to the limelight, made an outspoken defence of the 'Corinthian spirit':

> – They say that professionalism is the answer . . .
>
> – I only accept sport between amateurs. Professionalism, for me, is not sport. I've already had an opportunity to give this opinion at the club when they were trying to establish boxing there.
>
> – Do you think it will improve the decadent situation at which we've arrived?
>
> – Absolutely not. In any case my opinion shouldn't serve as a basis. I've been away from sport for a long time now – especially football. I don't know how this body of professionals will be organised. However, it's possible that they might achieve something useful.
>
> – And on the question of technique?
>
> – It must improve with the professionals, because they have a sufficient amount of time and with this they are submitted to constant training.
>
> – But in England the results . . .
>
> – When I arrived here professionalism over there did not yet exist on a grand scale. I only knew one or two professional players. In the north of the country, however, this class was already quite numerous. Four years ago I went to a football match in England, and I found that the game was played without enthusiasm, ending in a goalless draw. I said to a friend that I was surprised by the final score and some of the phases in the game. 'There in São Paulo,' I told him, 'we would have scored a number of goals.' 'These are professionals,' he replied. 'They don't want to get injured. It's the arrangement. They

need to earn a living.' This is why I'm against professionalism, which
in great part takes the shine from the game. The amateur makes an
effort because he plays for sport and he plays with enthusiasm.
- But here, professionalism is presented as a remedy for the general
state of hypocrisy, vexatious for the players themselves.
- If professionalism is to be adopted, it's preferable to do it openly.

(O Estado de São Paulo, 9 March 1928)

And that final thought was echoed by most of the participants of *O
Estado*'s survey. As regards 'shamateurism', enough was enough. As an
AA das Palmeiras player put it: 'It's really not fair to have this hidden
professionalism, very morally and technically damaging because the
individual who openly makes a living out of playing has to really
make an effort, whereas our imaginary professionals, with a guaranteed subsidy, don't take training seriously, giving the impresson that
they can't spare one single minute for exercises due to the number of
jobs they have outside sport.' Perhaps he hadn't witnessed paid players
in England playing out a goalless draw, but the point was made.

Incredibly, though, it was a further five years before a lasting
solution was found. The LPPF foundered because, in Waldenyr
Caldas's words, 'it was not a body that came from within the clubs, but
a group of sportsmen-cum-businessmen who were interested in
financial profit'; it was, in effect, a football agency. Ironically, it was the
exodus of Brazil's best players abroad – first to Europe, then to
Argentina and Uruguay – helped along by foreign recruiting agents,
that brought legalised professionalism in Brazil closer. Another boost
for the professional lobby was the disbandment of the Paulista Liga de
Amadores de Futebol (LAF) at the end of the 1929 season – and with
it Paulistano's football section.

Charles Miller's fleeting participation in the professional *v* amateur
debate was hardly going to impede the tide of change, but it was
nonetheless significant. *O Estado* prefaced their transcription of the
above interview by stating that despite Miller's reluctance to speak, 'his
words carry a veiled interest for football, where he has collected so
many laurels, raising the concept of Paulista sport'. There is almost a
sense in which Charles's dissenting words were the death throes of
what Caldas terms 'romantic football . . . sport for sport's sake'. And
appropriately, this *Estado* interview is among the handful of Charles's
personal cuttings that have survived. The issue clearly meant something to him.

We have noted how Miller suggested the name for Corinthians

Paulista in 1910. At the beginning of 1930, when São Paulo FC was formed by a group of directors from two former LAF clubs, Paulistano and AA das Palmeiras, according to Charles Rule, Miller 'gave a helping hand'. Charles's name does not appear in Mazzoni's detailed account of the club's foundation, but the fact that he lived within a hundred yards of Paulistano and was a regular visitor to the club meant that he was ideally placed to offer advice informally. It was at Paulistano that Charles had refereed until he was 50; and his daughter Helena can recall how happy he was when, returning home after one of those games, he declared: 'I can still run!'

When a framework for introducing professionalism was finally agreed in Rio in January 1933, however, Charles's reaction was to sever all contact with the game. Charles Rule, who stayed at Miller's house for several years, told me that his cousin would evade most questions about football: 'He always kept quiet except one thing. He said: "I was disgusted when professionalism started here." He said: "I taught the game as a sport and then it became business, all this changing of money and so forth," and he said: "I quit. I won't have anything more to do with the people."' But in the 1940s Miller was once more in the public eye: first for an event to mark the fiftieth anniversary of his return to São Paulo, and later for the visit of Southampton FC.

★ ★ ★

Seeing the eclipse of the amateur game he had pioneered was not the only blow that Charles Miller suffered in the late-1920s. 'Romantic football' was a thing of the past – and so too was romance in his private life. It was around this time that Antonietta, Charles's wife of 20 years, left the family home in the Rua México and went to live with the writer Menotti del Picchia. In the Brazil of the 1920s it was practically unheard-of for a couple to separate; and Helena Miller poignantly recalls how her own fiancé subsequently broke off their engagement because he disapproved of the separation.

It must have been especially difficult for Charles to accept the situation. As Helena affirms, he and Antonietta had been 'very happily married . . . and there was no apparent reason for them to separate'. It was a case, she says, of 'great artists . . . falling in love': Antonietta, the internationally acclaimed concert pianist; Menotti, one of Brazil's literary lights. Miller, according to Charles Rule, 'from that moment onwards became morose and very quiet indeed'.

Within the space of a few years Charles's past had disintegrated – and not just in Brazil. In 1927 Banister Court School closed down. The school buildings were sold, soon demolished, and when Charles next visited Southampton there was a speedway and greyhound stadium on the land where a large part of his youth had been spent. In one of the last issues of the school's magazine (vol. V, July 1923, no.80), there had been a touching, almost obituary-like, reminder of his influence on sport at Banister's and in Brazil:

> In the cricket matches between Brazil and the Argentine, in 1922, C. Miller played for Brazil and C. Lett for the Argentine. Miller has not lost his old skill, for in one match he made 50. Cricket in Brazil owes much to him and to Willie Rule, and he also introduced football there. He was certainly the best forward we have ever had in a football team. In cricket, some of our present eleven are fully equal to him. No one will be better pleased than he to read this.

In 1929, several months after Chelsea's visit, Miller, at the age of 54, was cricketing in Niterói. Had the school magazine not ceased publication, it would doubtless have recorded his innings of 73 for São Paulo City.

As the 1930s unfolded, Charles Miller would have been grateful for the escape that sport continued to provide. In a letter to his daughter who was studying in Rio, he writes, 'On Saturday afternoon I played tennis for two and a half hours, and on Sunday I went to Santo Amaro Golf Club and had lunch there and then played golf for over two hours.' (He would later refer to golf as 'my wise doctor'.) During the brief letter, mostly recounting family news, penned in May 1934, Miller's Anglo-Brazilian background is revealed. He begins the letter in Portuguese – and then abruptly switches to English, resorting again fleetingly to the first language. And there is a reference to a dance to mark King George's birthday: with melancholy he writes, 'I am looking forward to taking you to it, but shall be disappointed as no doubt you will not be here . . .'

A year later Helena was invited by her father to go to England. As the Royal Mail's agent in São Paulo – and a partner in the travel firm Miller, Goddard & Co – Charles was entitled, every two years, to an expenses-paid trip on one of the company's steamships. He had previously accompanied his wife on her concert tours in Europe, but in 1935 he showed his daughter the sights of Britain, taking her by car from London to Land's End and then up to Scotland. Helena remembers well their arrival in a bitterly cold England. 'Father bought me two overcoats . . .' she says, and then she starts to laugh, 'only for the temperature to shoot up the next day – but the coats were already mine!'

In Scotland Charles visited a number of friends – but by then there were no surviving relatives. Helena explains: 'During an earlier visit, father had left a note in the cemetery at his father's grave, and he got a reply from my grandfather's sisters. So he knew these "aunts". But when we went in 1935 they were no longer alive.' One thing that still amazes her is the fact that she understood the Scottish accent better than her father. 'Most of the time,' she says, 'I had to translate for him what they were saying – it was in my blood.' Charles found that amusing.

Another source of fun was the way in which Helena would receive money from her father for the hairdresser's or a meal – and then spend it on a concert or presents for friends. Miller 'knew what was going on and was amused by it all'; Helena then adds, solemnly, 'Father was a fine, good-humoured person.' With his daughter's penchant for mischief, it was as well he was.

On that trip in 1935, while Helena was attending a concert or shopping, Charles was more often than not at a sports event – 'tennis or football', according to Helena. But it appears he had returned to Brazil by the time Southampton played their golden jubilee match against Tottenham Hotspur in November, the day before his 61st birthday. Perhaps his name was mentioned in passing by the small group of St Mary's team-mates from the 1890s who were present at the club's anniversary dinner. Soon, though, he was helping in the preparations for SPAC's own 50 years celebration, his 'tenacious memory' of early club history being acknowledged in the souvenir booklet that was produced.

In 1939 Charles Miller made what was probably his final journey to England, taking with him his daughter as well as his son Carlos, his wife and children. Helena recounts how, at an airshow, she coaxed her father into going up in an aeroplane with her. It was the first time he'd flown; and after describing the fun they had she remarks, 'Father was such a good companion – for everything.' In London, however, were it not for Helena's sixth sense, the trip would almost certainly have ended in tragedy: both she and Charles narrowly avoided being among the victims of the IRA's first mainland bombing campaign. Helena remembers the incident as if it were yesterday: 'We were going to take the underground, and a few yards from the entrance I stopped at a shop window in which there was a bicycle, a racket and a pair of boxing gloves, with my father tugging at my arm and saying, "What's so interesting that it's made you stop?" At that instant, a bomb went off on the steps that we should have been taking at that very moment.'

Charles might have reflected on that miraculous escape as he cast his mind back on his life in an interview for the *Gazeta Esportiva* in March 1944. Indeed, it may well have been on that 1939 trip that, during a visit to The Dell to watch Southampton, Miller made up for missing the Saints' jubilee by staging a reunion of his own. He shared the story with the *Gazeta*:

> A few years ago, travelling to England, I was in Southampton, and I tried to make contact with old team-mates from my club. I was sitting in the stand, watching a game. So I asked some of the people around me if they could point out someone who had played in 1893 and 1894. While an elderly man was replying, I suddenly recognised two others who were there. I turned round and said: 'Hello, George! Hello, Alf!' The two men, a bit dazed, looked at me from head to foot and replied in unison: 'Hello, Nipper!' You can't imagine our joy! We talked about the old times, introducing some of the gossip of the period into our conversation.

It's more than likely that the two men referred to were George Carter and Ralph Ruffell ('Alf' being a transcription error) – both of whom were playing when Miller was first included in a St Mary's trial in 1891, both of whom attended the Saints' jubilee dinner.

The *Gazeta* headed their interview 'Charles Miller, Brazilian football's number one citizen', and the front page of the edition of 11 March 1944 is taken up by a photograph of the man. Apart from a potted career history, sport and professional, there are extracts from several publications including the one from William Pickford's *The Hampshire Football Association Golden Jubilee Book 1887–1937* that links Miller with the Corinthians. On Sunday, 12 March, fittingly, that link was given a Brazilian flavour.

Corinthians Paulista supporters at Pacaembú dedicated a banner to Miller; while on the pitch, in a pre-season tournament, their team won the Charles Miller Cup, put up by the Paulista Football Federation to commemorate Brazilian football's fiftieth anniversary. Before a crowd of 18,000 Charles, now aged 69, presented the trophy to a Corinthians official. He would have enjoyed watching what the *Gazeta* described as Corinthians' 'adventurous formation . . . with three centre-forwards'. And his presence at Pacaembú confirmed his parting remark in his *Gazeta* interview: 'Right up to today I belong to football, and when I can't go to a game I make sure I listen to it on the radio.'

* * *

Perhaps Miller was at Pacaembú in 1944 when Paulista champions São Paulo drew 3–3 with Vasco da Gama. Harry Welfare almost certainly wasn't. It appears that by 1938 he had stepped down from his coaching position at the Rio club. In that year Segundo Villadoniga, a Uruguayan, was signed by Vasco, and in his four years with them he remembers Harry as holding an administrative post which included paying the players. But despite the new back-seat role, Welfare's influence as player and coach continued to be felt.

In 1941 Max Valentim's *O Futebol e sua Técnica* was published, in which there was a nostalgic piece on Harry Welfare under the English subheading 'Thank You!':

> It is important to remember the BODY DRIBBLING and the DOWN-THE-CENTRE PASS that he taught to his inside-forwards and half-backs, tuning the mechanism that would permit him to penetrate the most solid backs, creating significant openings from where he found the net . . . And this MATCH-WINNER was responsible for Fluminense winning three consecutive championships – and its heaviest defeat in the 1940 season . . .

With Vasco having slipped in the ranking since their title win under Welfare in 1936, that 2–0 triumph in 1940 was a crumb of comfort in a year in which Fluminense claimed the Carioca crown.

Harry's impact on the Brazilian game as a player cannot be denied, and comments such as Valentim's can be backed up by statistics. In 167 starts for Fluminense (from 1913 to 1924) Welfare's strike rate was one goal per game, a record which makes him Fluminense's third leading scorer of all time. The difficulty lies in trying to gauge his merits as a motivator and tactician from the sidelines. Football folklore offers some clues.

In the 1980s, Carioca journalist Geraldo Romualdo da Silva singled out Harry Welfare in an article on the coach's authority – 'The rise and fall of *carte blanche*.' In a general reference to Welfare, he stated that his main contribution was that 'he made us aware that we were very far behind the new reality that he had brought from England'. Then, having established that Harry had 'the briefest of spells' as Fluminense coach followed by 'an expressive period at ambitious Vasco', da Silva gives a sketch of the English coach at work:

> Either because it was the fashion or because he hated having to expose his ugly physique of a retired weightlifter, Welfare did all he had to in long trousers and a casual shirt. Tireless in his varied gymnastics, he was accustomed to working hard at training, holding two sessions – morning and afternoon. In the morning, with long-distance walks and sprints, mainly for the wingers, who had to battle it out with the club's most important sprinters. For example, the Olympian José Xavier, Brazilian super-champion and South American record-holder in his event.
>
> Having always been more skilled and experienced than the others, he knew how to maintain, championship after championship, the best of Brazil panache. Also, he didn't let his young and sacrificed 'amateurs' have a rest. Another aggravating thing: in the week before a difficult game, watch out for his genuine and ferocious German shepherd – all the players, whether they were single or married, had to sleep at São Januário [Vasco's ground] from Thursday onwards, with a daily wake-up call at six in the morning. And whoever threatened to jump the wall – the eager guard dog sniffed out everything without sleeping a wink.

Da Silva went on to emphasise that a coach in Welfare's day wielded absolute power: 'Always respected. Always set in his protected domain of competence and omnipotence. Until he was considered surplus to requirements.' Perhaps Harry's greatest legacy during his ten years coaching at Vasco was the impressive number of star players he helped to bring on, among them Fausto and Jaguaré. But it seems that contrary to what da Silva would have us believe, these were two players who did not entirely see themselves as Harry's subordinates.

In *O Negro no Futebol Brasileiro*, Mário Filho strings together stories involving the Vasco players of the late-1920s and early-1930s, several of which feature Harry Welfare. One brings to mind the Scottish Wanderers' hair-raising experience in 1912. It is the incident in which keeper Jaguaré threatens Harry with a knife for leaving him out of the side for a game against one of the weaker teams: 'If [Vasco player] Pereira Peixoto hadn't been near,' writes Mário Filho, 'Welfare would have been dead.' Harry, the writer tells us, didn't make the same mistake again. Indeed, he would allow Jaguaré to doze off in the dressing-room until the players were due to go out.

The team-talk was another area in which Harry was obliged to tread lightly:

> Just before going out onto the pitch, Welfare would call his players together. It was the moment for instructions. Welfare would tell Mário Matos what he had to do, what Eighty-Four [the nickname for Carlos Paes] had to do. Players like Mário Matos, Eighty-Four, Baianinho, Santana, Mola, Tinoco, Brilhante, listened to Welfare. Itália soon turned his head, Russinho too – they didn't want instructions. Jaguaré was sleeping, and Fausto stood up in front of Welfare, stuck out his chest and clenched his fists.
>
> Welfare didn't dare to say do this or do that. If Fausto clashed with him, or anyone else at Vasco, Vasco would keep Fausto. The more he played, the more power he had inside Vasco.

This pre-match scene and the challenge to a coach's authority is reproduced, much later, in the popular anecdote that Simon Kuper relates in *Football Against the Enemy*: 'The Brazilian manager is outlining the opposition's game to his players, and when at last he finishes Garrincha asks him: "Have you told the other team all this? Then how do they know what they are supposed to do?"' As Harry discovered, players in the Garrincha and Fausto mould were best left to play in the way that came naturally to them. According to Mário Filho, 'Welfare was unable to name one centre-half who was as commanding as Fausto. Fausto stayed in the centre circle and the balls came to where he was. It was as if he attracted the ball.'

When I discussed Welfare's teams with Flávio Costa, almost inevitably he singled out Fausto. Although some sources link Welfare with the pioneering of the WM formation (3-2-2-3) in Brazil, Flávio Costa is adamant that Harry's sides played in the old 2-3-5 pattern – with Fausto as the 'pivot' in midfield. For Flávio Costa, it was the Hungarian Dori Kruschner, not Welfare, who first attempted to introduce the WM in Rio: 'When Kruschner arrived in Brazil [1937], Gentil [Cardoso] was talking a lot about the WM, but he never had the prestige to apply it. Kruschner was the one who tried to apply *futebol sistema* in Brazil'; Welfare, he says curtly, 'introduced nothing'.

Not long after Harry's first honours as a coach – the 1929 Carioca championship – four of his players, including Fausto, were chosen to represent Brazil in the first World Cup in 1930. But the squad was not the usual Rio–São Paulo mix. Due to a dispute between APEA and the CBD, only the Rio players travelled to Montevideo, and they were soon eliminated 2–1 by Yugoslavia. Fausto, 'The Black Marvel', later declared that his team-mates had lacked motivation – a weighty comment given that he was one of the discoveries of the tournament. His unhappiness, though, ran much deeper.

In June 1931 the Carioca league was put on hold while a party of Vasco players and officials toured Spain and Portugal. It was the second time a Brazilian club had journeyed to Europe. Harry would have been satisfied with the eight wins in twelve matches and contemplating the resumption of games in Rio with his team five points clear of its nearest rival. That was when he received some shattering news: both Fausto and Jaguaré would not be returning to Brazil. On 2 August a United Press telegram informed the club's supporters that the players had accepted an offer from Barcelona. América subsequently pipped Vasco for the title.

The decision by Fausto and Jaguaré – the first black Brazilians to be recruited abroad – to strike out for better conditions of employment in Spain strengthened the case of those calling for professionalism to be legalised in Brazil; and when official discussions began in Rio a year later, the Vasco president, not surprisingly, was one of the first to participate. Another factor that hastened the move towards change was the political upheaval that had recently taken place in Brazil. Caldas makes the point that: 'Football was completely in tune with the rhythm that the 1930 Revolution adopted to bring about transformations in the country.' From that moment the game became part of the culture, the most popular sport in Brazil and, more importantly, a symbol of national unity and identity.

By 1934 professional leagues were up and running; but, once again, in World Cup competition Brazil could not do itself justice. This time it was a squabble between the CBD and a rival national body, the Federação Brasileira de Futebol, that led to a weakened team being sent. Brazil, after making it all the way to Italy, were knocked out in the first round 3–1 by Spain. It was Europe's first opportunity to admire the skill of Leônidas da Silva – a privilege that Harry Welfare had already enjoyed.

Leônidas and another of the outstanding black players of that era, Domingos da Guia, had been snapped up by Uruguayan clubs after impressing in Brazil's victory over Uruguay in 1932. But by the beginning of the 1934 season they were back in Rio and playing for Vasco. We do not know what Harry considered to be the best-ever team that played under him at any one time. But if he had drawn up a list it most probably would have been the XI that started the 1934 season. There was Domingos at full-back, Leônidas in the forward line and Fausto (returned from Europe) occupying the centre of midfield – arguably the greatest Brazilian players, in their positions, of all time. Even though Leônidas made only four appearances, Vasco went on to win the 1934 Liga Carioca title.

Two years later Harry coached Vasco to a third championship success since their move to São Januário in 1927. One of the stars of the team was Feitiço. He had won six Paulista league medals and been a champion and leading goalscorer in Uruguay when he arrived at Vasco in 1936. He had also been on target four times when selected by Harry for the Rio–São Paulo XI to face Motherwell. The signing of Feitiço was one of the last examples of Welfare's ability to attract the best Brazilian players to São Januário.

It is a curious fact that while Harry was adding managerial success to his achievements as a player in Brazil, his family in Liverpool were kept completely in the dark. They weren't even sure of his where-abouts. As one of Harry's two surviving English relatives has informed me, it wasn't until the mid-1930s that efforts to track him down were successful: 'One of our generation who was in the Royal Navy and on a cruiser that was paying courtesy calls to South American ports managed to contact Harry and actually see him. This was made possible by enquiries made through the Naval Intelligence staff.' Such elusiveness is part of the enigma that surrounds Harry Welfare. And this has been confirmed by those who knew him in Rio.

When I asked Villadoniga to describe Harry, his first words were 'wonderful person'; he then went on to depict Harry as a 'gentleman' and emphasise the fact that he was 'withdrawn'. Flávio Costa similarly refers to Welfare as 'very reserved . . . a calm man'. However, on occasion he would overcome his English reserve. Villadoniga recalls meeting up with Harry and his Brazilian wife Flora in the restaurant at São Januário; Harry, he says with a chuckle, would consume copious amounts of beer. This bears out a comment by Mário Filho on Harry's Fluminense days: 'Welfare,' he wrote, 'drank more than the other players, but he was English and so he could take it.'

It was the 1940s and, with the war in Europe having concluded, it wasn't long before enquiries were made from Rio about the pos-sibility of a British team making a tour. When at last Southampton FC arrived in Rio in May 1948 Harry Welfare was on the verge of being appointed to a new post at the Rio Federation; in São Paulo, meanwhile, Charles Miller was poised to make his last official appearance on a Brazilian football field.

THIRTEEN

An Entirely Different Game

Although it seems strange, Brazilian football was more prepared to benefit from the lessons of an encounter with British football on the occasion of the visit of the Corinthians and Exeter City than the visit of Motherwell and Chelsea. The infancy of Brazilian football was in a certain sense British. The Corinthians' first game [in 1913] coincided with Harry Welfare's début. And Welfare's career helped to perpetuate the idea that the British were the masters of the game. When Motherwell and Chelsea came, the situation had changed completely. Harry Welfare was no longer playing, and Brazilian football, which had become isolated after 1925, lauded improvisation, moving more and more away from the classic model. Therefore, the defeat of Motherwell was seen only as a demonstration of indisputable Brazilian superiority. Nobody stopped to examine the British system of play. Not even when the Chelsea full-backs, ostensibly marking no one, taking just a step forward, made it almost impossible for the Brazilians to score.

Mário Filho in 'The greatest value of Southampton's
tour', *Jornal dos Sports*, Rio, 14 May 1948

Looking back, in 1948 they were light years ahead of us – in all aspects of the game. I don't care what anybody else says. In the passing, the movement off the ball, everything . . . They were like silk, they were . . . It was the first time we'd seen anything like it. Even in Europe, there wasn't anybody like it. You take Arsenal – the team, *weren't they? They were nothing like that at all.*

Bill Ellerington, Southampton, 16 July 1996

Exeter City's visit to Rio, 1914: ABOVE: Exeter players mingle with the Rio XI – (back): Sidney Pullen (seventh left), Harry Robinson (ninth left) and Harry Welfare (fourth right); BELOW: the historic game of 21 July at Fluminense: Exeter putting pressure on the Brazilian goal – INSET: Rolando (left) and Holt battle for the ball. Notice the spectators on the roof of the stand

A Paulista XI from the 1910s (front row from left): Formiga, Demósthenes, Friedenreich, McLean, Hopkins; Rubens Salles is in the middle row (centre)

A third successive Rio title draws near: the Fluminense side that defeated Andaraí 4–2 on 14 December 1919 – with two goals from Welfare, seated third from left, and directly in front of Marcos de Mendonça

'Celebrity Gallery', *Sports*, August 1915

Motherwell's Alex McClory depicted in Fluminense's in-house magazine *Tricolor*, June 1928

Heading for South America: Chelsea players on board the MS *Asturias*, May 1929

Charles Miller with his daughter Helena in the 1930s, the Rua México residence, São Paulo (courtesy Helena Miller)

Harry Welfare flanked by two Vasco players – Segundo Villadoniga (left) and Alberto Zarzur, Rio, c.1940

Southampton's tour, 1948: ABOVE: this cartoon by Orf appeared in the *Football Echo*, 1 May (courtesy *Southern Daily Echo*); BELOW: (from left) Bill Ellerington, Eric Webber, Stan Clements (in Botafogo's colours) and George Smith at Botafogo's training ground

Charles Miller kicks off Southampton's game against São Paulo, watched by (from left): Ted Bates, Charlie Wayman, George Reader and George Curtis, 25 May 1948 (photo: G. Santos)

Saints at the Hotel Quitandinha, Petrópolis, June 1948: (back): Alf Ramsey (fourth right), Rex Stranger (second right), Harry Welfare (first left) and George Reader (second left); Ted Ballard is in the front (sixth right)

Dressed for the part: Jack Barrick with the captains of Grêmio and Internacional before the Rio Grande do Sul championship decider, Pôrto Alegre, 1949

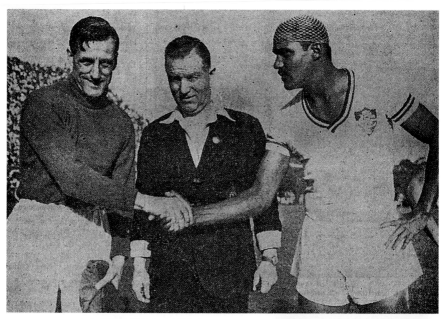

TOP: Arsenal keeper George Swindin (left) eyed by the Fluminense skipper. Jack Barrick looks on. Rio, 15 May 1949; ABOVE: pre-match pantomime in Brazil – *Daily Mirror*, 21 May 1949 (courtesy Mirror Group); RIGHT: Laurie Scott, Arsenal and England

With all the excitement down at the docks it was as if the English First Division champions had landed – not a team that had just narrowly missed promotion from the Second Division. In fact, four years earlier, a British embassy official in Rio had tantalisingly let it be known that 'Brazil will be the first country in America to receive a visit from Arsenal'. In May 1948 Brazilians had to make do with Southampton.

But what did it matter? The detailed newspaper reports that would follow the visitors' every movement were symptomatic of Brazil's high regard for British football. As respected columnist José Brigido put it: 'Whoever they are, they'll reflect the state of the English game . . . All of us – trainers, players, football directors, referees, linesmen and sports critics – must pay good attention to the way in which the English player "makes football".' But that remark, and others like it, soon sounded hollow.

The Rio *Diário da Noite* of 10 May 1948 set the tone for the ensuing press deluge – and today, the original cover of that edition serves as a reminder to one player, Ted Bates, of the actual impact made by him and his team-mates in Brazil. 'Southampton's arrival this morning mobilised our sporting world,' began the leading article. 'The *Andes*, carrying the delegation, docked early. But disembarkation wasn't until 9.30. There on the top deck, in the middle of the group, Carlito Rocha [president of tour sponsors, Botafogo] was preparing them to disembark. And wanting to get the players together at the front, he shouted: "*Jogadores, aqui na frente!*" Of course, nobody understood, but Welfare put things right by shouting: "Players. Come here, boys!"'

Another of those 'boys', Bill Ellerington, still savours that moment. 'You have to see it to believe it. It was like a hazy bluey-mauve atmosphere. It was magnificent. Like a sun coming up. And we sailed up there and when we got to our berth there were bloody streamers and, honest, we were just bedecked – and we were welcomed and [all these people] came on board. I don't think anybody knew what was going on.'

Forty-four years after their pioneering trip to South America, Southampton were the last British club to make the same journey by boat – and only because several members of the team were 'against air travel'. During the ten days at sea the players were 'treated like kings', encouraged at mealtimes by 'Saints-mad' waiters 'to go through the card'. Leaving the austerity in post-war Britain behind, and the rationing that was still in force, the players didn't need much prompting. Thankfully, as Ellerington recalls, they had a set training routine which, unlike the one devised for the 1914 Exeter tourists, included ball work: 'Up early in the morning. 6.30. Nice long decks to run, exercise. We even had footballs up – they put nets at the side and we played head-tennis and knocked the ball around. Then we went in and had a snack, had lunch . . . and in the afternoon, for about a couple of hours, not because we had to, we played head tennis . . .' So the players, although partly in holiday mode, were motivated – and blissfully ignorant of the Brazilians' brand of football.

Even in Rio, after a work-out at Botafogo's ground, a feeling of quiet confidence persisted. Southampton director Rex Stranger added a hasty PS to the first of several letters to the sports editor of the *Southern Daily Echo*: '13th. Had our trial 20 minutes each way last night by night lights. Absolutely marvellous. The team was really on top form and played like against Newcastle at home [Southampton had beaten Newcastle, one of the teams promoted from the Second Division, 4–2, on 13 March 1948]. To make up the opponents of the team we borrowed five forwards and a goalkeeper from Botafogo. They were good, very fast, clever, pass well in midfield, too greedy in the box. Our team made a great impression.'

That same evening of 13 May the Saints party attended a Rio league game at Vasco's stadium, the venue for their first match. Writing to his wife, Ted Bates gives a first impression of the Brazilian game from a player's perspective: 'These South Americans are very fast with the ball but very individual players and also they play very close and do not seem to have a lot of method. But they are very temperamental and charge and foul each other quite a lot. In this particular match both sides finished up with nine men a side. Two were sent off for fighting and the others were injured. George Reader said he was coming home, that's what he thought about it.' Brazilians would be thankful that referee Reader didn't carry out his threat to leave.

Refereeing standards in Brazil had plummeted to an all-time low, and in Rio and São Paulo there was already talk of hiring British referees for championship games. Reader's presence, therefore – suggested by Stranger – was both timely and fortunate. It would have been hard to find a better qualified official in England. A former Southampton FC professional, Reader was president of the Southampton Referees' Society and had recently lectured on co-ordination between referee and linesmen at an international referees' conference. The year before he had been given the plum refereeing appointment – Great Britain *v* The Rest of Europe at Hampden Park. The arrival of Reader in Rio also coincided with, and possibly influenced, Harry Welfare's appointment to a new post.

The Rio Federation's Referees' College was being restructured. Of the three administrative jobs that were created, one of them – technical director with responsibility for refereeing and rules – was given to Welfare. Certainly, Harry's help was invaluable during Reader's visit. Dubbed the tourists' 'diplomatic liaison' by the *Jornal dos Sports*, Harry served as interpreter when Reader lectured on 'standardisation and interpretation'; and, after it was decided that Reader would referee every one of the Saints' games, it was Harry who passed on instructions to his Brazilian linesmen.

Conveniently, Harry still had links with the club that hosted the games in Rio, Vasco da Gama, making him ideally placed to iron out difficulties on match days. But, in character, he remained in the background, distant, discreet: perhaps not even Reader was aware of his achievements in Brazilian football. Indeed, in letters to England and recent interviews, not one of the tourists mentions or remembers meeting Harry Welfare – a legend at Fluminense.

16 May
Southampton 0   Fluminense 4

> The extraordinary preliminaries before the match put the Saints off for quite a long time: due to start at 3.30 it started at 4.15. I should think at least 50 photographers were loose on the ground and three or four broadcasting microphones were being trailed around. I've since learned that without consulting anybody the kick-off was put back to 4 p.m. I was invited to ref. and I blew my whistle seven times before I had any chance of starting the game.
>
> The Saints were very quiet and subdued the first ten minutes because of the peculiar preliminaries and then hesitancy on the part of the inside-forwards lost us a good chance. Fluminense then played excellent football, fast, crisp and all players running well into position. After 21 minutes their centre-forward [Rubinho] nodded a good goal to the right of Black from an accurate centre from the outside-right. Three minutes from half-time the outside-left [Rodrigues] skipped through the defence and scored a good goal. Half-time: Fluminense 2 Saints 0.
>
> The Saints had their chances in the second half but gradually the opposition got on top and after 14 minutes the captain and inside-left [Orlando] scored a goal after drawing Webber out of position

and beating Ellerington. After 20 minutes in this half substitutes were introduced, Bates taking the place of G. Smith and Pereira the place of Orlando. This Brazilian player had not been on the field two minutes before he scored the fourth and final goal after a wonderful dribble. Saints were beaten by a better team on the day's play. The game was played in a good sporting spirit: I was agreeably surprised.

Echo correspondent George Reader would have been surprised, too, by all the attention he was receiving. For José Brigido, he had been 'secure, precise and irreproachable' and had given 'a masterclass in the use of the whistle'. The *Gazeta Esportiva* called for the Carioca and Paulista Federations to insist that all their referees attend Southampton's games, and suggested that if Reader continued to show the same 'class' he might be first on the list of the referees to be imported. Later, Mário Filho recalled the 'hand ball' – as Orlando was about to score – that Reader didn't blow up for because it was 'ball to hand': 'It was a shock. For almost half a century the Brazilians had played football thinking that hand to ball and ball to hand were the same thing.'

One thing that Reader highlighted in his letter to the *Echo* was the use of three different footballs: 'Our English T ball [the panels on the ball were in the shape of a letter T] for the first half (by arrangement); a Brazilian national ball at the beginning of the second half; and a white ball when the floodlights were switched on after about 20 minutes of the second half.' But even in view of the lighter Brazilian ball, this was not mentioned by Ted Bates in a letter home. He chose to emphasise the adverse conditions: 'The air was so humid after running anywhere it did not seem as though you could get any oxygen into your lungs.' And he summed up to a tee the implications of the defeat: 'If we have taught these people the game of football you can imagine the pleasure they get from beating us. They call us the English masters (or did) until we performed.'

For the next game, against Botafogo on 20 May, Bates and most of his team-mates wore the model of football boot used by the Brazilians: 'very soft leather and [it] does not come over the ankle . . . you put them in your hand,' says Bill Ellerington, 'and they almost take off they're so light.'

The crowd did not match the 50,000 or the record receipts of the tour opener, but the half-full São Januário did see the Saints give a much improved display. They may have been defeated again – 3–1 – but as the *Correio da Manhã* made clear, the result 'does not at all indicate what the game in reality was, for the scoring covers only the advantage taken by the Brazilians of the opportunities as they presented themselves, and at which Brazilians excel in view of their facility for improvising and their swiftness.'

It was a theme taken up by Rex Stranger: 'They are every man in the team greyhounds. The defence is as fast as any forwards, very strong, can kick from any angle with both feet off the ground.' He went on: 'They also have a knack of falling on their back and kicking the ball over their head, both at goal and the backs also in clearing their own goal. Every man in the team is running the whole time. When one of their men has the ball, there are at least two others running into the open spaces to receive it.'

It may have crossed Stranger's mind that instead of being out of their depth in Brazil, his players could have been better occupied passing on what they knew to American footballers. A tour he had set up to the United States had had to be cancelled. After ten days in Rio he'd seen enough to write sombrely: '[The Brazilians'] ball control is better than any team in England, and nothing short of the best international team is any good to send out here.'

Meanwhile, back in Southampton, readers of the *Echo* were being given a taste of what the Saints were having to endure. 'Fireworks – flashlights and football' ran one of the headlines. The correspondent was George Reader:

> Many of the happenings at the match [*v* Botafogo] were quite fantastic from a British point of view. For instance, there was a firework display at half-time. 'What a queer idea!', comments Mr Reader. Then, 'a very disconcerting feature is the great number of flashlight photos which are taken of all penalty-box incidents. These are apt to disconcert anybody, and more so, I should imagine, if one is not used to them.'

At the end of the piece, there was a reference to Botafogo keeper Oswaldo – 'one of the best I've ever seen,' wrote Reader, 'and all the Saints players agree with me. He is in the Frank Swift class. Four of his saves were, or appeared to me to be, miraculous. Although 6ft 2ins in height, he caught the ball like a first-class cricketer, and could leap like a cat. He would be a sensation in England.' As we shall see later, Brazilian goalkeepers also knew a thing or two about ball control.

★　★　★

On 22 May all but three of the tourists made the ninety-minute flight to São Paulo – for most, their first experience of flying. Travelling by train, it took Bill Rochford and Ian Black 16 hours to arrive; while George Reader remained in Rio to take charge of the showpiece of the Carioca calendar, Flamengo *v* Fluminense. Of Reader, Rex Stranger wrote: 'He is an outstanding success. Indeed he has covered our failure. As one Brazilian paper put it, "George Reader won the match which Southampton lost".'

But, despite the fact that they were struggling on the pitch, plenty of interest was being shown in them off it. Ted Bates described the scene at São Paulo airport: 'We had the usual reception as we got off the plane, photographers etc and the radio boy walks round, and we all answer a few things in the mike. They certainly do things in a big way out here.' One of those that greeted them was 73-year-old Charles Miller.

25 May
Southampton 2   São Paulo 4

As a special compliment, *Charlie Miller*, who was one of the first English footballers out here and is a well-known character and who was connected with the Saints in 1894 and 5 [*sic*], kicked off. Conditions were again strange: the lighting did not seem to me to be so good as in Rio, but there was heavy dew on the ground which made the ball slide a lot. The temperature was much better – as a matter of fact the Brazilians said it was cold!

The Saints got off to a very good start and produced some really effective football but São Paulo took the lead with a pile-driver by their inside-right [Lelé] from about 18 yards which gave Black no chance. In the 35th minute Ellerington equalised from a penalty for hands against their centre-half. Two minutes later São Paulo scored again [Bauer] but this was due to a lapse on the part of Black who obviously thought the ball was going outside: I should imagine this was due to the lighting – still there it was. Half-time: 1–2.

The Saints attacked again in good style and Wayman equalised with a very good effort after a scrimmage in the goalmouth. But São Paulo again took the lead after 15 minutes [Ponce de Leon]. Smith was then withdrawn, Scott came on to play inside-right and Bates went to right-half. The Brazilians sent on two substitutes, a new right-back and left-half, and seemed to benefit most by the change. Although the Saints tried really hard they couldn't get an equaliser and the Brazilians made the match safe ten minutes from the end by scoring a fourth [Ponce de Leon].

Reader's next remark confirms the shift in the visitors' pre-tour attitude towards Brazilian football: 'The Saints certainly have nothing to teach these teams on ball control, positional play and accurate passing. They play at a terrific speed which is good to see.'

Set against the Brazilians' speed and improvisation was what the *Gazeta Esportiva* defined as 'Southampton's clever football'. For instance, the offside trap was 'a tactical resource used with perfection and art'. But for Charles Miller, the Saints players had also, 'contrary to their normal game', run themselves into the ground at Pacaembú – trying to match the Brazilian tempo.

On 29 May the *Gazeta Esportiva* had a feature on Miller. Charles obliges with a comment that caught the mood – 'the speed of Brazilian football is winning' – but then he appears to take offence at some of the questioning. 'Do the Brazilians really play better [than the British]?' Answer: 'Your question is not agreeable, principally to someone like myself – very careful when I speak. But I have to say that Southampton are not making a bad impression, and winning or losing happens to everyone. But I believe Brazil could be among the best exponents of football in the world if some negative factors disappear in the life of the athlete.'

Charles went on to explain: 'Diet, physical development, preparation and others, constitute some of the deficiencies. With the speed that we have, nobody would beat us if we were to ally to this speed more intelligence and preparation.'

Later he sidesteps an attempt to get him to 'rate São Paulo's victory'. It is the authentic voice of the Anglo-Paulista, circumspect and scrupulous when caught between two traditions. But perhaps he goes too far in his criticism of the Brazilian game. Hadn't coaches like Fluminense's Quincey-Taylor introduced strict training routines as far back as the 1910s?

Rex Stranger was in no doubt about how far Brazilians were ahead when it came to preparation: 'Brazilian teams actually live in quarters on the ground, secluded from the outside world for four days before a match. And they devote themselves to individual training, breathing exercises, gymnastics, with great emphasis on jumping at suspended balls, sprinting and really first-class massage, and marvellous food. They have oxygen at half-time.'

Back at Pacaembú, on the same day the Miller interview appeared,

Southampton lost 2–1 to Portuguesa. Reader, who had given another 'meticulous' exhibition, felt 'this was a match we should have won' – especially as the Saints had been in front at the interval.

Writing home, Ted Bates preferred to tell his wife about the post-match visit to São Paulo Athletic Club: 'We all went to a British club here to dinner and a bit of a dance. It was a wonderful dinner and cooked in a very English way, as much as one could eat and also plenty to drink. We had a very nice evening in spite of being rather down-hearted at losing and finished up with a real good sing-song.'

The next day, the players' spirits were given a further lift. There were letters and messages from home, and the presence of the man who delivered them – Alf Ramsey. He had flown out from England having played one game for England B on an FA tour to the Continent. Ramsey recalled the welcome by his Saints colleagues as being 'sincere'. He went on: 'It was clear that being away from home for so long, and with a string of defeats behind them, had affected their morale.' As Bates wrote on the eve of the next game: 'I am fed up with saying we shall win so will say nothing this time except we are still trying hard to win . . . Maybe with Alf out here [our luck] will change.' It did – but not in the best of circumstances.

2 June
Southampton 2   Corinthians 1

At last we have won a match, but I don't want to play in many more matches like the one we had last night. It was an amazing experience. They did everything to us except knife us. We gave them a lesson in football and played some fine stuff but they were pushing, shoving, kicking, in fact doing every dirty thing you could think of and when we retaliated in the good old English way, did the crowd get mad. Towards the end there was almost a riot. Eric Day went down and as he was lying on the ground the full-back started to fight him. It was quite a scene. Of course the lads went in to help him. George Reader sent the full-back off the field.

Quite a few of the crowd swarmed on to the trainer's box and for a few minutes Bill [Dodgin] and Sam [Warhurst] were having a real free-for-all. But the police came to the rescue and cleared them off the field. You can't beat these football matches to increase the friendly spirit between the countries. I think Bill flattened about two to Sam's one. Things were getting very strained towards the end and I was quite relieved when the final whistle went. It was the nearest thing to a battle I ever want to see.

A word about the football. We played some grand stuff and should have won by a clearer margin. Alf missed a penalty. I played inside-left and supplied the two passes for our goals [scored by Grant and Curtis]. I think I can say that we all played really well and were easily the best team. These people are above the two other teams we have played in the League. It is really astounding that they cannot lose and they are very bad sportsmen. I will finish about the game saying it was the most amazing game I have ever seen or played in.

Ted Bates penned that account in his room at the Luxor Hotel in Rio – 'glad to see the back of São Paulo after the previous night's experiences'. But despite the 'incident', he and his team-mates had been well entertained by Corinthians at a banquet that went on into the early hours. Several days later the tourists issued a statement through the British Embassy in which the crowd disturbances were played down: 'Only two spectators came onto the field and two or three bottles were thrown. The police managed to control the situation with promptness and efficiency, and the game was allowed to continue.' As prospective hosts of the 1950 World Cup, bad publicity was the last thing Brazil wanted.

★   ★   ★

According to George Reader, Ramsey's appearance gave the team 'a wonderful fillip'; after the next game his praise was far more effusive. On 6 June Southampton defeated Flamengo 3–1, beating the Brazilians at their own game as implied in the *Echo* headline 'Fast and Clever Football'. Having faithfully recorded the details of the game, Reader noted the principal participants: 'Ramsey was outstanding: he played a magnificent game and he rallied his defenders and kept out the Flamengo forwards until the end. He was very popular with the crowd and he and Wayman [scorer of two goals] were the stars of a good side.'

The day after that win, Saints coach Bill Dodgin received a telegram from São Paulo. It read: 'Congratulations and all the best for [the game in] Juiz de Fóra. Kind regards to all, from the boys of SPAC soccer team.' In 1948 SPAC were celebrating their sixtieth anniversary, so the Southampton visit and the connection with Charles Miller were a convenient bonus. As well as the hospitality shown by SPAC, a group of Saints players and officials had been invited to Charles's residence in the Rua México. 'These British people in São Paulo,' wrote Ted Bates, 'really try to make us feel at home.'

But before the trip to Juiz de Fóra there was an unscheduled match to be played. Rex Stranger had turned down the chance of a rematch with Fluminense. Instead, the opposition would be provided by Harry Welfare's club – the reigning Carioca and South American champions. (In 1948 Vasco won a 'Club Champions Tournament' held in Santiago. This was a forerunner to the present Copa Libertadores de América.)

10 June
Southampton 1   Vasco da Gama 2

The preliminaries of this match were longer than usual. A terrific burst of fireworks greeted the arrival of the teams on the field – lots of them were too close to be safe. The Lord Mayor kicked off – and the usual radio commentators and photographers refused to be kicked off the field so that the match could start. The radio and press seem to be the deciding factors in this country about the time when a match shall commence!

Play at first was very even, each side seeming to be trying to weigh up the opposition, but excellent footwork by the Vasco left-wing resulted in their outside-left, a veritable box of tricks, scoring a good goal in the 11th minute [according to the Brazilian press it was the outside-right, Djalma, who scored]. He showed himself very fast and very tricky and cut in towards goal at every opportunity. Saints forwards, well led by Wayman and prompted by Curtis, played an enterprising game and Wayman scored a fine goal with a ground shot which went in near the post in the 24th minute after excellent combination between Scott and Day. From then until half-time the excellence of the Vasco defence was the feature of the game.

After half-time (when a full-scale firework display was put on and which left the playing pitch covered with acrid smoke and like a November fog!) the Vasco team took full advantage of the substitute arrangements and changed three players. Saints only substituted Ballard for Mallett who was feeling the effect of his thigh injury. Before the Saints could settle down, brilliant play by the Vasco left wing produced a second goal [scored by Chico] within 1½ minutes. The Saints half-back line was not strong enough to dictate tactics and only heroic efforts on the part of Ramsey, Rochford and Black prevented the Vasco team from scoring again. The Vasco defence showed its merit and would compare favourably with Arsenal's. Their two backs were ideal (all Vasco's defence are six-footers) and in the whole game did not concede one corner – not once did they kick out. The Saints forward line tried hard but could not get the necessary prompting from the half-backs.

George Reader completed his penultimate dispatch to the *Echo* by mentioning the attendance: 'I estimated the crowd at 50,000, but no figure was available as they only publish the gate-money! All the members of the home club – and there are thousands – are naturally admitted free.' Two years later, in Rio, before a crowd four times bigger than the Vasco gate, Reader refereed the World Cup final. It may not have been a dress rehearsal, but the Saints *v* Vasco game was Reader's last experience of Brazilian big-match atmosphere before he returned for the Finals.

Ramsey would also be back – a member of England's first World Cup squad. He was singled out by the *Gazeta Esportiva* in an article headed 'We saw another South[ampton]'. For those who had rashly proclaimed the demise of English football what was baffling was the visitors' 'speed, efficient marking and quick, accurate passing'. The 'star' of the team, Ramsey, was 'clever, solid, a legitimate barrier', not once allowing Vasco's 'infernal' winger Chico to get the better of him. It was a measure of the Saints performance that six of their opponents (Barbosa, Augusto, Danilo, Friaça, Ademir and Chico) would go on to represent Brazil in the 1950 World Cup final.

Not surprisingly, in his autobiography published in 1952, Alf Ramsey cited the Vasco game as 'one of the best matches in which I'd ever played' – and pinpointed what he felt were the 'most important things' about the tour. Before they left Brazil – after a tame 1–1 draw against an XI representing the state of Minas Gerais in Juiz de Fóra – the Saints had received various tributes extolling their 'sportsmanship' and 'conduct'. But for Ramsey, the 'good impression left behind' owed more to his team's attempts 'to play real football'. He then gave Brazil credit for confirming his belief 'that a defender's job was also to make goals in addition to stopping them'. What he'd learnt, he wrote, he'd later been able 'to try out with singular success' with Spurs and England.

Saints coach Bill Dodgin was another one who couldn't wait to try out in an English context some of the things he'd learnt in Brazil. In fact, so excited was he by the immediate success of his 'Brazil Plan' that he sent a cable to Rio: 'The Brazilians,' he wrote, 'were for us a veritable football compendium.' Asked to comment on this 'sensational' news, the Flamengo coach said it showed the British player's 'extraordinary capacity to assimilate', and that there were 'qualities' in the British game that the Brazilians had yet to assimilate. What these qualities were, though, he wouldn't say. Defensive ones, no doubt; the opposite of the 'always playing . . . to score goals' mentality that Ted Bates associates with Brazilian football.

One of the best testimonies to Brazil's unique approach to the game was given to me by Bates's team-mate Eric Webber, shortly before he died in December 1996. A centre-half, he recalled his first experience of Brazilian football – 'a bloke training against a wall':

> He's stood about three yards back from the wall – he's kicking this ball up against the wall, he's catching it on his knee, he's knocking it up in the air, on his head, dropping it back down onto his chest, from his chest back down to his foot. I stood there for five minutes watching this bugger and I thought, 'Christ, I hope he's not playing centre-forward.' [laughter] Oh dear! I said to one of their people who could speak pidgin English: 'Good player. Inside-forward?' 'No,' he said, 'it's the reserve-team goalkeeper.' Bloody hell! And there you have it in a nutshell. God Almighty, we had outfield players that couldn't have done it, never mind goalkeepers.

The Saints players may not have been able to reproduce some of the skills Brazilians took for granted, but at least, as coach Dodgin ensured, they could be schooled in aspects of South American tactics and training – and be kitted out like Brazilians. On 4 September 1948 the *Southern Daily Echo* reported that 'the Saints wore their lightweight Brazilian kit for the match against Cardiff City – the close-fitting club colour jerseys, and black shorts . . . The point about the goalkeeper's kit which impressed was the light texture of the material, but most of all the fact that the arms, elbows, etc., and the chest are padded.' And Bill Ellerington remembers that a supply of footwear was brought back – 'about 20 pairs of these little ankle boots'.

On his return to England, George Reader gave a talk on the Brazilian tour to a meeting of the Southampton Referees' Association. 'Brazilians,' he said, 'were crazy about football, and the standard of play was good.' The *Echo* report went on to say that 'never once did any player question any of [Reader's] decisions. The Brazilians appreciated the impartiality of British refereeing.' There is no doubt Reader was offered a lucrative contract to stay in Brazil – and Rex Stranger said he negotiated excellent terms for him. But Reader was not interested in 'sacrificing a career [in teaching] for a transitory contract'. Instead, four British referees were soon taking advantage of the 'fantastic system of payment' in Brazil, and continuing the reform process started by Reader.

Postscript – 'The aerial bicycle kick from Brazil'
Midway through the 1948–49 season George Reader received an action photograph from friends in Brazil. It shows Leônidas da Silva – winner of the Golden Boot in the 1938 World Cup – scoring for São Paulo FC at Pacaembú. On 29 January 1949 the *Southern Daily Echo* printed the photo – and a comment by Reader:

> I should have to think about what to do if this kick was introduced into English football. If an opposition player was near the kicker it would have to be classed as dangerous play. These Brazilians – great jumpers – bring off this kick when the ball is quite five feet off the ground. It has a great vogue out there, and I saw all the small boys trying to master the technique.

FOURTEEN

Refereeing Revolution

Apart from a close familiarity with the Laws of the Game, good refereeing calls for a sound knowledge of human nature, for firmness allied with rapid thinking, as well as immense reserves of tact and self-confidence. These qualities have already won British referees a magnificent reputation throughout the world.

Sir Stanley Rous's foreword to *The Football Referee*,
December 1949

Mr Reader, coming from Southampton, captured the Brazilian public. Suddenly, the referee, up to that moment always the villain of the play, was changed into the young hero.

Mário Filho, quoted in Willy Meisl's
Soccer Revolution, 1956

When Tomás Mazzoni is describing the 1938 World Cup in France he suddenly breaks away from the objectivity of his position as a historian. In an uncharacteristic outburst, passion takes over. 'Brazil,' he writes in his *História do Futebol no Brasil*, 'were the "slaves" of the championship.' And he backs up this assertion with statistics. Brazil, 'coming from afar', was the only country that was unfamiliar with the conditions; the team played more games than any other (five including two that went to extra-time), 'travelling 3,000 kilometres by rail during an eight-day period'; Brazil also had the toughest opponents.

Mazzoni now delivers his main gripe: 'Brazil was the team most penalised by the referees, suffering the punishment of three penalties (all converted), four goals disallowed and two dismissals.' It was an incident involving one of Harry Welfare's former charges, Domingos da Guia, that hastened Brazil's exit from the tournament.

It was semi-final day in Marseilles: Brazil versus the holders, Italy. Mazzoni, one of the travelling journalists, has detailed the seconds leading up to the 'monster-penalty' that would make it 2–0 to Italy. Corinthians legend Cláudio recalls seeing it on film: 'Domingos fouled Piola [Italy's centre-forward] off the ball and the referee gave a penalty. Now I can't tell you whether the ball was out or still in play – if it was out then it wasn't a penalty, the referee could only send Domingos off. So we lost 2–1.' For Mazzoni, the ball was clearly out.

Ten years later, with the next World Cup looming, hosts Brazil were starting to prepare. On 20 January 1948 the foundation stone of the Municipal Stadium in Rio was laid – the 'gigantic' Maracanã, the temple in which Brazilians hoped their team would be crowned champions. But, as Mário Filho wrote: 'For Brazil to be champions it was indispensable for them to know the laws of the game.' That was why George Reader, officiating to the letter, 'opened Brazilians' eyes'. No one wanted a repeat of 1938. Just how the CBD set about dealing with the 'vices and defects' of Brazilian referees is the subject of this chapter.

Not for the first time, Brazil were a step behind rivals Argentina. Even before the 1938 World Cup the Argentine FA had turned to an experienced Football League official in an attempt to solve the 'eternal problem' with local referees. Recently retired from the middle, Isaac Caswell, a Labour councillor from Blackburn, arrived in Buenos Aires in October 1937. His contract stipulated that he would 'referee international and representative games there, and give demonstrations on the field'. What it didn't state was that a knowledge of self-defence was advisable.

In its December 1938 issue, the *Football Referee* gave subscribers an update on Caswell. The title – 'Reffing in Buenos Aires – and the joys thereof!' – reflects Britain's smug detachment from the wider sporting world, the piece providing an illustration of the degree of fanaticism that British officials would later experience in Brazil:

> For the second time since he has been in Buenos Aires, Mr Isaac Caswell . . . has been attacked by spectators after refereeing a football match. He had to seek police protection.
>
> During the game there was some throwing of stones and Caswell was forced to hold up the play. This seemed to annoy the spectators and as he left the ground his car was stopped by the crowd, the windows being broken and the tyres cut. Mr Caswell was forced to

obtain the help of the police before he could escape the mob.

His first clash with indignant football spectators was in June this year when, after refereeing a match, he was assaulted in a train between Buenos Aires and La Planta.

Caswell, however, was undeterred and saw out his three-year term; and in 1946 the FA received an invitation 'to submit the names of ten referees for service in the Argentine'. Eight were to make the trip in March 1948; but from the outset there were problems. Writing in the *Vida Esportiva Paulista* of May 1948, Mazzoni tells us that 'from the word go, the British officials in Buenos Aires didn't like the crowd and the players. Discipline is not good.' And, while anticipating the arrival of British referees in São Paulo and Rio, he outlined why action needed to be taken:

> [Local referees] are victims of the passionate atmosphere, they have greatly lost the spectators' confidence, they've lost everything . . . And yet they're very well paid . . . But despite this regal remuneration refereeing hasn't improved, on the contrary it has got worse . . . The problem is no longer a technical one − of that there's no doubt − it has become one of moral order, of ethics . . .

In contrast, while touching on this point, George Reader diagnosed other possible reasons for the 'low' standard of refereeing in Brazil. He told members of the Southampton Referees' Association that '[Brazilian] referees used a lateral instead of a diagonal system; the linesmen had no authority; disagreement by players with a referee's decision often led to crowding round the referee; each club appeared to have its own "number one" referee and some clubs would not allow certain referees to officiate for them; and the system of payment was fantastic.' Later, we shall see how the 'diagonal system' was implemented in Rio.

There was still one other aspect of Brazilian refereeing that could be improved. The fact was the official in Brazil did not cut a convincing figure on the pitch − and when I mentioned the referees' episode to Cláudio that was the first point he made. He recalls the British referees coming to Brazil 'with a uniform characterisitic of a football player − that black uniform and everything, while the Brazilian referees wore tennis shoes, long white trousers and a yellow shirt. You can imagine in the rain, when the pitch cut up, it was difficult for them to keep their footing!'

So the picture we get is of an official who was downtrodden – both literally and figuratively. He was replaced at a stroke by men heralded as having 'high credentials in the art of refereeing' and was made to run the line for them. It must have been a humiliating experience not only for the individual but for the nation as a whole. As Tony Mason (1995) has written, with reference to the South American continent:

> It cannot have been easy for countries wrestling with their identities in a world still dominated by Europe to accept that their own nationals were not capable of controlling the leading players of the national game. On the other hand it was a clear sign to FIFA that a problem had been recognised and a solution was being sought.

In Brazil, one of the first – and perhaps the most famous – of the British referees to be recruited was Jack Barrick.

★ ★ ★

On the back page of the Rio *A Noite* of 15 May 1948 was a preview of the opening game of Southampton's tour – 'Combat of two tactics' the headline, under a photo of the visitors in Botafogo shirts at training. There was also a report and photo of one of Reader's lectures in which he'd tackled 'common refereeing controversies'. Curiously, though, an article on the imminent arrival of 'Mr Barrick' was relegated to the bottom corner of the preceding page.

Barrick had actually found favour with Carioca football before Reader, when taking charge of Vasco's games during their 1947 tour to Europe. This was duly emphasised by *A Noite*:

> One of the great successes of Vasco da Gama's tour was undoubtedly the officiating of the English referee Barrick. Carioca fans who followed the games on the radio noted, from the description of the commentator, the perfection with which the British official guided the encounter. Mr Barrick's name was considered for a post at the Rio Referees' College, as well as for controlling Carioca League matches. However, it wasn't possible to bring over the famous referee at that moment as he had commitments in England.

Given Welfare's links with Vasco, it would have been ironic if Barrick had been preferred for the job of technical director at the Referees' College. One of the reasons he had to put back his trip to

Rio was his appointment to referee the 1948 FA Cup final.

It had taken Jack Barrick 23 years to reach what he described at the time as his 'greatest ambition' in the game; and his selection for the final was, he said, 'a tribute to my county'. That county was Northamptonshire.

Born in 1900, Cyril John (Jack) Barrick had spent most of his life in the village of Brafield, five miles from Northampton. A centre-forward in his younger days, he played for Brafield and Rushden Town and was capped as an amateur by his county. Jack had taken up refereeing at the age of 24, when a serious knee injury forced him to give up playing, and by the early 1930s he had obtained the highest grade for a referee – aided by a 'natural ability to be in the right place at the right time and the fact that Northampton Town were supporting him'. That's the opinion of Jess Lay, a friend of Barrick and a former president of the Northampton Referees' Association.

Lay himself graduated to the Football League line, twice taking over in the middle as senior linesman. He is grateful for the help he received from Jack: 'It was hard going. Unless you'd got some inside bandwagon business you didn't get on as fast as the others. So where Jack could put in a word and say: "This lad's coming along. He should be given a chance", something to that effect, he did. He never minced words.' Jack was to recommend one of his Northamptonshire colleagues to those responsible for recruiting referees in Brazil.

On the several occasions that Lay was 'privileged' to line to Barrick, he found he had 'a strong sense of control without show ... [and was] fair in his interpretation. If he felt you weren't quite with it in some flag effort he would cover up for you. He'd have an uncanny way of showing that he'd changed his mind. He would take any comeback that came. He always defended his two men that helped him. He was very good like that.' He was certainly resolute when it came to defending his own decisions, as he showed after the 1948 FA Cup final (Manchester United 4 Blackpool 2), one of the most memorable in the history of the competition.

Jack had awarded a penalty to Blackpool in the 14th minute when 'Mortensen, going through, was brought down near the edge of the penalty area'. He recalled the incident in a column for the *Weekend Mail* in 1955. 'Was I sure it was a penalty? Yes, of course, I was! As I whistled, I saw my linesman running round to the goal-line, an arrangement we had previously made in case of an incident such as this. So it confirmed my own decision. Johnny Carey, United's captain, came up and said: "Inches our side, Mr Barrick." But I said:

"No. Definitely a spot-kick. There's no doubt about it." My linesman said afterwards that the incident happened two yards inside the penalty area. To me it had looked about 18 inches, but I was 15 yards behind the incident, which explains the difference.' You didn't argue with Jack Barrick.

But such frankness – some would call it arrogance – brought Jack into conflict with the powers-that-be. According to Jess Lay: 'He was admired from a referee's point of view. It was just the people who were in charge of football that probably resented him a bit because he was too outspoken to them and they objected to that.' One month before the 1948 final, the *Northampton Chronicle and Echo* had asked Jack, then aged 47, if he had any plans to retire. His reply, typically direct, was recorded in bold print: 'No, I first refereed in 1925 and I want to complete 25 years' service – two seasons more.'

Wasn't he aware, however, that the retirement age for referees had been lowered to 48? Maybe he assumed he would receive preferential treatment. In the event, just two months after controlling the Cup final, Jack's name was removed from the FA's list of officials. In view of the fact that he kept himself 'very fit' – and that there was a shortage of top-notch referees in England – it was no wonder he felt 'bitter'. He was forced to look abroad for work, keeping his career objective on track while showing the FA they'd been wrong to discard him. This, then, is the context for the negotiations which were taking place between Jack Barrick and the Rio Federation in May 1948.

★   ★   ★

We have noted how Harry Welfare acted as 'diplomatic liaison' during Southampton's visit to Brazil. When four British referees finally reached Rio on 9 July it was Harry who was at the airport to greet them. But whereas before his duties were mainly of an ancilliary nature, now his primary role was to represent the Rio Referees' College.

Even before the arrival of Jack Barrick and his three colleagues, Harry had been occupied with refereeing matters – filling the gap left by Reader. He lectured at the College and was responsible for organising the referees at the annual pre-season tournament in Rio. Also, at a general assembly of the Rio Federation, he put forward an item for discussion. It concerned the system used in England whereby a referee could let the players know when to leave for the pitch by means of a bell linked to their dressing-rooms. Players were to appear five minutes before the officials.

It is unclear whether Harry's suggestion was ever adopted, let alone how Brazilians would have reacted to the enforced punctuality implied. But it does show the thoroughness with which the refereeing issue was being tackled. Clearly Harry's brief was to study the whole function of the referee and make recommendations, not only to ensure that Reader's comments on standardisation and interpretation were being acted upon. In Barrick and co he had a 'first-rate' team of officials to assist him.

On his arrival, Jack Barrick announced that he and his colleagues, A. Devine, A.T. Ford and F.J. Lowe, had 'not come to teach' – an apparent denial of one of the reasons why they were being hired. But if the remark was intended to appease the critics of the scheme to import foreign officials, it wasn't long before it was shown to lack substance. Barrick for one lost no time in imposing his own inimitable style on the Brazilian game. In the opening round of the Carioca championship he was given the Vasco *v* Bonsucesso encounter to control:

> At corners [he] squats down, making a signal with his arm without whistling. This referee, indignant at [Vasco winger] Chico's violent foul on the Bonsucesso keeper Alvarez, grabbed him by the shirt and with energetic words threatened to send him off.

It was dramatic actions such as those depicted in the *Gazeta Esportiva*'s report that led Mário Filho to describe Jack as 'appearing like an interpreter of Shakespeare'. But then he'd always had a singular approach to refereeing. In Brazil that approach appeared exaggerated.

Unfortunately, the feeling that Brazilians were not up to the job of officiating was exacerbated right from the start. Four of the five first-round matches were controlled by the British recruits, and afterwards praise was heaped on them of the sort that George Reader had enjoyed. After four penalties had been awarded, including three by Ford, the *Gazeta Esportiva* wrote: 'The English referees will revolutionise Carioca football on the penalty question. They don't allow fouls in the area, and defenders need to be very careful.' After the third round of games the penalty total had risen to 13, just one short of the tally for the whole of the previous year's campaign.

The *Gazeta* also noted other differences in technique:

They don't whistle much, they run a lot, keeping up with play, in a diagonal, like Mr Reader. They don't whistle when they're restarting the game, for fouls or when the ball is out of play, nor do they count steps . . .

Local referees and linesmen needed practical training; and before the month was out Harry Welfare had arranged for an amateur game to be played at Botafogo's ground in which the English officials demonstrated how the diagonal system operated. As Mário Filho explains: 'The linesman . . . had to stay in an imaginary line with off-side. Between one linesman and the other a diagonal line could be traced, dividing the pitch.' The referee positioned himself along the diagonal.

Football League referees had been instructed to use the diagonal method of control in the 1930s, but the system was first developed at the beginning of this century. It was William Pickford, one of the architects of the pioneering Referees' Chart in the 1890s, who was responsible for its formulation. So given Charles Miller's connection with Pickford, the system might potentially have been introduced in Brazil before 1910. We do not know for sure, but if it was, it should have made life easier for Alex Hutchison, the Scot whose officiating fell foul of the Liga Paulista – and even his own club.

Forty years on, the four British officials soon had to put up with the effects of certain clubs turning against them – despite being backed by those running the game in Brazil. Barrick had to leave one ground in a car with tinted windows. *Gazeta Esportiva* columnist José Brigido deplored the 'threats of aggression' against Jack and his colleagues, and in supporting them he outlined their unenviable assignment:

> Without any shadow of doubt the English referees are doing a restoration job on refereeing, seeing to it that the Rules are observed with greater rigour and preventing the time of the game from being wasted by constant interruptions. The task that they've shouldered is enormous, on account of the level of sporting education of almost all of the players, directors and fans. It's a naked truth that must be said. An atmosphere corrupted over many years by cunning officiating, full of prejudice and complaisant attitudes, cannot be purified in a day.

The English referees also had to keep up with recent alterations to the text of the Referees' Chart. These had stemmed from the International Referees' Course and Conference held at the FA's London headquarters in March 1948. It was there that delegates from 28 countries gave approval to the diagonal system of control.

But even where it was argued that Brazilian players and referees needed to be familiar with the 'international rules', clubs had their own reasons to resist the imposition of a British referee. Palmeiras had reportedly refused to have their game with Santos refereed by George Reader because the club felt it would be discriminating against local officials. And for the deciding game in the 1948 Carioca championship – Botafogo 3 Vasco 1, refereed by Mário Viana – Mário Filho tells us that Botafogo 'did not want one of the Englishmen [to officiate]. Harry Welfare still had links with Vasco and spoke with the English referees in their language.'

In the case of the São Paulo Federation (FPF), before resorting to help from Britain, it was decided 'as a last effort' to upgrade the refereeing 'profession'. FPF Secretary José Ferreira Keffer explained that the reason referees were well paid was 'so that they could dedicate themselves entirely to [the profession], following a regular fitness programme and having a sufficient amount of time to devote to an intensive study of the Rules'. It was when this was deemed to have failed, just one month into the 1948 season, that the FPF decided to follow the 'Rio experiment'.

★   ★   ★

Early in 1949 both the Rio and São Paulo Federations were preparing to bring out referees from Britain. On 5 March the FPF's Official Bulletin reported that the vice-president of the organisation had been given powers 'to adopt all preliminary measures relating to the contracting of English referees by intermediary of Harry Welfare'. Shortly afterwards Harry, accompanied by his wife, boarded one of the Royal Mail's steamships, taking with him contracts for ten officials – five for Rio and five for São Paulo. Thirty-six years after arriving in Brazil, Harry told the press: 'I'm very excited about the opportunity to return to England.'

This 'official mission' took Harry to London for meetings with FA secretary Stanley Rous. There was also a trip to Merseyside which no doubt included a visit to Anfield. We know he went to Liverpool because Harold Welfare, whose father was Harry's cousin, recalls meeting him. Harold remembers Harry saying he was the manager of a 'sports complex' – presumably a reference to Vasco da Gama. As for

Harry's former club, Liverpool, they were then in mid-table in the First Division, the same position in which he'd left them in 1913.

By mid-May 1949 the FPF had received news that two of their five officials were on their way. 'Welfare's mission,' wrote the *Gazeta Esportiva*, 'has been crowned with complete success.' When they arrived in Brazil, Percy Snape and Harry Rowley talked of the need for 'standardisation' – just as their Rio counterparts had done. The *Gazeta* readership would have been surprised to learn that Snape, just like Charles Miller, was São Paulo-born and had been educated in England. But perhaps what might have intrigued readers more was the fact that both men, despite their vast and varied experience in the game, were part-time referees. Snape owned a textile business and Rowley worked for the National Coal Board.

On the eve of the Paulista championship, FPF secretary Keffer reiterated why the British officials were being hired: 'To create ... with their method, standard and conviction ... a new mentality, not only for Brazilian referees, but also for the public.' For him, it was not a 'definitive solution', but a 'remedy with immediate effect'. For the 're-education' process there were no half measures. As from the second round of championship matches – by which time Snape and Rowley had been joined by Wilfred Lee, Martin Storey and Godfrey Sunderland – the British held a refereeing monopoly.

As in Rio, during the previous season, the benefits of the scheme were soon apparent. Post-match protests at dubious decisions 'ceased almost completely'. On 1 July 1949 the *Mundo Esportivo* portrayed the popular mood:

> These days fans feel at ease to go to an encounter. They watch the game freely, not worried with keeping an eye on the referee. This is a blessing and a reflection on the appreciable providence of the acquisition of the Englishmen. Fans no longer experience a dreadful nightmare when they see their team lose, even when there are doubts over a decision that influences the outcome of a match. They are easily resigned. As the Palmeiras forward Lima says: 'The business of a team losing when it deserved to win is a thing of the past.'

But at the same time, in some sections of the press, the slightest mistake by a British official was being pounced on and analysed in detail, whereas his 'best virtues' were not commented on. For the *Mundo Esportivo* this smacked of 'injustice'. The *Gazeta Esportiva*, too, called for critics to be impartial. The British referees should be seen 'not as little Popes of infallibility, but as men like us, capable of making mistakes, even a lot of mistakes'. The *Gazeta*, however, felt that the new arrivals needed to be tougher on discipline.

Several months later, in September 1949, the *Gazeta Esportiva* returned to the theme of discipline in a series of articles. The sporting authorities in São Paulo had analysed the British 'mission' from a purely 'technical' angle; what was needed, urgently, was awareness of the 'psychological' aspect of the task. To this end, the *Gazeta* called for the British officials to be assisted in dealing with the unsporting behaviour of Brazilian players. Cases of players being hauled before disciplinary hearings were on the increase. Coming from a country where the game was played 'with a completely different mentality, how could they control, combat and wipe out indiscipline . . . if they weren't properly instructed?'.

The *Gazeta*'s analysis of the discipline question, provocative though it may have been, reveals what a precarious position the British officials and the Paulista Federation were in. While the British were encouraged to referee as they saw fit, clearly wanting to avoid controversy, any attempt by the FPF to introduce a tougher attitude to discipline would have met with hostility from the clubs. It was a no-win situation – but better, perhaps, to maintain the status quo rather than risk the backlash that was occurring in Rio.

There, adverse reaction to the refereeing of the British officials was becoming frequent. In October the situation had deteriorated to such an extent that the FMF accepted Mário Viana's suggestion that on match days two bodyguards be assigned to each referee – 'during the match the guards stay in the stand and only go up to the referee at the end of the game'. It must have been a testing time, not only for the officials, but also for Harry Welfare. After Arthur Ford had been badly kicked by a player in Juiz de Fóra, Harry 'indicated he was against the idea of sending more officials [there]'. But it appears this view was overruled.

Towards the end of November, a British referee was chosen to officiate in Juiz. When Ford and a colleague requested extra payments for games outside Rio, their demands were not fully met by the FMF. Welfare was powerless to break the impasse; and Ford and Dundas, after their contracts had been terminated, returned to Britain.

★   ★   ★

Jack Barrick, meanwhile, was still officiating in Brazil – but not in Rio. In June 1949 he'd signed with the Rio Grande do Sul Federation after being unable to agree terms with the FMF for an extension of his contract. But he too might have cut short his stay following a contractual wrangle with the CBD.

After his previous year's stint in Rio, interrupted by a return to London to officiate in the Olympic Games, Jack was invited by the CBD to take charge of matches at the South American Championship to be held in Brazil during April and May 1949. The problem arose over an ambiguity relating to two clauses in his agreement: one stated that the contract was valid for two months, the other that it was for the duration of the tournament. The CBD took the second line, paying Jack only for the games he controlled.

It was during this championship that Barrick – in the middle for 12 out of the 29 matches – came to prominence in South America. The *Gazeta Esportiva* reported that 'all participating countries wanted him for their games'; and subsequent offers of work included a lecture and refereeing tour in Chile.

But working in a team of referees who were 'reluctant' to use the diagonal system, Jack could not fail to stand out. José Brigido described the general level of refereeing as 'inferior', and he complained about the linesmen, 'militant referees [who] have displayed a disconcerting mediocrity, making absurd interruptions, often with the approval of the man in charge'. George Reader had noted that Brazilian linesmen 'had no authority'; now, it seemed, their South American colleagues had too much.

While in São Paulo on CBD duty, Jack gave an extensive interview to the *Gazeta Esportiva*. It appeared as a front-page feature on 22 April 1949 under the banner headline 'Jack Barrick tells his story and draws conclusions!'. In setting out what for him were the ingredients that lay behind successful refereeing, there were two things that predominated – 'vibrant personality and self-control'. For Jack: 'The referee, apart from the financial side, must like his work. His officiating will always depend on the disposition with which he comes onto the pitch.' Speaking his mind, in typical fashion, Jack reinforced the arguments of those who were critical of Brazilian referees.

The very next day, the *Gazeta's* editorial was headed 'Mr Barrick has spoken'; and it was suggested that 'all FPF referees needed to read and take seriously the words of this wise and intelligent Englishman'. Not only that, but the Paulista Federation should have a copy of the interview pinned to the wall in its boardroom. As opposed to Brazilian referees, who were like 'flies caught in a spider's web, Mr Barrick is an example of independence, honour, rectitude, and therein lies the secret of his perfect officiating'. Jack was no longer merely just another British import. In Brazil he had become the prototype of the ideal referee, of what Cláudio, when speaking of this period, defines as 'the uncorrupted man'.

But it remained the case that whereas Jack's strong personality was appropriate for refereeing, off the pitch it was liable to ruffle feathers. José Brigido also called for a wide dissemination of the Barrick interview, enthusing in English at the end of one of his commentaries: 'All right, Mr Barrick! We want your help! Help us to help you! Go ahead!' But soon Jack was publicly criticising the Rio-based CBD for showing inflexibility in their contract dispute, thus making a parting of the ways between him and the Rio Federation seem ever likely. For the new crop of British recruits his was a hard act to follow.

Perhaps player discipline might not have become so much of an issue in São Paulo had Jack moved there – and not to Rio Grande do Sul. But after the *Gazeta Esportiva*'s editorial, referred to above, that was never going to happen. During his eight-and-a-half-month tour in 1949, he ordered off 19 men in the 91 games he controlled. In Pôrto Alegre he was in charge for the state championship decider, and when he left, a local paper chose an appropriate metaphor to express its sadness:

> Mr Barrick's leaving opens a curtain on a black panorama for our football, which he has nearly retrieved from chaos. We shall be like the man who, delighted in Shakespeare plays for several weeks, has to turn back to clown jesters.

Jack, though, would be back; and besides, he let it be known that it was his ambition to referee in the upcoming World Cup. Just over a year before the tournament he offered the *Gazeta Esportiva* a view on the state of the Brazilian game, and the role of the British and Brazilian referees with regard to its future:

> What great football the Brazilians play! If certain illicit means that we see were abolished, this would be sufficient for there to be in Brazil the best football in the world. We don't understand a player pulling the shirt of another, or a full-back throwing himself into the goal, as a last resort, to stop the ball with his hands. There's none of that in England! In my country, no player other than the captain,

even if he has a respectful attitude, has ever addressed himself to the referee. It's a sending-off case. But I believe that with time and with the help of my colleagues and the national officials, some of whom are very good, we will achieve this. On that day Brazilian football will be irresistible.

Within days of this assessment being published, First Division Arsenal would encounter the good, the bad and the ugly side of football in Brazil. But they'd especially discover what Jack Barrick meant by 'irresistible'.

FIFTEEN

Masters Versus Pupils?

For the Englishman, football is an athletic exercise; for the Brazilian it's a game.

The Englishman considers a player that dribbles three times in succession is a nuisance; the Brazilian considers him a virtuoso.

English football, well played, is like a symphonic orchestra; well played, Brazilian football is like an extremely hot jazz band.

English football requires that the ball moves faster than the player; Brazilian football requires that the player be faster than the ball.

The English player thinks; the Brazilian improvises.

From Tomás Mazzoni, *A Gazeta*, June 1949, quoted in *Tom Whittaker's Arsenal Story*, 1958, p.227

Eventually, there was the Arsenal, who gave us the last lesson in tactical discipline, although, fortunately, no system will ever suffocate the Brazilian knack for improvisation . . .

Mário Filho, quoted in Willy Meisl's *Soccer Revolution*, 1956, p.72

My interview with George Swindin was drawing to a close. We had touched on the highs and lows of his career – being part of one of Arsenal's championship-winning sides of the 1930s, failing by a whisker to win an England cap – and had been discussing Arsenal's 1949 tour to Brazil. 'Did Arsenal learn anything out there?' I asked him.

There was a trace of hesitant admission in the reply. 'Individually, our players had quite a lot to learn. Tactics – if your ability is there, tactics come automatically. But it was the fact that these people were so good on the ball. This was the greatest thing. They could do something with the ball. They could get it under control quickly and move with it.'

Reminiscent of Eric Webber's story of the artful goalkeeper, George has his own enduring image which illustrates the extent to which Brazilian footballers are obsessed with ball control – and symbolises the hold the game has on the country:

> I saw a kid walking down the main street in Rio one day and he's got a ball on his foot and he was going [George paces down his living-room, juggling an imaginary ball] . . . The ball never touched the floor! And he must have walked a hundred yards and the ball was still going up and down. You couldn't believe it! In the main street in Rio! Crazy, isn't it?

And just as Southampton had found, 'craziness' was what awaited the two parties of Arsenal players and officials when they alighted at Rio airport in the second week of May 1949. Accompanying the tourists, the *Daily Mirror*'s John Thompson would write: 'In over 20 years of following our national game I have never known such enthusiasm for it. Nothing else matters here.'

First Division Arsenal had been forewarned, to a degree at least. Southampton manager Bill Dodgin was returning as a guest of tour sponsors Botafogo. He'd emphasised Brazil's 'great football qualities' to the Gunners' secretary-manager Tom Whittaker – and the 'magnificent hospitality'. George Swindin remembers their arrival: 'There were a lot of people there with flags and bunting. Oh yes, it was fabulous. There was no doubt about it. There'd been a lot of publicity given to it which got these people to the airport.' But no sooner had they been hailed as '*A maior máquina futebolistica do mundo*' – 'The greatest football machine in the world' – than Arsenal were put on the defensive.

In his autobiography, Tom Whittaker explains how he'd had to call a press conference in order to counteract a 'lying attack' by certain Brazilian reporters. 'Among many other highly colourful things I and the players were supposed to have said were: "English football is the Best in the World; Arsenal will win every match; Brazilian football is Third-Rate; Arsenal are Soccer Masters, says Manager"; and so on in similar strain.' As Plymouth referee F.W. Reeve had discovered in 1924, there were no bounds to the methods employed by news-hungry reporters in Rio.

Following the friction there was a publicity stunt. Before Brazil's match with Paraguay in the final of the South American Championship, Whittaker and some of his players made an appearance on the pitch. After Brazil's 7–0 victory, their first success in the competition since 1922, Whittaker's comments were reproduced verbatim. 'I've just seen one of the best teams in the world,' he told the *Gazeta Esportiva*. 'They play quickly and with an efficient work-rate. It's hard to mark them and this makes them a very difficult team to beat.' He was particularly impressed by the Flamengo inside-left Jair – 'a very skilful player who could be part of any team in the world'.

For George Swindin, however, there seemed no undue cause for concern. Arsenal's last line of defence, and captain for the tour, he recalls attending the international match at Vasco's São Januário stadium. 'I didn't see anything really that frightened us. I thought there were some very clever players. I thought: "I think we could cope with them." And it proved to be so.' Initially it certainly did. But thereafter, Arsenal found results hard to come by.

15 May
Arsenal 5   Fluminense 1

> The 60,000 crowd which paid more than £13,000 to see last night's match in Vasco da Gama stadium went home after a game which was packed with fine excitement. They exploded thousands of fire-crackers to prove their enthusiasm despite disappointment at their own team's failure.
>
> We had seen Arsenal with crisp, clean tackling, with wing-halves who knew the value of the cross ball. It was English football at its brightest – cohesive and precise. Long passes by Douglas Lishman [scorer of four goals] time after time, and his imaginative moving into position, stamp him definitely as an England star of tomorrow.
>
> At centre-forward, Don Roper, who scored the first of the five goals, looks far more at home than he did on the wing at Highbury. He had the Brazilians worried all the time. His powerful shooting and pace will win many League games for Arsenal. But it would be unfair to single out individuals on this occasion. Every man was a success.
>
> (*Daily Mirror*, 17 May 1949)

John Thompson's report was entitled 'A little whiff didn't do Arsenal any harm'. 'Tired by the sultry heat and fast pace of the game', several players had had oxygen treatment at half-time. Another thing they experienced after matches and training was a form of massage: a hosing down with cold water. 'It knocked me flying,' said full-back Laurie Scott. He got 'little black bruises' where the water hit him. It was all part of what Scott describes as Brazil's 'modern facilities – everything was being studied from A to Z before they did anything out there'.

It is no surprise, therefore, that Brazilians at once set about trying to dissect the visitors' style of play. *O Estado de São Paulo* put Arsenal's use of the WM into a historical context:

> It's interesting to note that the English adopted the technique of keeping a third back, naturally the centre-half Daniel. This player cancelled out every effort in his sector. A veritable barrier. Chapman's style, that Dori Kruschner tried to play without success at Flamengo, was shown in all its splendour. If Southampton weren't successful [playing it], the same can't be said of Arsenal.

Success, moreover, had been achieved without three key players. Centre-half Leslie Compton and his brother Denis, the regular left-winger, were cricketing with Middlesex; while club captain and left-half Joe Mercer had stayed behind to look after his grocery business. These three players, George Swindin feels, 'could have made the difference to us in Brazil'.

For despite Arsenal's comfortable victory and presenting football that, according to one headline, '...delighted the eyes and warmed the heart', it was clear that already there were lessons to be learnt. Laurie Scott, who was nursing an injury for most of the tour, recalls a moment from the opening game. 'Suddenly, a bloke comes dashing through and he's had a shot at goal and the ball went wide. And we started looking round to see who we'd got to blame for this. We couldn't find it. We found out it was their full-back. See, they didn't care. I never went up there like that. I used to go down the sideline, yes, but never [like that]. Anyway, we got a bit of a shock and then we had to start thinking again before the next game.' The words of a former England international.

According to Scott, it resulted in Jimmy Logie – the inside-forward who, in the manner of Alex James, 'did all the donkey work in the middle of the field' – coming back an extra ten yards. 'So, roughly, we had four wing-halves instead of three.' Who would have thought they'd just won handsomely – 'Arsenal's visiting card', as the *Gazeta* had summarily announced it?

★ ★ ★

A couple of days after the tour opener the Arsenal party made the first of two trips to São Paulo. They had flown over from Europe in two parties. As George Swindin explains: 'At Arsenal this had always been a policy that the club flew in two halves. When we went to Paris [for the annual friendly against Racing Club] we went in two planes.' Now, though, they were split up into three groups, probably because of the air disaster in Italy, just days before, in which AC Torino's entire squad had been killed.

Only the previous season, the Italian champions had visited São Paulo. When they played Palmeiras, the team that represented the Italian colony in São Paulo, gate receipts were broken at Pacaembú. On 18 May 1949, Arsenal's first game in São Paulo drew an even bigger crowd, the £15,000 taken at the turnstiles a South American record. Palmeiras, as they'd done against Torino, managed to draw 1–1.

For full-back Walley Barnes and his team-mates, playing under lights for the first time was just one among a number of novelties:

> The 16 lamps at each corner were extremely effective, but didn't always allow the goalkeeper a perfect view of the ball. The strangeness of the artificial lighting, the white ball and the continual firing of photographers' flashbulbs during the game were not all we had to cope with, however. In addition the Palmeiras players, mostly of Italian extraction, were both livelier and tougher than our previous opponents.

For John Thompson it had been:

> an unsatisfactory and scrappy game, [and] the penalty which decided the result was itself unsatisfactory. It was awarded for hands by red-headed Scot, Alex Forbes. From where I sat on the touchline near the corner flag, it looked as though Forbes was only protecting himself. Said referee Jack Barrick, from Northampton: 'There was no question about it. Forbes definitely handled the ball.'

Barrick's typically obdurate comment came after he'd controlled the second of six games allocated to him on the tour. Both he and Arsenal were on show. And, judging by some reports, this was tantamount to being on trial.

Two pieces in the São Paulo press, both published on 20 May, put the state of euphoria over Arsenal's visit sharply into perspective. An editorial in the *Gazeta Esportiva* called for an end to the Brazilian 'mania for overestimating [opponents] – they are not invincible'. Brazilian club sides were advised by Tomás Mazzoni 'to impose their school. The English have a style that is practical, brief, almost ugly. We play with a great deal of improvising. We are more imaginative and less calculating than they are.' As for the weekly *Mundo Esportivo*, one headline set off a series of biting attacks on Arsenal and English football ('they taught the world and now they're living on past glories'). It ran '*Eles jogam futebol para inglês ver*' – a play on the words of a popular saying, meaning that Arsenal may look the part, but it's really a deception.

But how perceptions differed. For anyone reading John Thompson's dispatches in the *Daily Mirror* it was as if Britain's soccer prestige was 'brighter than ever'. He reported that a number of South American countries were 'anxious' to see Arsenal before they returned to London. Two soccer chiefs had even flown from Montevideo 'to plead Uruguay's case'. All requests, though, would have to be turned down. Meanwhile, as part of the preparations for their next match Arsenal players had studied a film of the Palmeiras game. 'It was an example,' wrote Thompson, 'of Arsenal thoroughness.'

22 May
Arsenal 2   Corinthians 0

In the first half the Corinthians showed superiority in their rapid passes, and their technique [was] completely unknown to the Arsenal. Another important factor was the tremendous heat and sun through-out the entire game, to which the British players are not accustomed.

Corinthians attacked all of the first half, giving Arsenal's players few chances to reach the locals' goal. Arsenal's defence played a wonderful game not letting the locals score, which I might say was a very difficult task, for the locals were constantly near the goalposts. The most outstanding player in the British defence was Swindin. The Corinthians' best man was the centre-half Touguinha. The first half ended with a tie of zero.

> The second half brought us a considerable change on behalf
> of both teams . . . Corinthians began to play a slow and
> uninteresting game. Arsenal started to attack and after a few
> minutes Forbes kicked a high one and Lishman put it in,
> [opening] the score for Arsenal. The public had not expected the
> goal against the locals, so they started cheering wildly for the
> Corinthians to tie the game. To their astonishment the Arsenal
> made another goal when McPherson shot another ball and
> Vallance put it in with his head.
>
> (*Times of Brazil*, 27 May 1949)

One member of that Corinthians side can still recollect what a
frustrating afternoon it was, trying to find a way past George Swindin.
'It was different from any other game,' says Cláudio, the right-winger,
'because, to give you an idea, at corners we didn't have a keeper and
two defenders, we only left the keeper [in the goal]. And on that day,
with two defenders [on the goal-line] it made things a bit difficult for
us; and we were doing our utmost to score, the ball hit one, it hit the
other and it just wouldn't go in.'

This defensive ploy was already part of Arsenal's armoury when
George Swindin joined them in the mid-1930s. It was part of a system
where the emphasis lay on 'safety first'. Having had 'the whole run of
the penalty area' at Bradford City, George recalls his initial resistance
to having two full-backs on the goal-line, one either side of him. 'I
didn't like it at all because it restricted me. I was an agile person and
they were getting in my way.' But the system had paid off for Arsenal
in England – and it was paying off in Brazil. George Swindin explains
how the WM worked:

> The inside-forwards came back to reinforce the defence and the
> wingers came back as well, leaving one man up the field. It more or
> less amounted to the fact that the nearest man to [the ball] when it
> broke down went back immediately to help the defence. If one of
> the inside-forwards was a bit far up, then the winger had to come
> back and do his bit. You had to work in conjunction with one
> another and not get drawn out too far so that it left them with a free
> run on to goal.

However, as José Brigido reminded *Gazeta Esportiva* readers, in
Brazil the WM:

had never been employed with the necessary wisdom. The tactic was transformed into a spoiling game, lacking vitality, under the denomination of a 'closed defence', reducing football to the condition of a game that was cold and without vibration. In their opening game, however, Arsenal demonstrated that the WM doesn't have to be used rigidly, so much so that several of their players didn't even keep to their positions. We battled against this rigidity at the time when it was fashionable to speak of a 'closed defence'.

Not that tactics were high on everyone's list of 'all the possible angles to be studied'. For Cláudio, the number-one lesson Brazilians learnt was 'English discipline' – and the discipline of sides visiting Brazil from Continental Europe. (Botafogo president Carlito Rocha was quoted as saying that Arsenal's discipline, 'both on and off the field', was magnificent.) But today it is a quality that is sadly missing. Cláudio laments what he sees as 'very violent' play in the European games that are transmitted in Brazil. It is an 'ill', he reflects soberly, that came from South America.

* * *

25 May
Arsenal 0   Vasco da Gama 1
Back in Rio, it was the turn of Vasco da Gama to take on Arsenal. Just as it had been during Southampton's tour, this proved to be the 'match of the series'. That's how George Swindin remembers it. Result-wise it was a turning-point. Before a crowd that produced gate receipts that surpassed even the Palmeiras game, Vasco, as the *Gazeta* put it, 'made Arsenal capitulate'. The only goal of the game, coming near the end, was memorably captured by the *Gazeta*'s man on the spot:

> At precisely 22.40 ending an irresistible Brazilian attack, right-wing Nestor, in a magnificent move, shot inside the English goal! A marvellous play, in which the fabulous Ademir, with his recognised class, also intervened. Besides, it was down to the 'blue devil' to block Swindin's vision, giving Nestor the chance to enter and score, without appeal! 1–0 for Vasco! The crowd goes mad! What we're seeing here inside São Januário is an apotheosis, a frenzy! Nestor, extremely emotional, falls to the ground, while Ademir and Heleno jump on top of him in wild joy!

The reaction of the crowd was depicted in John Thompson's *Mirror* piece: 'Women in the stand kissed each other and cried with joy. On the terraces men flung fire-crackers among their neighbours.' There was also a reference to the goal celebration: 'When they disentangled themselves Nestor stayed on the ground, knocked dizzy by his friends' embraces. He had to have treatment before resuming.' Quite simply it had been 'one of the most stirring soccer occasions' Thompson had ever known, the quality of the football 'unforgettable':

> The contrast in style and method was fascinating. Arsenal's defence, at its best, looked as well drilled as a King's guard. Vasco played in attack as though they could conquer the world. Their approach to the penalty box was the most sparkling I have seen for years, their swinging passes crisp and beautifully timed. What a great team they are, and what a team Arsenal are to have stood firm against them for so long!

As a pointer towards the relative standard of the game in England and Brazil, in the run-up to the World Cup, Arsenal's performance did not augur well – and Thompson knew it. He was sorry the England selectors hadn't been there: 'The experience would have dispelled any complacency there may be about our chances in the World Cup next season. Make no mistake. Brazil will start favourites.'

Ademir and several of his Vasco team-mates would, of course, figure in the World Cup campaign. And so would the player who had caught Tom Whittaker's eye in Brazil's win over Paraguay, Flamengo's Jair. He too shone for his club against Arsenal; but the match was marred by violence on the pitch, a single incident leading to five minutes of chaos.

29 May
Arsenal 1   Flamengo 3

> Whittaker described the brawl which caused police to charge on the ground in the second half, as the worst incident he had seen in 30 years' football. 'A full report will be made to the Football Association when we return to England,' he said. 'The Flamengo players need to be taught the way football should be played. They are clever, and I cannot understand why they need to stoop to such tactics – deliberate fouls which blotted the game from start to finish.'
>
> The incident started when Bryn Jones, one of the quietest players

in British football, went to play the ball after the Flamengo goal-keeper had saved. Jones told me: 'A player came at me from behind and squeezed my throat. I could hardly breathe.' Flamengo and Arsenal players crowded round and substitutes from both teams from the touchline joined in as police waving truncheons dashed on the field.

An identity parade was held after the game but said Whittaker: 'There were so many police it was impossible to identify the culprits.' The miracle was that Arsenal players did not retaliate. Footballers can seldom have had such provocation.

(*Daily Mirror*, 31 May 1949)

Judging by accounts in the Brazilian press, however, there was another side to what happened. For *O Estado de São Paulo* it was after Flamengo had taken a 2–1 lead early in the second half that 'illicit methods' began to be used. First, 'the Carioca players used their hands a lot, not only to keep the ball but also to grab hold of their opponents by the shirt'. This led to Arsenal responding, 'in irritation, with body contact of a more violent nature'. Bryn Jones's late challenge on débutant keeper Garcia was one excess too many.

Whittaker mentioned 'deliberate fouls' by the Flamengo players, but in the *Gazeta's* report the blame fell squarely on the visitors. Commenting on the referee, the *Gazeta* wrote: 'Mário Viana's offici-ating was correct as far as the technical part went, but he failed to repress the violent play practised by members of the Arsenal side.' One might assume that had Jack Barrick been in the middle the game would not have been allowed to deteriorate. Ironically, it was the Arsenal camp who had suggested that Viana control the game – 'It's the best demonstration of confidence that Brazilian referees deserve from us.'

But worthy though the gesture may have been, Arsenal must have known there was an element of risk involved. Laurie Scott remembers how Brazilian officials measured up to, say, Barrick: 'My goodness, there was a big difference. They used to stand for anything . . . It seemed at times they were scared to give a free-kick or a foul to anybody.' Scared to the extent that, as Walley Barnes relates, Mário Viana had 'a six-shooter in a shoulder holster under his blouse, which he wore throughout the game'. It was he who later called for bodyguards to be assigned to referees in Rio. Could it be that when trouble finally got out of hand, Viana, a police officer by profession, motioned to his police colleagues to assist him?

Whatever the reason for the 'police intervention', Botafogo and the CBD took 'energetic measures' to restrict access to the area surrounding the pitch for the one remaining tour match in Rio. The aim was to make the Arsenal *v* Botafogo match on 1 June an occasion of 'the greatest sportsmanship'. To this end, Botafogo president Carlito Rocha decided that 'the first Botafogo player to overstep the mark, either through indiscipline or disloyalty, will be taken off'. The threat worked wonders, for each of Rocha's players later received a cash bonus for playing 'so well and so cleanly'. The reigning Rio champions, after twice falling behind, drew 2–2 with Arsenal. And in the effort to clamp down on indiscipline, Jack Barrick, restored to the middle, had had one of the Rio Federation's new recruits, Bill Martin, running the line.

It was on the day of the Arsenal *v* Botafogo game that one respected columnist expounded his view on what could be learnt from the visitors' style of play. For José Brigido writing in the *Gazeta*, the 'English key' consisted of 'playing hard and using first-time passing'. Counter to Mazzoni's insistence that Brazilian teams should 'impose their school' on Arsenal, Brigido was now calling for São Paulo FC, Arsenal's last opponents, to do as Vasco had done – namely to adopt aspects of the British style. When Brazilian players released the ball early, 'the efficiency of our football appears'; and as regards a tougher approach: 'We know this too, but we don't use it because Brazilian football is more art and show, unnecessarily disappearing, at times, in personal exhibitions that bring no advantage to the team.'

Corinthians' over-elaborate approach work was a case in point. Arsenal had been let off the hook. While emphasising 'English discipline' as the major legacy of the Gunners' visit, Cláudio uses Brigido's argument as to why they were difficult to beat: 'The English,' he maintains, 'were hard but fair, and they played first-time football really well.' With the World Cup just round the corner, it was a taste of what Brazilians could expect from participating European nations.

★   ★   ★

In São Paulo it wasn't only the football fraternity who were looking forward to Arsenal's return. The São Paulo Athletic cricket club had revised its fixture list to accommodate a match with a team from the Arsenal party. Charles Miller, most probably, would have attended both the cricket and the football. Perhaps Archie McLean was also among the group of SPAC members who went across to Pacaembú.

About to return to Scotland after retiring from Coats, he could relive his brief association with Arsenal as a trialist in 1908. But just as it was back then, the experience was a losing one.

4 June
Arsenal 0   São Paulo 1

> There is no doubt that Arsenal played a mediocre game, which is not surprising when one considers that they have played seven games in three weeks, both in São Paulo and Rio.
>
> The São Paulo team dominated throughout, Swindin's, and later Platt's, goalkeeping averting a larger score. Another factor for the low score was the inclination of the São Paulo forwards to try to position the ball before shooting, thus allowing the Arsenal backs to rob them and clear up-field. The only goal of the match came about halfway through the second half, Teixeirinha scoring with a fast low shot which Platt had no chance to save.
>
> For São Paulo, the best players were Mauro, Rui, Leônidas and Teixeirinha. For Arsenal, Swindin gave a perfect exhibition in the first half and his substitute, Platt, brought off some fine saves. Barnes played well at back but his colleague, Wade, did not impress. The only member of the team who had his inspired moments was Roper, but he could not inspire a ragged forward line.
>
> (*Times of Brazil*, 10 June 1949)

If this was a 'British' version of the match, then it is not difficult to imagine the reaction of the Paulista press. As usual the *Gazeta Esportiva* were the most overtly ecstatic. The huge front-page headline read: 'No team has ever dominated so much for so little', and below photographs of the goal and a joyful Teixeirinha, Tomás Mazzoni's commentary begins. The match tipped the balance of results in the Brazilians' favour; but more importantly it had been won through 'ninety minutes of conspicuous superiority' – São Paulo 'attacking with eight men', Arsenal showing 'only defensive merit'.

When Mazzoni's seminal *História do Futebol no Brasil* was published a year later there was a section on Arsenal. While stressing the financial success of the tour – record gate receipts for Brazilian football – the author returns to his pet theme. 'We played better because we imposed our own school which the English found strange and didn't accept.' The point had already been made in *Gazeta* editorials, and the visits of Arsenal and Southampton contrasted. Whereas 'South[ampton] "took in" Brazilian football, after several defeats, and then achieved balanced results', during Arsenal's tour, 'it was the Brazilians who had "taken in" English football after that initial thrashing . . . transforming defeat into victories.'

So Brazilians benefited from Arsenal's play, admiring 'the solidarity of [their] defensive system and the manner in which the team fights back'. The scale of Britain's shortcomings, however, was made frighteningly apparent. In his penultimate dispatch (*Daily Mirror*, 6 June 1949), John Thompson took up where he had left off in his Vasco report. He had Tom Whittaker as an ally. The Arsenal manager stated candidly what needed to be done:

> Clubs here spare no expense in looking after the welfare of their players. The medical side is far in advance of what it is in most British clubs, and I admire the completeness of their coaching, massage and training staffs. They have obviously made a careful study of what a player needs to make him fighting fit.
>
> Worthy of imitation, too, is the manner in which leading clubs foster the interest of youth in all kinds of sport. Vasco, Botafogo, Fluminense and other clubs here have members who joined as schoolboys and will be members all their lives.

But how were such views to be disseminated in Britain – and, more vitally, to what extent would they be embraced and acted upon?

In November 1949, John Thompson began a series of 'Letters from England' for the *Gazeta Esportiva* on 'British football and the World Cup' – another lesson in guarding against insularity. In his first offering he once again made plain his high regard for the Brazilians' 'speed and marvellous ball control'. Tom Whittaker had 'offered to help the English team in its preparations for playing in Brazil, lending them the film of the Arsenal *v* Palmeiras game'.

'I remember,' Thompson writes, 'that, seeing the film for the first time in Brazil together with the Arsenal stars, I noticed that the players turned into fans. So enthusiastic were they that eventually one of them turned it off.' Then, in order to show 'the importance placed in Great Britain on the Brazilians' capacity to dominate the ball', he cites a comment by George Swindin: 'The way they "kill" the ball, when it's coming down, and instantly take it under control is indeed remarkable.'

Fifty years on, there are signs that at long last action is being taken to remedy resistance to skill among those involved in developing the

British players of tomorrow. A schoolteacher from George's native Yorkshire is in the process of setting up a network of soccer schools in Britain that will teach Brazilian coaching and training methods.

But first to the 1950 World Cup. It was to be the beginning of a painful learning process for the England national team; for the Brazilians, however, pain of a different kind was produced.

SIXTEEN

Reasons to be Tearful

Some of our clubs are still training as we did in the days of Queen Victoria. I am an old man, but young enough in coaching ideas to appreciate that the modern first-class player must be able to control a ball with any part of his legs or body – knees, hips, thigh – and must also have that touch and feeling of the ball so vital for the precise pass or scoring shot on the run, turn, volley or half-volley.

To attain all these things, one MUST HAVE PLENTY OF BALL PRACTICE.

I have been advocating this during my 50 years in football, but trainers are still jogging their players round 15 to 20 laps a training session. It's all wrong. Speed, plus stamina, minus skill, equals mediocrity.

Jimmy Hogan, quoted in the *Sunday Empire News*,
23 July 1950

There will be more physical contact [against Norway] than against Brazil, I'm sure of that. The Brazilians have such terrific skill that it's hard to get tackles in. There's no space between them and the ball, so it's all about jockeying them. That was alien to us, but there's nothing like the same level of skill in the English game and that's why you see so many tackles being made week in, week out. This game [against Norway] will suit our guys much better, they'll see more of the ball.

Scotland's John Collins, quoted in *The Observer*,
14 June 1998

Ticket-holders were still fighting their way into the unfinished Maracanã stadium when George Reader's whistle set the 1950 World Cup in motion. 'To add to the confusion,' wrote the *Sunday Empire News*'s W. Capel Kirby, 'as the game was starting pigeons were released and flew round the stadium bowl with rockets exploding amongst them, a twelve-gun salute boomed out, and fireworks set up a barrage reminiscent of London at the height of the air-raids.'

Somewhere in the reserved seats, there was a party of England players and officials, visiting the venue where a day later, 25 June, they would begin their own assault on the trophy. Suddenly, the anecdotal experiences of Brazilian match-day mayhem as related by two of their number – Alf Ramsey and Laurie Scott – did not seem so far-fetched. Before kick-off, the Brazilian players 'paraded the running track, bowing to sections of the crowd', exuding a supreme confidence that was reinforced by a message in the Rio sky.

Tom Finney remembers 'a little trailer aeroplane passing overhead which had the score before the game started – Brazil 4 Mexico 0. I thought it was very coincidental that that was how the game finished, because Brazil scored and got 4–0 in the lead and then just passed the ball around.' But even though Brazil appeared to be taking it easy, perhaps playing for a prearranged payout for a 4–0 win, for Finney and his England team-mates it had been 'a real eye-opener'.

'Looking back at that game,' he says, 'I often think now when I see the present game played, even though it was going back to the 1950s, they played every bit as good as some of the present sides. As far as I was concerned, it was a real education for me as a player to see the skills that they displayed on that particular game, despite the fact that Mexico were not the strongest of sides.'

That England's best were trailing behind to foreign soccer skills had been exposed, not for the first time, during a friendly at home to Italy in November 1949 – a game which Finney and co were fortunate to win 2–0. In one of his letters to the *Gazeta Esportiva*, John Thompson, of the *Mirror*, wrote that 'it was patently clear to the 72,000 spectators that the Italians are better footballers and I'm certain that, should the two sides meet in Brazil, their superior ball control would bring them victory'.

In a subsequent dispatch, Thompson reveals that club managers in England who had seen the Italy game were calling for 'a general revision of training methods', so as to raise their players' skill level. He quoted a convert to the Brazilian way, the former Southampton boss, Bill Dodgin:

In the World Cup, in the very difficult games in Brazil, our faults on the matter of ball control will be much more in evidence than on the occasion of the bad match against Italy at Tottenham. In relation to other countries, we are only advanced in finishing and team work. When they grasp these points, unless we concentrate on reconquering the art of playing good football, with the same dominance of the ball as the Italians and the South Americans, there will be nobody to outplay them.

In fact the FA sounded out both Dodgin and Tom Whittaker for their opinions on the South American game. But the creation of a Technical Committee, 'to examine the developments and practices in football', came too late to have a bearing on England's first World Cup excursion. All the same, when the time came to set out for Brazil, Tom Finney recalls that the mood in the England party was 'very buoyant', sustained by a belief in the country that they had 'a great chance of winning the World Cup'. There was a similar feeling in Brazil.

National coach Flávio Costa, on a scouting trip to Europe, was left in no doubt about England's potential. He had seen them defeat Scotland 1-0 in Glasgow (15 April 1950) and, impressed by their performance, had cut short his itinerary to return to Rio. 'It was especially the teamwork,' he explains. 'I didn't mark down any particular player. No. But I made a note of the English team as a whole. Before, I'd watched Portugal *v* Spain (2–2, 9 April 1950). The team I feared most, though, was England.'

British sides had been treated kindly when it came to World Cup qualification. FIFA decided that the top two countries in the 1949–50 Home Championship would go into the draw. Once England and Scotland had both beaten Northern Ireland and Wales, it seemed the issue had been resolved. But the Scots, for reasons best known to themselves, were keeping to an agenda of their own: only a first-place finish would ensure their presence in Rio – and that meant coming out of their game against England with at least a draw. No wonder Flávio Costa hurried home after seeing the Scots go down. 'They [Scotland] had most of the pressure,' wrote Tom Finney, 'we carried more danger and punch.'

But in Brazil, the killer punch deserted the England forward line – and how. England had begun their World Cup campaign against Chile in Rio – 'they were just an ordinary run-of-the-mill side,' says Tom Finney, 'and we won comfortably 2–0.' There was then a 300-mile flight inland to Belo Horizonte for what should have been another straightforward victory. Fate revealed otherwise. According to Finney: 'It was "we mustn't take things for granted", although we were just considering the USA as a team that were really [there] to make up the numbers. They were a nonentity as far as everybody was concerned.

'It was one of those games. It was a poor pitch; but having said that we struck the woodwork on five or six occasions, and the longer the game went, desperation crept in from our point of view because we were expected to win comfortably. And they scored, and I think they had roughly a couple of attacks and scored from one of them, and then of course pulled everybody back and it was a question of stopping us from scoring. The longer the game went it was obvious to each and every one of us it just wasn't our day.'

Harry Keough, a full-back for the USA in Belo Horizonte, takes a similar view, while highlighting the contribution of one of his side's foreign imports. 'In our opinion a number of factors helped us in the game against England. One was Eddie McIlvenny, a Scotsman who knew the English style and intercepted a lot of their passes in midfield. The pitch also helped us. It was bumpy and although the grass was not long, the ball seemed to 'sit up' on the surface. Consequently, a lot of scoring chances went high and wide – and England suffered most because they had more chances!'

But for Laurie Scott, there are absolutely no excuses for his colleagues' failure to find the back of the net. He was watching from the sidelines as he'd done for most of Arsenal's matches in Brazil. 'It was a terrible performance. You'd never seen anything like it. You wouldn't believe it, that they were supposed to be the best players in the country. Well, they were the best players in the country, no doubt about it. But they never clicked.'

Certainly, in tone, Scott's comments are much closer to those of the attendant British reporters. Forget the circumstances of the defeat; it was a national disgrace. W. Capel Kirby in his *Empire News* column was particularly scornful:

> The kings of football, the masters, the technicians superior, the professors, the magnifico English, would today like to dig a deep sandpit in Copacabana Beach and bury themselves.
>
> And to think that a short time ago American soccer authorities were pleading with the FA to return home via the United States to play a propaganda 'how to play' demonstration in New York.
>
> Now we're the laughing stock of the Americas. Whatever happens in the vital game against Spain tomorrow afternoon [2 July

1950] it's no good dismissing the Belo Horizonte travesty as a fluke.
It's more than that; it's the biggest-ever blow to our sporting prestige
and it's most unpleasant when one's abroad to suffer taunts and jibes.

Against Spain, England would have to win to have any chance of
making it through to the final pool. But they weren't the only
favourites with their backs to the wall. Incredibly, hosts Brazil had
failed to take both points from the Swiss in São Paulo, prompting calls
for coach Flávio Costa to be dismissed. The 2–2 result, wrote Capel
Kirby, 'plunged another nation into mourning'.

★ ★ ★

We have seen how George Reader's officiating spared the blushes of
the Southampton players during the poor start to their tour to Brazil;
'Mr Reader won the game which the Saints lost', insisted one of the
reports. At the 1950 World Cup, Reader and four British colleagues
could hardly be expected to cover for the shortcomings of the
England team. But what they could do was reinforce the high opinion
in which British referees were held.

Predictably, of the 22 matches in the tournament, ten were controlled by British officials; and it was surely more than coincidence that
every one of those ten matches featured at least one South American
team. In the run-up to the World Cup, the *Football Referee* had
reminded prospective officials of the dangers they might face in Brazil:

> The [Maracanã] pitch upon which the closing stages of this cup will
> be played is surrounded by a deep moat to prevent crowds
> interfering with the teams, and we have seen how excitable these
> South American football crowds can be. The sponsors of the
> competition over there anticipate trouble, and they will get it unless
> the arrangements are approached in a rational manner.
>
> In South America, differences can bring revolvers and razors into
> action, and we want no world football cup if it is to be a case of any
> country not wishing to reach the final. The first consideration in this
> matter should be the referees, and, if possible, the appointment of
> officials who are either linguists or who can make themselves
> understood to both teams.

So FIFA's 'rational' approach was to go for quality – i.e. a majority
of Britons – and to issue each official with guidelines which included

a football vocabulary in five languages. If the South American countries had had their way, one of the first names to be pencilled in would have been that of Jack Barrick.

Returning to England in December 1949, Jack still held hopes of being nominated by the FA for FIFA's referees' panel. But when the selection was finally made he was overlooked. Jack would doubtless have interpreted this as a snub – and what made it all the more difficult to swallow was that Reg Leafe, one of his linesmen in the 1948 Cup final, had been chosen ahead of him. To add to his disappointment, the World Cup final, which he aspired to be part of, was scheduled to take place on 16 July, his fiftieth birthday.

But although he was absent from Rio, that personal landmark still produced the 'finest memory' of his refereeing career. In 1955 Jack told the *Northampton Mercury*: 'Before a match [in Rio Grande do Sul] they played a record of 'Happy Birthday to You' in English over the loudspeakers and 95,000 people stood up and tried to sing along with the record, although few of them understood a word of English. It brought tears to my eyes.' To mark the occasion he was presented with a silver whistle.

To compensate for missing the World Cup, Barrick derived much pride from the fact that in 1950 Brazilians regarded him as 'the world's number one referee'. As Capel Kirby reported, Jack remained 'the big noise in refereeing circles' in Pôrto Alegre – and with a salary of £320 per month, by far 'the highest-paid referee in soccer'. He also was still called on to take charge of Brazil's top games. In March he refereed the deciding match in the Brazilian championship at Pacaembú ('Mr Barrick's officiating was one hundred per cent impartial, a job worthy of the importance of the encounter,' concluded the *Gazeta Esportiva*); and he was back there in May for the first in a series of matches between World Cup contenders Brazil and Uruguay.

It was after the third game, which Brazil won 1-0 to take the Rio Branco trophy, that Jack narrowly avoided being attacked by one of the Uruguayan players. Jack may have had wide support among national federations in South America, but even he was not immune to the fits of violence that outsiders feared. He reported the incident to the CBD:

> Immediately after the conclusion of the game I awaited the goalkeeper of Uruguay, who had been acting as captain, when number 9 of Uruguay came near and attempted to kick me. However, he did not succeed because my English friend, Mr

> Simpson, my interpreter, intervened and unluckily received two
> kicks, one on his thigh and the other on his buttocks. Such conduct
> is not only violent, it is disgusting.

The comments, in English, are preserved in the CBD Boletim
Oficial for May 1950; and it is typical of Jack that he should voice his
disapproval in such a forceful way. Even so, if action was taken, it did
not prevent the assailant, Miguez, from participating in Uruguay's
World Cup campaign.

As expected, the band of British referees led by George Reader
more than made up for England's World Cup fiasco. In August 1950
the *Football Referee* was able to boast that 'from all reports received it
appears that the only referees who measured up to world class were
the contingent sent from the British Isles'. While criticising the low
standard of refereeing of foreign officials, the publication referred
specifically to England *v* USA, 'when reports show that hand balls,
unfair tackles, etc., were allowed to go unpunished'. This explains the
out of character remark by the then England manager Walter Winterbottom that 'the refereeing [in that game] was a farce'.

It was also the reason why countries such as Brazil continued to
offer attractive contracts to experienced British officials. In 1952 there
were three of them handling championship games in Rio; of the
others, meanwhile, Harry Rowley had signed for the Paraná
Federation. By 1956, however, the number of British recruits stood at
two – a decline reflected in other South American countries.
Recalling his playing days in São Paulo, Cláudio says that by the mid-
50s Brazilian match officials had improved to the extent that 'there
was more discipline, referees perhaps had a greater back-up and they
entered into a system of officiating that was much better'.

Jack Barrick had actually commented on the improvement in
discipline in Brazilian football when he returned to England for good
in December 1950. His legacy is laid out in the pages of a book,
translated into Portuguese and published in Pôrto Alegre, containing
250 questions and answers about football. Jack prepared the book 'so
that the public could have a better understanding of the spirit of
football and to give them an idea of the problems that the referee
continually has to solve'. In the introduction, the president of the Rio
Grande Federation contributed a lasting encomium:

> On the Latin fits of anger he imposed conscious calm, phlegm and
> even British humour. The crowd itself, lavish in aggressive effusive-

ness, put up with the educational influence of Mr Barrick. He knew how to impose himself like someone who honestly goes about his work. He conferred on the function of referee a dignity that had been ignored. The sport and its practice will no longer be a grotesque spectacle, but a constructive competition.

★   ★   ★

Perhaps the outcome of England's game with the USA might have been different had a British official been in charge. But the fact remains that, for faults on and off the pitch, England had only themselves to blame. The Luxor Hotel on Copacabana beach had been an adequate base for Southampton and Arsenal; but for England? Says Tom Finney, 'It's like Blackpool right the way through ... We got very little sleep, it was very very noisy and certainly the last place that one would have taken an international side to prepare for a World Cup.' There had also been a personnel problem.

On the eve of the tournament, Capel Kirby reported that the FIFA commitments of the chief England selector, Arthur Drewry, were interfering with his duties as FA member in charge. This left team manager Walter Winterbottom overworked: 'He is dealing single-handed with transport, hotel room and food difficulties, all of which places a heavy responsibility on him when he should be dealing with the much more vital problem of team tactics for the job in hand.' For it wasn't as if England had an entirely settled side.

After the Scotland game, there had been a sudden and unexpected vacancy at centre-half caused by Neil Franklin's decision to accept a lucrative offer to play in Columbia. To lose such an 'oustanding player ... at that vital stage' was, says Tom Finney, 'a great blow for England'. Drewry also had to pronounce on whether there would be a place in the starting line-up for Stanley Matthews – a last-minute, public-pressure-induced selection. That he wasn't in the original party was 'a shock to us all as players', recalls Sir Tom. But Drewry, absent from England's twice daily work-outs, left it until the crucial match with Spain before recalling Matthews.

In marked contrast, Brazil's preparations were state-of-the-art, taking their usual practice of 'concentration' to extremes. While England were commuting between a seafront hotel and Botafogo's training ground, the Brazilian squad were secluded at a luxury training camp set up at a millionaire's property on the outskirts of Rio. Flávio Costa had a back-up team which included three chefs and two doctors, and such was the attention to detail that during the players' leisure time, to help to alleviate the ban on wives, entertainers broke their schedules to visit the camp.

Brazil's players were focused and they had fun – ingredients sadly missing from the France 98 finalists. Barbosa, the keeper in 1950, has said that 'it was so relaxing [there] that we'd suddenly remember: "Today we've got a game, so let's go down there and thrash those gringos and get back up here and release paper balloons and light a bonfire [a reference to Brazil's annual Festa Juninha]".' In the second phase of the tournament the Brazilians began by doing just that: 7–1 *v* Sweden, 6–1 *v* Spain. These results reveal just how far England had slipped behind their rivals; for in the space of a year, they had been beaten by Sweden (3–1) – and now Spain.

Elimination from the 1950 World Cup had come despite the introduction of Matthews and two other changes to the forward line. FA Secretary Sir Stanley Rous gave an apposite summing up after the 1–0 loss to Spain, saying: 'We were the better gentlemen, they were the better players.' England could win full marks for spirit and sportsmanship, but when it came to performing . . . Charles Buchan later wrote, 'their failure to score against the fiery Spanish defenders was another pathetic example of weak finishing after grand midfield work.'

Capel Kirby was one who saw the need for urgent action: 'The more one looks at the sorry show in retrospect, the more it has made me realise that the repercussions of a disastrous entry into world football competition will be far-reaching. Let us face the fact that defeats by the United States and Spain are not going to be isolated cases unless the whole structure of our international set-up is radically overhauled – beginning *now*.' That was the *Empire News* of Sunday, 9 July 1950. A week later the diatribe continued: 'Our methods are outdated and about 25 years behind the times. Moreover, our players are not craftsmen, although they think they know it all, and fall easy victims for the time-worn ballyhoo that the English are still the world's Soccer masters.'

In his report of the World Cup, Chairman of Selectors Arthur Drewry took a mixed view, on the one hand acknowledging the South Americans' ascendancy, on the other ignoring that there were lessons to be learnt. He noted that the Brazilians' game was 'attractive to watch, differing in many respects from that seen in this country', that they played 'football of bewildering skill' against opposition he had previously ranked as good and that there was an 'enthusiasm for training, practice and disciplined coaching ... at all levels throughout the country'.

Drewry then concluded by reiterating the need for an FA Technical Committee to be set up – 'in order that this country can marshal the advantages we possess to maintain a premier place in world football.' In other words, it was a case of looking for ways of making better use of the resources available so England could retain her position at the head of football's top table. The obvious implication was that improvements would come from within. But barely had the soul-searching begun than there was more bad news from Brazil.

In mid-1951 Brazilian football was still desperate for antidotes after its previous year's 2–1 loss to Uruguay in the World Cup final. When George Reader ended the contest, Flávio Costa says, 'there was no booing. There was nothing. There was sadness, silence. Brazil's defeat was greeted by silence.' *Placar* (October 1994) describes it as 'the greatest national tragedy of all time, comparable only to the death of Ayrton Senna'. As Wales international Walley Barnes noticed when he arrived back in Rio with Arsenal, there was 'a decided apathy towards football'. Maybe there was; but wins against top British club sides could at least help to expunge the tragedy of 16 July 1950.

So it was that Arsenal, and weeks later Portsmouth (league champions in 1949 and 1950), returned from visits to Rio and São Paulo with just one victory in a combined total of twelve games. But according to Walley Barnes, Arsenal's poor results were not due to 'a deterioration in our standard of play, but rather to a spectacular improvement in the play of our opponents'. The Brazilians had not only thoroughly assimilated Arsenal's system of defence, 'they added ideas of their own which made them superior to any sides we had ever met previously.'

However, Barnes later berates the Brazilians for their apparent reluctance to entertain further tours by British clubs: 'Could it be that they feel they have nothing more to learn from us, and will they continue to play blithely along the lines that proved successful in 1951?' And in his autobiography published in 1953 he goes on to make what with hindsight is a tragicomic observation. 'I am confident,' he writes, 'that the powers-that-be are constantly seeking new ideas for the improvement of our football generally, and there is not so much danger of our becoming set in our ways so that we are liable to be beaten by the unorthodox.'

In May 1954 the Hungarians handed out a second lesson to England – six months after whipping them 6–3 at Wembley. It came in the guise of a 7–1 thrashing, prompting freelance correspondent Willy Meisl, who at the time made it a personal crusade to investigate British football's 'fall from glory into mediocrity', to declare 'England's soccer has learnt nothing, but forgotten much'. For Meisl, the lessons could be summed up in three words: 'Brain beat Brawn.'

★   ★   ★

For Willy Meisl, writing in the mid-1950s, the soccer style of the future would involve the setting free of individuality, fresh opportunities for all-rounders ('a really fine footballer will be almost equally good in several positions and far from bad in all of them') and the importance of proper training. The penultimate paragraph of his excellent *Soccer Revolution* is a prescription for change, an appeal to the leaders of the game in Britain:

> We must free our soccer youth from the shackles of playing to order, along rails (in ruts) as it were. We must give them ideas and encourage them to develop their own. Hard tackling we have always known, they need not study it. We must show them many of the world's best teams and stars to let them see whether they can pick their brains and imitate their movements, later perhaps to add some new twists to thoughts and tricks thus acquired. Then they will produce something new or at least original, therefore it will be effective for some time.

What underpinned Willy Meisl's blueprint for the future was the emphasis on ball practice. Several years later, Tom Finney takes up the same theme in the wake of Brazil's first world triumph, and like Meisl he vents his frustration at so-called soccer reformers: 'Can we, in Britain, profit from this Brazilian lesson? Of course. Do we wish to learn from Brazil? I doubt it, although I feel it is essential that we should.'

In *Finney on Football* (1958) the dead-ball technique of Didi and the versatility of full-back Nílton Santos are used to illustrate the deficiencies of British players – in much the same way as the talents of Roberto Carlos and Cafu might serve the same purpose today. For it's a painful fact that the author's overall point, put despairingly, is as relevant now as it was back then:

> A free-kick that dips or swerves must be more dangerous than a straightforward one. A ball trapped dead must be easier to control

than one which bounces a yard in front of the player. A man with a body swerve must have a better chance of beating an opponent than a player without a body swerve. These are the points which have guided the soccer education of foreign footballers. They list the basic skills, work on them constantly, and do not stop working until they have mastered them. Nothing slipshod about it. Scientific methods of learning, supervised all the time, bring success.

It may have taken 40 years, but finally the Finney formula is being acted upon. In 1997 a youth coach from Leeds, having utilised individual skill routines from Holland, decided to investigate the training methods behind Brazil's success. During a self-funded visit to Rio and São Paulo, Simon Clifford discovered a form of football which does much to ensure that development of basic skills is not left to chance.

In the BBC documentary *A Whole New Ball Game* Clifford presents the merits of *futebol de salão* – football on a basketball-sized court. 'It's a five-a-side game so there are fewer children playing and the children in the game are getting more touches. The game's all about passing and moving, and the Brazilians have played it for years. It's played with a small ball with one other difference – it's heavily weighted to encourage passing, creativity and better control of the ball.'

As he watches a group of 15-year-old Paulistas being put through their paces, Clifford notes: 'The children are using their feet very quickly, using a small ball that's on the floor. This is what kids need at the beginning to become masters of the ball before they move on [to a bigger ball].' Rivelino and Zico are graduates of the game, and the latter, at his soccer school in Rio, tells Clifford: 'Ten years, eleven years, only ball, ball, ball; and after 14 years it's okay tactics. First, basic techniques – movement, pass, look – only this; but tactics after.' Meisl's message again.

Former Scotland international Gordon Strachan appears to have a similar outlook. After Scotland's last game at France 98 he analysed their weaknesses for *The Observer* (28 June 1998), pinpointing the main hindrance to future improvement – the dearth of young players with flair. The problem, he feels, is particularly highlighted when the opposition is from South America or Africa:

> Players from these parts of the world seem to get much greater encouragement to express themselves and take chances on the ball. You could argue that this is sometimes taken to extremes and causes

them to become vulnerable, but they recognise that even the most well-organised defences are going to have problems in dealing with opponents who keep wanting to beat two or three players.

One of the differences between Scotland and Morocco on Tuesday [23 June] was that you had to look long and hard for anyone in a Scotland shirt to produce the unexpected. That is not to say Scotland have no particularly skilful players. John Collins is definitely in that category. But one or two in your team is not enough. If you're going to play with imagination, everybody must be on the same wavelength . . .

. . . Sadly, from what I have seen of the [Scotland] Under-21 team, I cannot offer much hope of a dramatic transformation in the near future. It has to be viewed as a long-term project and, for me, one of the keys lies in managers and coaches encouraging young players to follow the examples set by the South Americans and Africans. This will involve addressing how players are developed in Scotland, as schoolboy players and professionals. As a professional footballer myself, I was fortunate not to have received any formal football coaching until I was 13 or 14. I just played and concentrated on enjoying myself.

Since founding the UK Confederation of Futebol de Salão, Simon Clifford has been inundated with requests for membership from all over the British Isles, and by the end of this year at least ten Brazilian Soccer Schools will have been set up. If there's a sense in which a challenge is being made to the FA's so-called Centres of Excellence, this has not prevented Glenn Hoddle and a host of Premiership clubs from turning their attention to Leeds. In January 1999 a group of Clifford's coaches will be studying for the Brazilian Coaching Licence – in Brazil.

Nothing short of a total shake-up will do if the English game is to finally rid itself of the timeworn mentality that big is beautiful, that brawn is capable of overcoming brain. It was only in March that there was fresh personification of this when England and Brazil met in a schoolboy international at Wembley. *The Observer* (15 March 1998) emphasised that England's 6ft 4in striker 'physically dwarfed the much slighter frames of his Brazilian opponents . . . But the sublime skills, if not physical strength, came from the Brazilians.'

28 July 1998. I receive news from São Paulo of the death of Charles Rule. What, I once asked him, would his illustrious cousin have made of Brazil's dominance of world football? 'He would have said: "Good

show. I'm glad that my game took on so well here and that despite the fact that it's professional they are good players." ' And the thought of British footballers reshaping the *chaleira*? The idea had still to be hatched.

Epilogue

'GRANDAD' LIKED THE 'OLD ONES'
Only yesterday was the columnist informed that Charles Miller, the introducer of football to Brazil, who now at almost eighty years old rarely leaves his residence in the Rua México, was at Pacaembú following with interest the South American veterans competition.

Charles Miller thinks that the veterans are still youthful, at least when it comes to class. He couldn't believe that Domingos [da Guia] was already old, that he had already retired.

'I've never seen a better game,' he commented.

Última Hora, 4 March 1953
(a cutting found in a wallet in Helena Miller's
possession which belonged to her father)

[Charles Miller] died [on 30 June 1953] in the Samaritano Hospital. [The next day] there was an important game in Pacaembú. And when the cortège went past, the teams came out and saluted the cortège.

From an interview with Charles Rule,
November 1994, São Paulo

THE 'TANK' HAS DISAPPEARED!
Nobody played the compact and positive football of Harry Welfare, with the great show of a goalscorer, in the authentic English style. Today he would have been a centre-forward . . . a tactic for springing traps . . . But he would have scored a lot of goals in the same way, owing to his decisiveness in favouring

216

shooting. Old Welfare died aged 78. The last time we heard anything about him it was that he had expressed a wish that before dying he wanted to see Pelé play. We don't know if his last football wish was realised, because he [Pelé] was a long way from Rio.

If Brazilian football knew, today, how much it owes to past players of Welfare's class, it would be observing three days official mourning!

Tomás Mazzoni, writing in the *Gazeta Esportiva*, two
days after Harry Welfare died on 2 September 1966

Archie McLean's name – because of his fleetness of foot, he was known professionally as O Veadinho *('The Little Deer') – is revered in Brazilian sporting circles; and on one memorable occasion, when he was making a sentimental return visit to Brazil in 1966, this talented Scot received a standing ovation from the large crowd of spectators attending a game at Pacaembú stadium.*

From *Our First Fifty Years: 1924–74*,
The St Andrew Society, São Paulo

Appendix One

Letters written by Charles Miller published in the *Banister Court School Magazine*

1) from Vol.III. No.31, March 1904

S.Paul's Town [*sic*] is, as you know, situated about fifty miles west of the seaport of Santos, and 3,000 feet above sea level or Santos. The railway between Santos and S.Paul's belongs to an English company and is managed by Englishmen, and it is said that it is one of the best organized and kept roads in the world. The trains leave Santos and run on level ground for about fifteen miles, then are pulled up the side of a mountain or serra for seven miles to the height of 3,000 feet, and then on level ground to S.Paul's. The pulling of the trains up and down the serra is worked by endless cables on the grip system. The present population of S.Paul's is anything between 280,000 and 300,000 inhabitants, the greater part being Italians. The whole town has an European appearance, as you will see by a few photo cards I am sending you. Electric-cars or trams run all through the town and out into the suburbs, six miles or more. The force for the electric power is supplied by a large waterfall fifteen miles out of town; nearly all the factories are worked by electricity from the same fall. The centre streets of the town are paved with wooden blocks, the same as the High Street in Southampton, I am told. The climate is very much as in England, very changeable. For instance, it ought to be pretty hot now, being midsummer, but for the last week the thermometer has not been over 73°F., not even summer heat.

Now as to sports, which no doubt will interest you most. With cricket we have not been able to do very much, except, of course, amongst the English. We have a very nice ground, pavilion, and three tennis courts, which most clubs in England would be proud of. We play five cricket matches with Santos and two with Rio; the latter being 300 miles away it's difficult to arrange more. The Rio matches are State or County matches, State of S.Paul's *v* State of Rio, generally a two or three days' match, according to how the holidays fall. This country being of Catholic religion we get all Saints' days as holidays. In November, 1902, Rio, S.Paul's, and Santos sent a Cricket XI. to Buenos Ayres [*sic*], eight from Rio, two from S.Paul's, and one from Santos. We went down by the Royal Mail Steamer *Danube*; it took us five days from Rio. We played four matches – lost three, and drew one. In Buenos Ayres they play on grass, which made a vast difference to us, being used to matting. I was elected captain on board, greatly to my surprise; I expected a Rio man would be picked, as there were eight of them. Willie Rule went with us to umpire. The English colony in Buenos Ayres numbers 30,000, so that they can put a very strong team in the field, having such a large number to pick from. We took down very weak bowling, four of our best could not go. In 1901 Buenos Ayres sent up a team. We beat them in S.Paul's by an innings and eight runs, and they were beaten in Rio three times by an innings. We hope to receive a visit from them this year.

Football: You will be surprised to hear that football is the game here. We have no less than sixty or seventy clubs in S.Paul's city alone. Two years ago a Brazilian by the name of Antonio Casimiro da Costa [*sic*], educated in Switzerland, and myself formed a League. He gave a silver cup. Five clubs entered. We won in 1902–3; both years we drew with a club called "Paulistanos", all Brazilians, same number of points. As goal average does not count, we had to play off an extra match. We always get two or three thousand people to a League match, but for the final we had 6,000. The Brazilians scored the first goal, and you never heard such a row as the spectators kicked up; we scored twice in the second half. A week ago I was asked to referee in a match of small boys, twenty a side. I told them it was absurd them playing twenty a side; but no, they wanted it. I thought, of course, the whole thing would be a muddle, but I found I was very much mistaken. They played two half-hours, and I only had to give two hands. The youngsters hardly spoke a word during the game, kept their places and played well; even for this match about 1,500 people turned up. No less than 2,000 footballs have been sold here within the last twelve months; nearly every village has a club now.

We have also a very nice Golf Club, with a limited number of playing members, which is forty.

CHAS. W. MILLER.

P.S. – I enclose a photo of myself taken in football things. As we could not get all the players together at the same time, we had to have them taken separately and then have the group made up. I will send you the group when ready.

★

2) from Vol. V. No. 37, April 1906

CAIXA, No. 579,
S. PAULO, BRAZIL.

Some time ago I promised to send you a photo. of our last year's football team that won the League Championship; Mr. Coupar has kindly offered to take the photos; he sails to-day by the SS *Magdalena*, bearer of this letter, so if you do not receive it within two days from receipt of this letter please send down to the Royal Mail office for it as I have asked Mr. Coupar to ask one of the officers on board to have it sent to you or to place it in the Royal Mail office to be sent for.

Please accept the photo. from Willie Rule and myself. The game represented on the photo. was the final game last year. You will note that the photographer was able to catch all three goals, two made by us and the other by the C.A.P. It looks very much as if we shall have to play an extra match this year again with the same club. The C.A.P. have 16 points and one more game, and we have 14 points with two more games.

We did our best to have the Southampton team up here, but they could not come. I went down to Rio specially to see them. I think we could have given them a pretty good game. Mr. Lupton H.B.M. Vice-Consul, went to England last March on a holiday, and I was appointed his substitute as Acting Vice Consul during his absence.

CHAS. W. MILLER.

Appendix Two

Goals and games for Miller and Welfare: their championship-winning seasons in Brazil

1) CHARLES MILLER
(source: *O Estado de São Paulo*)

1902

8 May	SPAC	v Paulistano	4-0	1 goal	
13 May		v Mackenzie College	3-0	1	
8 June		v Internacional	3-0	1	
29 June		v Paulistano	0-1		
20 July		v Germânia	4-0	2	
3 August		v Germânia	3-0	1	
24 August		v Internacional	0-0		
20 September		v Mackenzie College	4-4	2	
26 October		v Paulistano	2-1	2	

1903

21 May	v Mackenzie College	2-0	1	
24 June	v Paulistano★	0-2		
5 July	v Internacional	5-0		
19 July	v Germânia	4-1	1	
2 August	v Paulistano★	4-0	*(scorers not named)*	
9 August	v Germânia	1-1	1	
27 September	v Internacional	3-0		
25 October	v Paulistano	2-1		

1904

12 June	v Germânia	1-0	1	
19 June	v Paulistano	1-1	1	
29 June	v AA das Palmeiras	5-0	1	
10 July	v Germânia★	3-2	1	
24 July	v Paulistano★	0-0		
31 July	v AA das Palmeiras★	3-0	*(scorers not named)*	
7 August	v Internacional	5-0	1	
15 August	v Mackenzie College	1-0	1	
18 September	v Internacional	4-1	1	
28 September	v Mackenzie College	5-0	1 *(2 goals unattributed)*	
30 October	v Paulistano	1-0	1	

★Miller's name appears in the SPAC line-up on the day of the game, but not in the match report

2) HARRY WELFARE
(source: *Campeonato Carioca: 96 Anos de História, 1997*)

1917

18 November	Fluminense v	Botafogo	1-2	
25 November	v	Vila Isabel	4-1	2 goals
9 December	v	Bangu	11-1	6
23 December	v	Flamengo	2-2	
30 December	v	Andaraí	7-2	3

1918

14 April	v Andaraí	4-3	1
21 April	v Bangu	9-3	3
3 May	v Mangueira	2-0	
12 May	v São Cristóvão	3-2	1
19 May	v América	2-0	
26 May	v Vila Isabel	6-1	
23 June	v Flamengo	3-0	1
30 June	v Carioca	6-0	2
14 July	v Botafogo	0-0	
21 July	v Bangu	4-2	3
28 July	v Andaraí	1-0	1
15 August	v Vila Isabel	0-1	
15 September	v América	4-0	
20 September	v São Cristóvão	2-2	1
29 September	v Botafogo	2-1	1
6 October	v Flamengo	2-2	1
8 December	v Mangueira	2-0	1

1919

8 June	v Carioca	4-0	1
22 June	v Mangueira	8-0	4
13 July	v Vila Isabel	4-1	3
20 July	v Botafogo	2-1	1
27 July	v São Cristóvão	0-2	
17 August	v Bangu	4-0	1
24 August	v Flamengo	3-1	
31 August	v Andaraí	6-0	3
7 September	v América	3-2	
5 October	v Carioca	5-1	2
26 October	v Mangueira	3-1	1
9 November	v Bangu	3-2	
16 November	v Vila Isabel	2-1	
23 November	v Botafogo	5-2	1
30 November	v São Cristóvão	4-3	1
14 December	v Andaraí	4-2	2
21 December	v Flamengo	4-0	1
28 December	v América	4-1	1

Bibliography

Adamson, Richard, *Bogotà Bandit. The Outlaw Life of Charlie Mitten: Manchester United's Penalty King*, Mainstream, Edinburgh, 1996

Assaf, Roberto and Martins, Clóvis, *Campeonato Carioca: 96 Anos de História, 1902–1997*, Irradiação Cultural, Rio de Janeiro, 1997

Banister Court School Magazine, 3 Vols – 1893–1903, 1904–1913, 1914–1927, Banister Court School, Southampton

Barnes, Walley, *Captain of Wales*, Stanley Paul, London, 1953

Barrick, Cyril J., *Sabatina de Futebol: Perguntas e Respostas*, Coruja, Pôrto Alegre, 1950

British Presence in Brazil, Paubrasil for Lloyds Bank, São Paulo, 1987

Buchan, Charles, *A Lifetime in Football*, Phoenix House, London, 1955

Butler, Bryon, *The Football League 1888–1988: The Official Illustrated History*, Macdonald Queen Anne Press, London, 1987

Caldas, Waldenyr, *O Pontapé Inicial: Memória do Futebol Brasileiro (1894–1933)*, IBRASA, São Paulo, 1990

Capel Kirby, W. and Carter, Frederick W., *The Mighty Kick*, Jarrolds, London, 1933

Chalk, Gary and Holley, Duncan, *Saints: A Complete Record of Southampton Football Club 1885–1987*, Breedon Books, Derby, 1987

Clark, Sylvia, *Paisley: A History*, Mainstream, Edinburgh, 1988

Coelho Netto, Paulo, *História do Fluminense*, Rio de Janeiro, 1952

Coelho Netto, Paulo, *O Fluminense na Intimidade* (Vols. II and III), Rio de Janeiro, 1969 and 1975

Creek, F.N.S., *A History of the Corinthian Football Club*, Longmans, London, 1933

Dimand, Dora, ed., *Club Athletico Paulistano: Um clube que cresceu com a cidade*, PROAL, São Paulo, 1970

[Ellaby, Christopher G.], *Early History of Banister Court School* and *Banister Court School 1884–1892*, Banister Court School, Southampton [n.d.]

Ellis, Arthur E., *Refereeing Round the World*, Phoenix House, London, 1956

Ferrier, Bob, Wright, Billy and Winterbottom, Walter, *Soccer Partnership*, Heinemann, London, 1960

Figueiredo, Antônio, *História do Foot-Ball em S. Paulo*, O Estado de S. Paulo, São Paulo, 1918

Filho, Mário, *O Negro no Futebol Brasileiro*, Civilização Brasileira, Rio de Janeiro, 2nd ed., 1964

Finney, Tom, *Finney on Football*, Nicholas Kaye, London, 1958

Finney, Tom, *Football Round the World*, Museum Press, London, 1953

Forsyth, Roddy, *The Only Game*, Mainstream, Edinburgh, 1990

Fry, C.B., *Life Worth Living*, Eyre & Spottiswoode, London, 1939

Gannaway, Norman, *Centenary: A History of Hampshire Football Association 1887–1987*, Hampshire Football Association, 1987

Gannaway, Norman, *Association Football in Hampshire until 1914*, Hampshire County Council, 1996

Gibson, Alfred and Pickford, William, *Association Football & The Men Who Made It*, Vols I to IV, Caxton, London, 1905–1906

Grayson, Edward, *Corinthians and Cricketers*, Sportsmans Book Club, 1957

Hutchinson, Roger, *Empire Games: The British Invention of Twentieth-Century Sport*, Mainstream, Edinburgh, 1996

Inglis, Simon, *League Football and the Men Who Made It: The Official Centenary History of the Football League 1888–1988*, Collins Willow, London, 1988

Joy, Bernard, *Forward, Arsenal!*, Phoenix House, London, 1952

Kuper, Simon, *Football Against the Enemy*, Orion, London, 1994

Lever, Janet, *Soccer Madness*, Waveland Press, Prospect Heights, Illinois, revised ed., 1995

Mason, Tony, *Association Football and English Society: 1863–1915*, The Harvester Press, Brighton, 1980

Mason, Tony, *Passion of the People? Football in South America*, Verso, London, 1994

Mazzoni, Tomás, *História do Futebol no Brasil 1894–1950*, Leia, São Paulo, 1950

Meisl, Willy, *Soccer Revolution*, Phoenix House, London, 1956

Miller, David, *Stanley Matthews: The Authorized Biography*, Pavilion, London, 1989

Mills, John R., *Charles William Miller: 1894–1994, Memoriam Clube Atlético São Paulo*, Price Waterhouse, São Paulo, 1996

Neiva, Adriano and Varzea, Paulo, in *Concurso Comemorativo do 60.o Aniversário da Introdução do Futebol em São Paulo: 1894–1954*, Federação Paulista de Futebol, São Paulo, 1954

Oliver, Guy, *The Guinness Book of World Soccer: The History of the Game in Over 150 Countries*, Guinness, London, 1992

Peskett, Roy, ed., *Tom Whittaker's Arsenal Story*, Sporting Handbooks, London, 1958

Pickford, William, *The Hampshire Football Association Golden Jubilee Book 1887–1937*, Hampshire Football Association, 1937

Ramsey, Alfred, *Talking Football*, Stanley Paul, London, 1952

Rodrigues, Nelson and Filho, Mário, *FLA-FLU . . . e as multidões despertaram!*, Europa, Rio de Janeiro, 1987

Sant'Anna, Leopoldo, *O Futebol em S. Paulo – Notas Crítico-Biográficas*, São Paulo, 1918

Sebe Bom Meihy, José Carlos and Witter, José Sebastião, eds., *Futebol e Cultura – Coletânea de estudos*, IMESP/DAESP, São Paulo, 1982

Storti, Valmir and Fontenelle, André, *A História do Campeonato Paulista: 1902–1996*, Publifolha, São Paulo, 1997

Taylor, Rogan and Ward, Andrew, *Kicking and Screaming*, Robson Books, London, 1995

Tulk, William, Ferris, Cyril and Andrews, Reg, eds., *São Paulo Athletic Club: 1888–1938*, São Paulo, 1938

Valentim, Max, *O Futebol e sua Técnica*, ALBA, Rio de Janeiro, 1941

Varley, Nick, *Golden Boy: A Biography of Wilf Mannion*, Aurum Press, London, 1997

Walvin, James, *The People's Game: The History of Football Revisited*, Mainstream, Edinburgh, 1994

Young, Percy M., *A History of British Football*, Stanley Paul, London, 1968